## SEVEN NORTH

The smart thing to do ~~...~~ to say how flattered I was that he should value my opinion, but how I just couldn't do justice to this wonderful case right now. The Chief Res could tell the story to the house staff any way he wanted. That being the obviously smart thing to do, I said, "I'll see what I can do."

It was the kind of case I never could walk away from, with everyone else so eager to avoid it . . .

The whole explanation would be something simple, something obvious and easy to clear up, as most hospital incidents usually are, if you take the time to go through the records carefully, and to listen.

But this was a Vietnamese and that thought kept rumbling around my skull in a low unnerving undertone. Nothing that had to do with Vietnam was ever simple or obvious or easy to understand or ended the way you thought it would.

# Seven North

# Neil Ravin

NEW ENGLISH LIBRARY
Hodder and Stoughton

*For Carl Ravin, M.D.*

First published in the USA in 1985 by
E. P. Dutton, Inc./Seymour Lawrence

First NEL Paperback Edition September 1986

NEL Books are published by
New English Library,
Mill Road, Dunton Green,
Sevenoaks, Kent.
Editorial office: 47 Bedford Square, London WC1B 3DP

Typeset by Hewer Text Composition Services, Edinburgh

Printed and bound by Cox & Wyman Ltd, Reading, Berks

**British Library C.I.P.**

Ravin, Neil
  Seven North.
  I. Title
  813'.54      PS3568.A84

  ISBN 0-450-39032-2

# 1

They thought they really had me this time. Why, I have no idea. If there's one thing I'm not likely to miss, it's an insulinoma. Christ knows, they could've given me half a hundred other things and I would've floundered miserably. Great high drama at the medical centre, a clinicopathologic conference: presented me the case as an unknown, in front of an auditorium full of medical students, house staff and all the old tenured farts who crawl out of their holes once a month hoping to see a young smart-ass blow the case.

Mrs. Bromley, my secretary, says I reacted most inappropriately to the whole thing. She meant I didn't want to do the conference at all. I thought that was a most appropriate reaction. But it's good press, she said. Puts your name in lights, she said. Once I read the history I thought I knew the answer, which is what had me worried. They never choose straightforward cases for those conferences. It always looks like something obvious, but turns out to be something sneaky, something you wouldn't think of in a million years. Life isn't all that sneaky, said Mrs. Bromley. But a CPC isn't real life. Oh, it's a real case all right, but it's show biz.

I've had enough high drama to last a lifetime. I didn't move to a sleepy town like Washington and go into private practice to live a fast life and engage in high drama. But Mrs. Bromley ordered me to take the case. She occasionally intimates she just might leave if things don't pick up, so I hustle around, digging up new patients, and things are busy for a while and Mrs. Bromley's happy and there's peace at the office. The moonlighting pays the rent and her salary, but she gets bored if we slow down in the office.

And Mrs. Bromley's essential. She's English, excessively efficient, and sounds great on the phone. Without her I'd never keep track of where I was supposed to go and things would fall apart. She said to do the CPC and I did it.

So there I was, sitting on the stage while a resident presented the case of a Mrs. Gladys Best, who was referred from the psych ward for a medical workup. Mrs. Best was delivered into the hands of the shrinks because she was sitting around the pool at her place in McLean, when for no apparent reason she exploded into a wild rage and started throwing glasses at the maid and the gardener. This wouldn't have caused much comment but her husband happened to be home and he became most upset about the glass smashed all over the pool deck.

Mrs. Best wound up on the psych ward at Saint George's. It took the shrinks two weeks to figure out that there was something different about her – namely that in her lucid intervals, she wasn't crazy at all. In fact, she was quite alarmed by her own outbursts, although she had no explanation for them, and she got pretty depressed sitting on the psych ward with all those insane people.

The shrinks worked her up for her depression but couldn't get past her explanation that she was depressed by the ward and by the psychiatrist. They replied that she was obfuscating, and probably she'd still be there, but one morning she had the good sense to slip silently into coma and when they couldn't wake her, they called a medical consult who knew enough to evaluate coma with a blood sugar which turned out to be vanishingly low, and she woke up as soon as they jolted her with an IV bolus of fifty-percent glucose.

There were a few red herrings among the lab findings, like the negative CAT scan, but basically I knew she had to have either an insulinoma or some other source of insulin. You don't just drop your blood sugar to nineteen by getting depressed and not eating breakfast. I went through the whole parade of possibilities for the fans, just the way you're supposed to, eliminating them one by one, making it sound difficult, and finally said it was an insulinoma after all, which of course it turned out to be.

2

A small one. They had a hell of a time finding it at surgery. They had the belly open, looking right at the pancreas and still couldn't see it. The negative CAT scan was what was supposed to fool me. That's why they all looked so smug before the conference and thought they had me. Fortunately, I went to medical school before CAT scans.

Everyone was very amused about the shrinks calling her paranoid and bipolar manic depressive and all the other things they called her, when, in fact, she had a real disease. I resisted the strong temptation to play to the audience and milk that angle for a few laughs. But ever since I opened my own office, I've been eating humble pie. It's astonishing how the guy with the real tumour is indistinguishable from the legions of walking worried who cross my threshold complaining of spleen-swelling and feeling pins and needles all over. And there's nothing to keep one of those from getting a real disease. Nothing looks so clear in the office as it does in the auditorium. So I couldn't be too smug about Mrs. Best's psychiatrists.

Right after the conference my bladder commanded a performance at the nearest urinal and one of the medical residents came into the bathroom. He said they had all been thrown off insulinoma by the negative CAT. It's really tough on these guys when their CAT scans let them down. They have to rely on what they know.

I ran down to the vending machine room near the library. There were two third-year medical students standing close to one another in front of the Coke machine. They depressed the hell out of me with all their respect. I know it's a Catholic hospital, but I wear no collar and they're no school kids. They jumped away from each other as if boy and girl shouldn't have the hots for one another. The girl tried to regain her composure by asking me something about proinsulin levels. They'd been at the CPC. I don't remember what I told her.

They made me feel very old. They're asking me questions very professionally, thinking they're covering; I'm hoping for their sakes they're screwing in broom cupboards, when up comes Fred O'toole, the Chief Resident, who asked me to do the conference in the first place. He says, "Nice job."

3

I was almost beginning to believe Mrs. Bromley was right about doing the conference. I hadn't heard so much commendation since I recited the Hippocratic oath in pig Latin, fourth year in medical school. Then the Chief Res said, "Dr. von Dernhoffer wants to see you." Dr. von Dernhoffer was the Chairman of the Department of Medicine. "Now," said the Chief Res.

# 2

The wooden doors to Dr. von Dernhoffer's office would have admitted a pair of elephants. The room itself was a little smaller than Madison Square Garden. We sat opposite each other on couches in front of his desk, after the Chief Res had formally introduced me. I had just gone through an identical introduction downstairs, in the auditorium, before the CPC, but Dr. von Dernhoffer seemed to enjoy it, so I shook his hand again, as if it were the first time.

I know I should have counted myself among the honoured, being introduced to the Chairman twice in a single morning. Dr. von Dernhoffer did not deal personally with just anyone. I knew that for a fact because he had asked me to handle problems for him three times before over the past year and he'd never seen fit to call me about any of them himself. He usually had the Chief Res deal with me. The last time, he had a slightly more senior faculty member call me. That case had been a little more delicate, so it rated a higher ranking emissary. A year on the clinical faculty and three successful missions and he'd never seen fit to make my acquaintance personally, until today.

Then again, I could see why the Chairman might not be eager to socialize with me. The three cases had been messy affairs: missed diagnoses, semi-horror shows that did nothing spectacular for the self-image of the hospital or the Department

4

of Medicine. The last one in particular was not a case anyone in the department liked to talk about – a Zollinger-Ellison syndrome who kept coming to the Emergency Room and vomiting blood all over the interns. They kept admitting him, missing the diagnosis, despite all the times the case had been presented to all the different faculty members, and finally they called me, "on the Chairman's orders," to look into it. I looked into it and found enough diagnostic oversights to heap into a compost pile and grow malpractice suits by the bushel. So having me sitting there on his silk couch was like socializing with the town undertaker. Nobody likes the guy who sees you at your worst moments.

A secretary appeared from somewhere and got everyone coffee, and we sat there looking at each other over the rims of our cups. I decided to wait for the Chairman to speak, and while he was arranging his thoughts I priced his oak desk, the china lamps on each end, the green Oriental rug overlying the peach wall-to-wall carpet. Since I'd set up my own office I noticed things like that. The Chairman's office cost the hospital plenty, but then again image is supposed to be worth something in Washington. You can't have some senator's wife come in to be reassured that your Cardiac Care Unit is going to take good care of her husband and have her sit on a Sears couch. Not in Washington. Wrong message. Besides, hospital money doesn't cost anyone.

The Chairman looked good in his office. White hair, clear skin, light grey suit, the shirt not quite pink, not quite white, and a subtle grey tie. He looked comfortable here. He made me uncomfortable. He had his secretary hovering and his Chief Resident on chair's edge and gave the impression that there were great and urgent demands on his time, but he was relaxed and going to give me some of it.

I was trying to decide whether this was the little post-conference conference where you got congratulated for upholding the tradition of clinical acumen at the CPC, or a belated, if grudging, word about the way I'd bailed out the staff in the case of that Zollinger-Ellison patient, when von Dernhoffer said, "I suppose you've heard about our little trouble on Seven North."

I looked at him, trying not to look too confused, and then to the Chief Res whose face was about as revealing as a West Point cadet's. Then I looked back to the Chairman of Medicine and said, "No."

"It's in all the papers," said the Chairman, waving at the newspaper on the coffee table between us.

"It made Eyewitness News last night," said the Chief Res.

"Did it?" said the Chairman, not at all pleased. He waited for me to speak. He took a sip of coffee, but I still didn't know what he was talking about. Then he said, "You did a very nice job this morning."

He said that almost graciously, as if it didn't hurt him at all to have to admit it, as if he would have rather seen me get it right than fall flat on my face for once, the way his full-time faculty had been known to fall on three sad prior occasions. He was smiling now, as if whatever little resentments he held for me were gone, and as if whatever had run in Washington's one and almost only newspaper was gone too, evanescent as a bad burp.

"Hypoglycemia isn't an easy topic," he said. "So much misinformation." He looked me over. "Especially in the popular press."

"Well," I said, "newspaper reporters, what can you expect? They're writing about sewer installations one day, hospital stories the next."

"Yes," chortled the Chairman. He allowed himself to be amused by that. He looked to the Chief Resident, to be sure he was also being amused, and the Chief Res hurriedly pulled up what was supposed to be an amused smile. It looked more like a grimace.

"I've been looking over your file," said von Dernhoffer. "I know we've asked you to clear up a few little matters for the department in the past." He swallowed when he said that, face sour. "But I'd forgotten you did your fellowship with Fulton, at Hopkins."

I was still trying to guess where he was leading but couldn't. Whatever it was, it was special enough to arrange a personal audience. Even the admiral's wife assignment hadn't rated that. She'd had a pituitary tumour nobody knew how to work

6

up, and he sent the Chief Res for that. He never even sent a thank-you note. I would have settled for one of those "Dictated and signed in his absence" notes. But no. What would a note have cost him? I was thinking about all this when I heard him say, "Most of your publications were in glucose metabolism." He was smiling a smile which did not put me at ease, which in fact had just the opposite effect. I had the feeling I was being set up. But I had to agree: most of my publications had been in glucose metabolism, in the days I was still publishing, before I heard the call of private practice, devoting myself to full-time patient care and personal financial independence.

"I think you might be just our man," said von Dernhoffer. Broad smile now, as broad a smile as a tight face like that will allow. Showed me all his too-white capped teeth. "If anyone can settle this, it has to be you. I know you've commented on the necessity for the rigorous diagnostic approach." He was still smiling, but his brows were narrowing. "So this ought to give you a chance to give us all another valuable lesson in clinical rigour."

Another valuable lesson – he said that with just enough irony to let me feel the heat, but not so much as to sound out of control. He looked very pleased with himself and he beamed and winked at the Chief Resident.

"Well, then," he said, standing up, "why don't we have Fred fill you in? Whatever you need, of course, you'll have. Whatever we can do. We'd like this brought to a conclusion as quickly as possible."

"Who would like what brought to a conclusion as quickly as possible?" I said.

He went on as if I'd said nothing.

"Of course, your faculty status will have to be elevated to a rank commensurate with this job," he said.

That was supposed to be some sort of carrot. Whenever you apply for membership on the staff of a university hospital they appoint you to the faculty of the school of medicine, the "clinical faculty" it's called. That entitles you to tell all your patients you're on the faculty of medicine and it gets you into the medical school library, and it gets you gym privileges. I wasn't even sure what title they had given me. It was probably Clinical Instructor. Buck private. Mrs. Bromley would know. Now they were going to make me some sort of clinical professor. It would make my mother proud, but it would do me about as much good as a commission in the Afghan army.

I could see I was being ushered out, everyone was standing, and I didn't like it.

"Just what is it you wanted me to do?"

The Chairman looked startled. "Why, the hypoglycemia case," he said. "Don't you understand?"

"I'm just a humble local medical doctor," I said. "Why don't you spell it out?"

We all sat down again.

The Chief Resident, Fred, explained: Last Thursday, just exactly a week ago, a patient had been admitted with pneumonia to Seven North. He had recently begun on insulin for diabetes, and also had some heart disease, angina, and a few other problems, but nothing very acute. He died suddenly, unexpectedly, the next day. Nurse goes in to see how he's liking his dinner, and he's not breathing. "At post, there was some question of a hyperacute MI," said Fred, "but you know they can't tell for sure. But what they found was a blood sugar of twenty-four. Of that there was no doubt."

I whistled. The normal blood sugar is around one hundred. A sugar of twenty-four could shorten your life abruptly if it got there quickly enough and if it had fallen from high enough, especially if your coronary arteries weren't ready for it, if they were clogged to begin with and your heart couldn't take the sudden stress. I could see why they were worried.

"The nurse gave him the right dose?" I asked.

"He was on a single dose: ten units NPH in the morning. She insists she gave him no more. She logged it in as ten. They had her show how she draws up insulin, and she did it right."

"They?"

"The Director of Nursing and our Pathologist-in-Chief, Mel Turner, have been looking into this, up to now," said the Chairman.

"The Medical Examiner wasn't interested?"

"He turned the case down."

8

"The Medical Examiner wasn't interested, and your in-house people haven't come up with anything?"

"Of course," said the Chairman, "the first thing we thought was that he received the wrong dose of insulin."

"When did you find out about all this?"

"The patient died Friday," said the Chief Res. "The post was done Saturday morning. The blood sugar came back from the lab Monday afternoon."

"And the newspaper story appeared yesterday," said the Chairman. "Like many of our patients, this man happened to be a man of some prominence. A refugee."

The Chairman gave a newspaper lying on the coffee table between us a short shove in my direction. I left it there.

"Why have me do the investigation?" I asked. "You must have someone on the faculty. In Pathology, or Endocrine."

That was a little slap. I knew very well who they had in Endocrine. When I first moved to town every doc told me Saint George's had nobody worth anything in Endocrine. The local docs had been pushing von Dernhoffer for years to build that section of the department but he just made noises about the general excellence of the Department of Medicine and never hired anyone. The truth was, one of von Dernhoffer's old cronies, an octogenarian named Pffiefer, was the endocrinologist in residence, chief of the Section of Endocrinology and its only member. Whenever anyone in the hospital needed an endocrine consult they had to ask Pffiefer, so Pffiefer had a captive practice, and a very lucrative little fiefdom it was. But Pffiefer could probably smell lawsuit all over this case and didn't want any part of it.

"I thought," said the Chairman in his most untouchable tone, "it might be best to have someone who has a little more independence from the institution." Then he added, with a little smile, "Someone with your credentials."

That last line was supposed to melt my heart instantly. I had credentials. That was supposed to be like telling a starlet she had talent.

"The patient's been dead a week," I said. "How am I supposed to figure out what your own faculty couldn't figure out when they had the case fresh?"

9

"You've been quite vocal, in the past, about certain . . ." von Dernhoffer searched for the word ". . . shortcomings, in the clinical approach of one or another of the staff. This ought to be a fine opportunity to demonstrate the value of a systematic, rigorous approach, by a well-trained practitioner."

He was almost enjoying himself now. He had me in a nice spot. Either way, he'd come out smiling: if I solved his case for him, it would look good for his department. If I stumbled around and sank in the mire, he'd have shown me I wasn't such a boy wonder after all, and anyone can miss a diagnosis once in a while. The smirk was creeping across his face and I was asking myself why I was being so polite. The worst he could do was throw me out of his department, and I'd have to go looking for another teaching hospital where I could admit my problem patients.

"Your own faculty endocrinologist's begged off the case," I said. "And he probably knew more about it when he turned his back than I do now."

Von Dernhoffer's face was unreadable, but the Chief Resident's forehead was popping out in little beads of sweat.

"Of course," said the Chairman, "if you feel this case is beyond your capabilities and training," and he looked at the Chief Res, his pipeline back to all the interns and residents on all the medical wards, "we wouldn't want to put you in a position where you felt overmatched."

Then there was that smile again. He was serving me up a powder keg and daring me to swing. I'd been less than humble reviewing foul-ups in his domain before, and now he was smiling.

The smart thing to do was to plead a busy practice, to say how flattered I was that he should value my opinion, but how I just couldn't do justice to this wonderful case right now. The Chief Res could tell the story to the house staff any way he wanted. That being the obviously smart thing to do, I said, "I'll see what I can do."

It was the kind of case I never could walk away from, with everyone else so eager to avoid it. And what else did I have to do? It wasn't like my practice was overwhelming me. It had

10

some interesting possibilities. It would probably turn out to be something simple, but it had possibilities.

Von Dernhoffer smiled his sly little smile and winked at his Chief Res and turned me towards the door.

"I'll need a letter from you," I said, "stating that I'm investigating this case, as your personal agent, and how you'd appreciate whoever I show it to doing whatever I damn well want them to do."

"Whatever you need," he said, grinning. "I want you to have a free hand," he said. Then to Fred: "You'll tell Sally to type up the letter. Dr. Benjamin Abrams will run this case just the way he thinks things ought to be run. He is entirely in charge."

The Chief Res smiled. Dr. Benjamin Abrams would have nobody to blame but himself.

"It's going to be a little tough, starting a week after he died," I said.

"Oh, I'm sure you'll overcome adversity. You'll have everyone's cooperation."

He didn't say, "We're all rooting for you," for which I was grateful. I was annoyed enough as it was. Annoyed at him, and annoyed at myself for not having the good sense to get out of this.

3

When we reached the outer office, the Chief Res drew me aside and spoke in a low voice. He said, "Dr. von D.'s all bent out of shape over this." He handed me the newspaper and the patient's medical chart and he told the secretary to type up my letter. I sat down and read while he dictated and the secretary typed.

## NO CAUSE FOUND FOR DEATH
## OF FORMER VIET GENERAL

BY STEPHANIE SHAW

Nguyen Duc Dhieu, former commander of the elite South Vietnamese Ranger Unit and once third in line in the Saigon government, died here Friday August 19 after a brief illness.

A spokesman for St. George's Hospital said the General had developed a fever and cough several days prior to his admission for pneumonia. He was found dead in bed Friday evening. An autopsy was done but results have not been released. Informed sources say preliminary findings revealed a low blood sugar "incompatible with life" suggestive of a medication error. The hospital spokesman refused to speculate on the cause of death until an investigation has been completed.

General Dhieu fell from power in the last weeks of the war, when he was accused of complicity with the enemy. He was charged with having connections with the Viet Cong, the guerilla wing of the North Vietnamese Communist Government.

He was forced to flee without the benefit of official Government evacuation priority designation, and he escaped Saigon in the waning days of the war with his wife and children aboard a small boat, surviving storms at sea, attacks by pirates, and a variety of adversities before making his way to this country and receiving asylum.

He settled in Arlington's Little Saigon, across the river from Washington, the city he had visited as a top official many times during the war. He owned a dry cleaning store and a laundromat.

Now Dr. von Dernhoffer's little case had all my attention. The newspaper article was a lot closer to the truth as I knew it than newspaper articles about medical subjects usually get. The reporter had even managed to get a few facts straight: the patient died with a blood sugar which might be incompatible with life. (Some pathology resident had talked to the press. I wondered how that had happened.) The patient had died shortly after admission, which made it a Medical Examiner's case, if the Medical Examiner was interested. But the Medical Examiner wasn't interested, and I could only guess why that might be. Anyway, that left the investigation up to the hospital, to von Dernhoffer, and he was falling all over himself to unload it on me.

What wasn't clear was how sick the General had been when he was admitted, whether or not anything happened to suggest his illness was a lot worse than first suspected, and whether or not he could have died from his pneumonia or from the heart disease the reporter apparently didn't know about.

There were a few more questions the medical chart would answer: Was there any reason he might have been more sensitive to his usual dose of insulin, so the same dose would provoke a more intense response and send his sugar plummeting? That can happen in renal failure. Was the sugar low when he was first admitted, or did it suddenly drop from a relatively stable normal level? If things had changed suddenly, it was more likely the sugar was the culprit, but if he were a brittle diabetic and used to sudden swings in his sugar levels the low sugar might not have anything to do with his death.

The secretary handed me the letter and I tucked the chart under my arm and went off to find a lift to the car park.

I thought about all the people I had to talk to and tried to visualize my schedule for what was left of this week and for the next week coming up. I had to be at one moonlighting job or another every afternoon, as far as I could recall, and that left mornings for snooping around the hospital. Mornings were when I usually saw patients at the office. Mrs. Bromley would know when I didn't have any patients scheduled. Von Dernhoffer wanted quick action, but then again, he wasn't paying my salary.

And I thought about General Dhieu having survived battle, storms at sea and all the picturesque things the reporter mentioned, only to meet his fate between the clean sheets of a Saint George's hospital bed, and I wondered why. I hadn't spent long in Vietnam, but I'd heard of Dhieu. I'd heard he was tough for an ARVN and comparatively efficient, as their officers went, which wasn't saying much. And I thought about the nurse who gave his insulin and what the little old biddies in nursing administration must be doing to her in their frenzy to keep their own noses clean.

The whole explanation would be something simple, something obvious and easy to clear up, as most hospital incidents usually are, if you take the time to go through the records carefully, and to listen.

But this was a Vietnamese and that thought kept rumbling around my skull in a low unnerving undertone. Nothing that had to do with Vietnam was ever simple or obvious or easy to understand or ended the way you thought it would.

4

I stayed at my office long enough to pick up my mail and the pile of telephone messages and long enough to answer Mrs. Bromley's questions about the CPC.

"So you *did* get it right," she said, very satisfied, triumphant even. Satisfied for me, triumphant for her bullying me into it. "And were the fans ecstatic with your performance? Standing ovation?"

"The Chairman of Medicine was most impressed."

"But what about the private doctors? Will they send you patients with whatever it was this patient had, since you are now a world authority?"

"I hope they don't. I truly do."

"But why? Don't you like . . . what was it? That tumour that produces insulin – insulinoma?"

"Insulinomas are cute enough," I said, "but nobody sends you insulinomas. They send you hypoglycemics."

"And what's wrong with hypoglycemics?"

"Hypoglycemics are people who think they have low blood

14

sugar," I said. "Your average patient with hypoglycemia has read every *Cosmopolitan, Mademoiselle* and *Redbook* article on the subject and can attest that she has all seventy symptoms listed in those unassailable sources. Furthermore, she has previously seen four doctors and has had five glucose tolerance tests."

Mrs. Bromley was enjoying all this immensely. She was sitting at her desk, sipping tea and smiling.

"And she will tell you that she has altered her diet dramatically, but still gets hypoglycemia and is about to lose her job, husband and mind from the sudden drops in her blood sugar, which kill ten thousand brain cells every time."

"How do you know how many brain cells are killed?" she asked.

"That's just the point," I said. "You can't possibly know. There's no way to count dead brain cells in a living patient, or even in a dead one. But the hypoglycemic knows. She's read all about it in *Redbook*."

"I see. And are they always women?"

"Almost always. And last, but certainly not least, she will accept no other explanation for her symptoms, like, heaven forbid, there is nothing wrong with her, save acute and chronic neurosis, *mishuginosis* and *gornisht mit gornisht*."

"So they are not satisfactory patients?"

"They are a thorn in the flesh. If anyone calls and says she wants an appointment to see Dr. Abrams about her hypoglycemia, Dr. Abrams is out of town, out of business, died last week, whatever you like, but I'm not available."

Mrs. Bromley said, "I understand." And she gave me one of her looks.

"I know things are slow. I'm not turning patients away," I pleaded. "I answer all my calls. But at hypoglycemics, I draw the line."

"So you got no consults from your triumph?"

"Not exactly," I said. "The Chairman liked my talk so much he gave me a little case to work on."

"Well," said Mrs. Bromley, interested, happy and triumphant again. "That sounds interesting. So some good did come of it."

"That," I said, "remains to be seen."

"What did he have for you?"

"A dead patient."

"What can you do for *him*?"

"Very little," I said. "But I might soothe some feelings of the hospital staff, if it turns out not to be their fault the patient got that way."

"And what has all this to do with hypoglycemia?"

"The patient's blood sugar, at autopsy, achieved a world class lowness. The Chairman wants to know if that had anything to do with his dying."

"People *die* from hypoglycemia? I thought they just got neurotic and shed a few brain cells."

"The brain lives on oxygen and sugar. It can't make either. It can be most unforgiving if deprived for long."

"And how does it express its displeasure?"

"By throwing a seizure – a grand mal epileptic fit. Or by dying, if the seizure goes on too long."

"Not at all good," said Mrs. Bromley, sipping her tea at me. "And how do you go about discovering what happened to this unfortunate patient of the Chairman's?"

"By talking to people, by reading the patient's chart, and then by talking to people again."

"And when do you have time to talk to people? I presume this cannot be done over the phone?"

"No, I have to be at the hospital. I was hoping to start this afternoon, if I can get out of clinic on time. I could make it back to Saint George's before everyone goes home."

"You mean, before five o'clock?"

"Yes," I said sheepishly.

"Fat chance of that," she said. "You've not got out of that worthless clinic before five-thirty since you started working there. And they only pay you till three-thirty."

"How's tomorrow look?"

She looked at the schedule book. "Afternoon's out of the question, of course. You've got your downtown clinic. At least they pay you for your time at that one. . . . Morning . . . " she looked at the schedule, and shook her head, "morning's hopeless. Patients from nine to noon."

"Monday?"

"Monday morning's clear," she said. "They *paying* you for this?"

"Not in dollars."

"In what, then?"

"In the only currency a doctor really needs: gratitude."

Mrs. Bromley laughed. She really was amused. "And that's the only currency you'd ever collect, if I left you to your own devices." Then she looked at the schedule book again. "I don't suppose you could do your snooping around at night?"

"No, I've got to talk to people who work nine to five."

"I thought hospital people worked all hours. A city that never sleeps."

"I've got to talk to administrators."

"Oh, that *is* different," she said. "Too bad."

"Why?"

"If you snooped at night, I could tag along."

"You'd be bored to tears."

"Oh, I doubt that. Not with a dead general and the question of foul play."

"I didn't say anything about a general."

"Didn't have to. Crikey, it's in the paper. Cause of death unknown. Low blood sugar. At Saint George's. Who else could it be?"

"You're always ahead of me," I said. "Maybe I should just stay here and answer phones, and send you over to Saint George's."

She liked that idea, but I left too quickly for her to seal the deal. I ran out the door and down to my car. The sooner I got to the clinic, the sooner I could leave. But Mrs. Bromley was right about my chances of getting out early enough to make it back to Saint George's. This was my inner-city clinic, the Martin Luther King, Jr., Clinic, and I was lucky to get out of that one before six. In fact, that particular Thursday I was there until six-thirty and had a raging headache by the time I left. I was in no shape to poke around Saint George's asking questions about a dead ex-general, even if there had been anyone there to answer them.

17

# 5

After my bath my headache was better and I settled down in my rocker, poured myself a Drambuie, turned the stereo to the golden oldies radio station, WXTR, and opened General Dhieu's chart. First, I went to the nurses' notes.

The nurse who gave the General his insulin had signed off the dose as ten units, as prescribed, at seven A.M. Her sign-off note at three-thirty was the standard nursey stuff: patient did ADL (activities of daily living) for himself; then she noted the blood pressure, pulse, temperature; patient offered no complaints.

The next note was from the evening shift nurse. The handwriting was more hectic. The patient got his dinner tray at five o'clock, and the nurse, checking at five-thirty, found him slumped behind the tray, food untouched, pulseless, blood pressureless, ashen and quite dead.

The doctor's notes didn't add much. They had tried to resuscitate him for forty minutes, drugs used, EKGs obtained, all the usual.

The medical student's admission note described him as a "merchant," and never mentioned Vietnam or the fact that he was a general or on which side he fought. That medical student was just a year or so into college when the war ended. It probably didn't mean much to him.

The intern's admission note mentioned the General had a scar on his abdomen from "prior surgery." The General wasn't too clear on what kind of surgery. If it was trauma, they might have relieved him of his spleen. Spleens come in handy when you get pneumonia. Spleenless people sometimes die from little old run-of-the-mill pneumococcal pneumonia, whereas most patients get by with a sprinkling of penicillin. That was interesting, but not conclusive. Apart from that, it was all pretty standard.

His pneumonia was right middle lobe, and he wasn't especially sick – normal blood pressure, one temp of 102, Thursday night. No renal failure. No reason he should be especially sensitive to his insulin.

He had had all the usual Vietnamese diseases: malaria, for which he took a little quinine whenever he got a recrudescence, tuberculosis, the usual things. Lots of notes the day he was admitted, fewer thereafter. Nothing unusual. Nothing jumped out at me.

I sat there sipping Drambuie and flipping the pages of the General's chart, listening to the stereo. They were playing "Woodstock" on XTR, the Joni Mitchell version. They usually give the year the song came out, but they didn't this time. They didn't have to. Nineteen sixty-nine. They had played that song all the way over to Vietnam on board the *Yakatak*. The corpsman had the album. And someone had it at Walter Reed, when I was being put back together. I liked one line, and I listened for it: "And I feel to be a cog in something turning." Sitting there with the General's chart on my lap, in a suburb of Washington, D.C., I got that same old feeling, hearing that line. Don't ask me why.

## 6

Friday morning there were actually three patients scheduled for the office.

"Banner day," said Mrs. Bromley. "Things are picking up, or heating up, I should say." It was not immediately obvious what she meant, but I didn't stop to ask with the first patients sitting there staring at me.

There were two people in the waiting room, both looking

me over, and I knew only one, so I guessed the other, a young woman in a blue suit, was a new patient.

I took the lady I recognized back to my office. She was the nice wife of a foreign service officer, and she had been found more or less dead on the floor at Saint George's emergency room, the result of a little thyrotoxicosis which put her heart into overdrive. I had fixed her thyroid with a blast of radio-active iodine.

The next patient had arrived when I was with the first. When I went out to the waiting room he stood up to shake my hand and I noticed the young woman in the blue suit still sitting in her chair, staring at me. I really had very little to do for the patient, just adjust his blood pressure medication and listen to his jokes. He was a professor at American University. He said, "You know what Henry Kissinger says about why faculty politics are so vicious? There's so little at stake." I took him back out to the waiting room.

The same woman was still there, still looking me over. I thought she had to be my next patient, but she was not. My next patient was Mrs. Simpson. Mrs. Simpson was five feet tall and weighed two hundred pounds and wanted very badly to have a thyroid problem so I could give her pills and make the fat melt painlessly away. But she did not have a thyroid problem, and the pounds did not melt, nor did they go painlessly. Twenty minutes with Mrs. Simpson was a week in a hair shirt in a hot August. I took her out to the waiting room and the same woman was still there, eyes raised expectantly, as if I should know her.

She had to be a drug salesman. She wore that blue suit and she looked eager. I retreated to my office, swung into my swivel chair and thought about ways I could get past the drug salesman and get downstairs to the coffee shop for lemonade and oatmeal cookies. I owed myself that lemonade for seeing Mrs. Simpson and the oatmeal cookies for having been civil to her. I was thinking about this when Mrs. Bromley appeared in front of my desk.

"Oh, no you don't," she said. "You were plotting your escape. Cookies and lemonade, I'll wager. Not so fast. You've one more yet."

"One more?" I whined. "Can't be. You said three."

"I told you things were heating up."

"What's heating?"

"Your good press. I told you that CPC would be good press, and here it is, in the flesh."

She handed me a business card: Stephanie Shaw, reporter, Washington's Big Time Newspaper. "She called early. Phone was ringing when I got in. Said she had to talk to you, *would* you call? I said you were not reliable in that respect and she'd better come by. Here she is."

"What's she want with me?"

"Not sure, really. She's been pumping me while I've been trying to pump her and neither of us has got very far. You've been appointed to some commission, I gather. I think it's about the dead general."

Stephanie Shaw was dressed for success in her navy blue suit and white shirt and a bow tie. She wore too much makeup and carried a hand-held tape recorder. She had written the article about General Dhieu's death. Someone in the Chairman's office had told her I was in charge of the commission investigating the affair. She wanted to know what I knew. She kept emphasizing that she was a newspaper reporter as if I was supposed to stand up on both hind legs and bark. I suppose she got that reaction a lot in this town. She asked me again what I knew.

"Nothing solid," I said. "When I know for sure, I'll write it down for you."

"You can call me."

"And I'll put it in my report to Dr. von Dernhoffer and you can ask him for a copy."

She didn't like that.

"Who else is on the commission?"

"What commission?"

"That's investigating General Dhieu's death."

"Damned if I know."

She liked that even less. Her pale skin was flushing right through her makeup.

"Look," I said, "when I know something with enough certainty to stand behind it, I'll put it on the record, in my report. Until then you're just wasting your time trying to get me to tell you what I don't know."

"Just let me ask," she said, "is it usual for a patient with pneumonia to die within forty-eight hours of his admission to the hospital?"

"That depends," I said.

She waited for me to continue, but I just stared at her. She finally gave in and said, "On what?"

"On how sick he was. On complicating conditions. On a lot of variables."

"Did General Dhieu have complicating conditions?"

"That's confidential medical information. I can't discuss it."

"Is a blood sugar of twenty-four normal in a patient who dies suddenly?"

"A blood sugar of twenty-four is not normal in any patient, as you well know, or you wouldn't have asked the question. Now if you're asking whether or not the blood sugar was explicable, or whether it contributed to his death, those are other questions."

"*Can* you explain it? Did it kill him?"

"When I know, it'll be in my report. But now at least you'll know what to look for."

"Have you ruled out foul play?"

"I haven't ruled out anything. All I know is the patient is dead and they've asked me to look into it."

"What qualifications do you have to do this investigation?" she asked. She was trying to get aggressive. It wasn't really a question.

"Why don't you ask the man who appointed me?"

"Are you board certified in internal medicine?"

That, I surmised, was supposed to make me roll over with all four paws in the air. Reporters had learned there were ways to intimidate doctors, and they had learned to ask about board certification, although I'd never met one who had any idea what passing the old boy's club exam really meant. My certificate was about six feet from her head on the wall, but I said, "Ask the man who appointed me." I stood up and watched her fumble with her tape recorder. Then she stood up and left.

22

Mrs. Bromley appeared in my doorway, moments later. "How exciting. Am I going to be your press secretary? When does Dan Rather arrive?"

"I think we may have to wait another week for fame to come knocking at our door."

"Oh, no. You're going to be a celebrity."

"Did Miss Shaw tell you that?"

"No, she asked me one or two more questions on her way out, which I tried not to answer."

"Good," I said. "Then you have the concept of how to deal with a free but commercial press."


# 7


Saturday morning I discovered what had been bothering Miss Shaw.

### WIDOW SAYS COMMUNISTS KILLED DHIEU IN HOSPITAL BED

#### BY STEPHANIE SHAW

He was once the third most powerful man in the South Vietnamese Government. He survived a direct hit on his helicopter, thirty parachute jumps, assassination attempts with hand grenades and machetes, but Nguyen Duc Dhieu may have finally been reached and killed as he lay in a hospital bed in Washington, D.C., the city he had often visited during his years in power, the city which offered him safe haven after the war.

Speaking through her attorney, Mrs. Dhieu claimed that evidence has surfaced suggesting her husband did not die of natural causes, and that he may have been killed by a fatal injection of insulin.

Dr. Ludwig von Dernhoffer, Chairman of the Department of Medicine at St. George's Hospital, where Dhieu died Friday, said yesterday that he has appointed a local expert in insulin and hypoglycemia to investigate the cause of death. The chief investigator, Dr. Benjamin Abrams, Clinical Assistant Professor of Medicine, has published research in this field. Dr. Abrams would not comment on charges that the General may not have died of natural causes.

That's where I stopped reading.

Mrs. Bromley was right: things were heating up. I could only guess how they had heated up. Maybe the reporter called the pathology resident who did the autopsy and found out about the sugar and asked the widow if she had heard about the sugar. Or maybe the pathology resident had called the reporter. Or maybe the General's private doctor told the widow as soon as von Dernhoffer told him.

If I were a private doc, I would have done that. Try to be above-board. If there was a mistake and too much insulin was given, better to come right out with it and throw yourself on your patient's wife's mercy, and hope she likes you enough not to call her lawyer. Or maybe the old lady was just paranoid enough after all those years in Vietnam to ask a few questions on her own when her husband died unexpectedly.

It didn't much matter to me. I'd read the chart and narrowed the possibilities: either the General got more than his normal dose of insulin or there was a mistake on that sugar. Nothing else worked. He wasn't sick enough to die from his pneumonia. His diabetes was well controlled. His angina was stable, and although his heart could simply have crumped out like anyone's with bad coronary arteries and the new stress of pneumonia, it didn't fit the picture. His pneumonia hadn't put him under that much stress. They put him in the hospital to rehydrate him with some IVs and something dramatic happened.

I pulled on my sweatpants and my T-shirt and my jogging shoes and went out for a run.

Of course, the fact that he had an intravenous line was a

little worrisome, if you want to consider the widow's contention. With an IV in his arm anyone with a syringe full of insulin and the knowledge of how to inject it into the IV line and a lack of fondness for the General could have sneaked into his unguarded room and pushed a hundred units of regular insulin into his IV line and the General would never have felt a pinch. If he were asleep, anything could go through that line and anything could be put into it without waking him.

I turned around at the entrance to the David Taylor Naval Research and Development Station at the big sign that says U.S. GOVERNMENT PROPERTY. NO TRESPASSING. That sign is one and four-tenths miles from my house, and I run a loop which turns there and then takes me back down to Trav's Tavern at Glen Echo. I turned around there and headed home to my shower, thinking about the General.

Running cleared my head, and helped me see things in terms of the cold undramatized facts. The problem with the IV scenario was that it didn't fit the facts, at least as I could discern them from the chart. The fact is, the General was admitted on a Thursday morning, and an IV was inserted. The order discontinuing the IV was written Thursday evening, and the nurses signed it off Thursday evening, so presumably the IV was pulled then. The General didn't die until the next evening, a full day after the IV was pulled. Even if someone had slipped him delayed action insulin, he would have been feeling the effects by Friday morning and certainly he would have been complaining or showing signs of trouble by Friday afternoon. But he had blood drawn that morning, and he'd been seen at rounds by house staff, and he'd been checked by two shifts of nurses and nobody had noted anything wrong.

Most of the questions would settle themselves Monday when I talked to the nurses and I heard the stories directly. Doctors and nurses write notes in medical charts because it's required, but they're too busy to care much about what they put down. The answers would come Monday.

Of course, I knew I couldn't put General Dhieu out of mind until then. After my shower, I read Stephanie Shaw's article again. Then I phoned the newspaper and asked for their library. I wanted to read some back issues.

"Our library is not open to the public," said the librarian.

"That's what I like about newspapers," I said. "Unwavering concern for the public's right to know."

"That's what the public libraries are for," said the librarian. "They've got back issues on microfilm."

The librarian at the public library said it was all true, and an hour later I was seated in front of one of the six microfilm viewers of the Bethesda Public Library, watching years zip by. Not only did they have ten years of newspaper articles microfilmed, they had an index, which did not list the General by name but which did have entries under "Refugees, Vietnam."

I was immediately distracted by the early headlines, from 1975. These were all glowing and Christmas-warm: FLEEING VIETNAMESE WELCOMED TO NEW HOMES IN AMERICA. Then came the items about Texas and Louisiana fishermen Ku Klux Klaning Vietnamese immigrants who had the temerity to want to do some shrimping in the gulf and compete with the good white Christian Americans there who had a hard enough time feeding their families without a lot of competition from immigrants. Then an article about a benefit at the Kennedy Center attended by Ted Kennedy and a galaxy of Washington glitterati, all for the resettlement programme. And there was a very catty article about Mrs. Henry Kissinger attending a local resettlement meeting. She said she thought she might be able to answer phone calls at the resettlement centre, but the Kissingers would not be taking in a Vietnamese family. The Kissingers' house in Georgetown was "rather small," she was quoted as saying. "There's not enough room." They had sharpened their claws at the local desk that day.

Then I noticed a headline in the index about a general who had been deported from Paris and was resettling in the Washington area. I got that microfilm from the floor-to-ceiling microfilm file and popped it into the viewer. It was General Dhieu, all right. Stephanie Shaw would have done better to spend a little more time in the library. There was more to the General than his fall from power and his harrowing escape. He had been chief of the "notorious" (that was the newspaper's word) South Vietnamese Central Intelligence Organization, which apparently extracted information in some unappetizing ways. He had been accused of selling government positions – provincial chief, battalion commander – to friends, and there was mention of sales of heroin on the black market and an especially disagreeable item about his selling Army munitions to the Viet Cong. Evidently, the General had been something of a wheeler-dealer. What really impressed me was that the French deported him. That had to be a distinction in itself – to be so obnoxious even the French won't tolerate you. U.S. government sources admitted that CIA officials had arranged for his rapid entry into the United States.

The index had no more listings about former South Vietnamese generals for that year, except one, but he wasn't my general. This was a brigadier, who was now a maitre d' at a local Georgetown restaurant. The next year's index had one more article on General Dhieu. It said he had resettled in Arlington's Mekong Delta, and opened a dry cleaning store in Little Saigon. There had been threats on his life, but he had refused to change his name. "I have done nothing to be ashamed of," he was quoted as saying. "I am not a Nazi."

I had heard of Little Saigon, and knew it was across Key Bridge from Georgetown, but I'd never been there. I didn't eat in Vietnamese restaurants, either. I had never read a novel about the war, never gone to a veterans meeting, never seen *Apocalypse Now*. Since I got back, I hadn't even eaten rice. Not out of any antipathy, you understand – it was just that I'd put it all behind. I was having enough trouble looking ahead without looking back.

Now, however, it was time for a visit to Little Saigon. I had to see the General's store. It was up the hill from all the glassy new buildings in Rosslyn, on the Virginia side of the river.

Driving down Wilson Boulevard was a strange and dis-orienting trip. All along the road were stores with the familiar Viet names on their signs, with Viet faces in the doors and along the sidewalks, but the stores were former Woolworths and Elk Lodges, and all this within spitting distance of the

Arlington Cemetery, just mortar distance from the Watergate, the Kennedy Center, and the Mall across the river.

I parked near the Mekong Center, a block of store fronts with names printed in English and Vietnamese: Saigon Department Store, Dat Hung Jewellers, Pleiku Imports, Quangtri Market, Vietnam Custom Laundry. That was my mark. That was the name in the newspaper article. Stephanie Shaw called it a dry cleaning store, and it might have done some of that, too. There was a young girl, maybe fifteen, it was always hard to judge, behind the counter, might have been Dhieu's daughter. She was talking on the phone in rapid, animated Vietnamese, to a girlfriend, I thought. She wasn't coy enough to be talking to a boy. She put whoever it was on hold and asked me in accentless English, "May I help you?" I bought some spot remover and left.

I don't know what I hoped to learn by going to General Dhieu's store. The girl had spun me around, put me into a tailspin. The whole street had. Funny, the little details you forget. They seem so important when you get reexposed: the nasal quality of the language, the smallness of their bodies. I'd felt like an ungainly giant the whole time I was over there. And I got that same awkward feeling again in the General's store, with his daughter, or whoever she was.

And there was the wary look in her eye – maybe I was imagining that, maybe not. But she was old enough to remember Americans, to have learned how careful you had to be with them.

I walked into the Saigon Department Store. It was humid in there, and cluttered and bare, and I was the only non-Asian. I don't know why it was so humid, but the air was the trigger, spinning me back, as if I'd stepped through some door in time. I was so light-headed I had to sit down. There was a rattan chair. An old woman watched me without looking directly at me, from behind a sales counter.

My clothes were soaked with a sudden sweat, and breath came hard, and I put my head between my knees until it all passed.

No one bothered me.

I lifted my head and tried to focus. The clerks had melted

28

away and the store appeared empty, except for an American customer, a blonde woman, looking at a silk vest, fingering it carefully. I stood slowly, finding my balance, and walked towards the bright daylit door, and out onto the pavement, and back to my car.

In the car park, two Vietnamese men stood talking and smoking. They were old enough to have been soldiers in the war. They were smiling. One had a peculiar bronze-grey cast to his skin, like a patient with hemochromatosis. They noticed me looking at them and I saw or thought I saw in their eyes the same look I'd seen in dark eyes in Saigon when American soldiers stumbled out of a bar with hands all over some Saigon Sally, lurching and singing, and headed for an upstairs room on some side street.

I walked to my car and watched those two watch me while I started it up. Then I drove down Edgewood Street to Wilson Boulevard, down to Key Bridge and across the river to Washington, checking my rearview mirror only a dozen times.

# 8

I'm usually late to the office Monday mornings, which might create problems if there were ever any patients waiting. This Monday, I was keen to get to Saint George's and start on General Dhieu's case, so of course there actually was a patient waiting, and Mrs. Bromley looked meaningfully at her watch when I came through the door.

"Don't tell me." I said, "We have a bona fide patient, and I'm late."

"This time, however, you really will feel remorse."

"He's left?"

"No, but it would have been your loss if she had. Lovely young thing. Looking at your walls right now."

29

"When did she make the appointment?"

"Called bright and early, just as I arrived. Doesn't surprise me a bit," said Mrs. Bromley. "I shouldn't be surprised to have the phone ringing off the hook, now that you're famous."

"Oh? You saw Saturday's paper, then."

"Didn't everyone? The phone will start ringing now."

"You've lived in Washington too long, Mrs. Bromley," I said. "You're starting to believe in fame."

"Oh, I don't believe in its intrinsic worth," she said. "But I respect its value."

She handed me the chart she had already prepared, with the entry form all filled out by the patient, and I said, "I've got to get to Saint George's. Buzz me in twenty minutes on the intercom and tell me I've got to move on, another patient, emergency, anything. Just get me out of the office."

"You're not going to want to hurry through this one," she said. "But as you wish, professor."

I took the chart and hurried down the hall without reading it.

The lovely young thing was standing looking at the photo of the Viet peasant behind my desk and she turned when I came through the door. Obviously she hadn't come because of weight problems, hirsutism, acne or anything cosmetic. She had absolutely no cosmetic problems. Her skin had never known a pimple. Her hair was shiny dark and prematurely grey-streaked. She smiled a dimpled pretty smile and looked very spare and fresh. It was a look I've always liked: too prim and untouched to be true. She wore shades of light grey, to complement her eyes, and it worked well. Her neck was thin enough to show a goiter, if she'd had one, and her eyes were not at all proptotic, although they were large and alert. Her voice was low but not hoarse and I decided she wasn't a thyroid case. She said, "Dr. Abrams, I presume," and shook my hand. Her grip was warm and firm.

"Sorry to keep you," I said, meaning it.

"That's okay, I like Borodin."

We had Prince Igor playing on the office system, and I was impressed she hadn't called it "Stranger in Paradise."

She sat down with wonderful grace and it hit me suddenly that she was a ballet dancer. Probably hadn't menstruated

30

for a year. That's why she was here. The dancer's carriage is unmistakable. Then I opened the chart Mrs. Bromley had given me and saw *hypoglycemia* on the entry form and felt very sad.

"I like your cartoon," she said, nodding to the Mankoff from *The New Yorker* I had framed on the wall: a field crowded with prosperous men in three-piece suits and women in evening dresses holding martinis spread out under a banner, WOODSTOCK REUNION. She laughed an ironic, biting laugh. "That's really perfect." Then the sharpness drained away and she smiled and said, "This is probably nothing. But I asked my gynaecologist if he thought it could be hypoglycemia and he couldn't be sure it wasn't."

"Who's your gynaecologist?"

"Jerry Finney," she said. "Jerry thinks I'm a neurotic female," she laughed. "But then again he thinks all females are neurotic. He's probably right about me."

There was hope then. At least she had the basic concept of hypoglycemia. With great reluctance I asked what specifically made her think she had hypoglycemia. She told me about waking up at night with nightmares and sweats and running to the refrigerator.

"At first I thought: It's just a hangover. But there was never a hangover like that. The headache maybe, but the heart going wild, the panic – that was no hangover. I've had enough to know."

It turned out the night all this happened she had gone to bed drunk, so all bets were off.

"I guess I really tied one on at Mr. Smith's."

"Who's Mr. Smith?"

"Not who, what. It's a bar. And a restaurant, in George-town. Went to bed that night pretty wasted. Didn't even get undressed. I woke up after a dream.

"Couldn't remember the dream," she said. "Just knew it was truly horrific. And the craving. Christ, I ran right to the kitchen, drank a gallon of orange juice and ate everything that wasn't tied down. You'd have thought I was a starving Biafran. Scared hell out of me. That kind of fright used to send me to confession and get me fifty Hail Marys."

31

She paused and her eyes went opaque. "I don't go to confession any more," she said. "I called my gynaecologist. Asked him for somebody who'd know about hypoglycemia."

I questioned her closely about morning headaches and whether she got her symptoms after a prolonged fast. She waffled. She never fasted longer than overnight and she thought she got her symptoms mostly during the day, usually after eating.

"But I eat all the time," she said, "so I guess it's hard to say."

I asked if she'd gained weight.

"Yes," she said. "Is that significant? It's really remarkable. I never gain weight. But the last two months I've gained five pounds. Made my roommate so happy."

"Why's that?"

"She's got a weight problem. I eat all the time and never gain a pound. Drives her crazy. Try not to eat in front of her, but she buys the groceries, and she knows where the food goes. She's always cooking me meals and just dies seeing me eat and never put on weight. But, as I said, lately I have. Why's that important?"

"I didn't say it was."

"But you asked."

"I'm asking about evidence for increased insulin levels. Insulin levels rise, you tend to eat more and to store more of what you eat."

"You're talking about that tumour that makes insulin?"

I knew she'd read all about it.

"An insulinoma," I said. "If you get hypoglycemic symptoms when you haven't eaten for a long time then we're talking about possible fasting hypoglycemia – the main thing to rule out would be insulinoma."

"How do you do that?"

"Put you in the hospital for a three-day fast. Draw lots of blood sugars and insulin levels."

"Sounds like lots of fun," she said unhappily.

"Before that, we'd have to document a low blood sugar. I'm not going to waste everyone's time without some blood sugar numbers."

She asked how I proposed to do that and I told her she'd have to get blood drawn during an episode when she was having symptoms. She said that'd be a problem, since she usually had her episodes at work.

I looked at the form Mrs. Bromley had had her fill out: under "Employment" it said "Management consultant" and under "Employer (or Department if Federal Employee)" she'd written "Billings Institute."

"What does a management consultant do?"

"Whatever the job requires," she said.

I guess I deserved that.

"Doesn't the Billings Institute have a nurse sitting in an infirmary who can draw a blood sugar?"

"I'll have to ask."

I asked her a few more insulinoma questions and probed a little about her drinking habits. Sounded like she got more than a few of her calories in the form of alcohol. Her past medical history was significant only for an abortion. I asked her what she used for contraception now. "Abstinence," she said.

She smiled when she said that, but it didn't look like a cheerful smile and I decided not to risk pushing her on the topic. I didn't think that tough-cookie exterior would hold together if I pressed her on the abortion, and it didn't seem crucial to her hypoglycemia, at the time.

Then I did a review of systems, which I hate slogging through because it's boring and tedious, especially when I'm eager to get to the social history. But you miss things when you get impatient, and besides, Mrs. Bromley had designed and typed up this beautiful history form for me, with all the review of systems questions and little yes/no boxes beside each one, so I went through it. Maureen Banting surprised me: she denied almost everything.

Most women with hypoglycemia have what's derisively known as a very positive review of system. In other words, no matter what symptom you ask about, they've got it, and more, and furthermore, they're sure it's caused by the hypoglycemia. The absence of other complaints made her hypoglycemia symptoms sound more authentic.

Her family history was negative, but she did have five brothers and she laughed and said, "The Pope's got no complaints with our family."

We finally got to the social history, where I usually get the most useful information. She was born and raised in Brooklyn, went to Catholic schools until she packed off for Mount Holyoke.

"Daddy never really understood it wasn't a Catholic girls' college. All he knew is they were giving me a free ride, and the principal at Holy Redeemer called him up to say how pleased he was I'd been admitted."

But she stayed only two years.

"Had this little behaviour problem," she smiled, all dimples. "I liked the boys."

If Daddy had been surprised to learn the college was not Catholic, Maureen was astonished to learn there were no men.

"It never occurred to me to ask. I'd never seen the place before I arrived with my foot locker and there were all these girls in white dresses floating around and *no men*."

She spent a lot of time hitchhiking to Amherst, but she didn't find any men there either.

"Full of boys who gossiped in French and had identity crises."

So she went down the road to U Mass.

"Now *that* was more my idea of college, all these guys back from Vietnam, sitting around coffeehouses, despising Robert McNamara, talking revolution."

Suddenly I wanted her to stay. I could forgive the hypoglycemia. I just wanted to keep her there, talking.

She left Holyoke for Bellvue School of Nursing. Two years later, she was on her way to Vietnam, with a gold bar on her collar.

"What year was that?"

"Seventy-three."

Her abortion was in 1973.

"You were there too," she said, nodding at my Viet peasant on the wall. "Friend of yours?"

"Never really knew."

She smiled. She had very white, straight teeth.

"Where were you?" I asked.

"Saigon, mostly. Binh Thuy, too," she said. "Where were you?"

"Sitting offshore, most of the time."

"Navy?"

"Coast Guard."

"Coast Guard?"

"Guarding the coasts of Vietnam. Making the beaches safe for democracy."

She laughed a pretty, knowing laugh and looked at me for a moment, thinking. "I didn't know there were any Coast Guard over there."

"It was worse than that," I said. "I was in the Public Health Service."

She laughed again. She really had very pretty teeth. "So you thought you'd be safe on some Indian reservation?"

"That was the plan. But the PHS provided the docs for the Coast Guard. And the Coast Guard guarded the coasts."

"When were you there?"

"Sixty-nine."

"So you were out in seventy."

"No, I got out in sixty-nine."

"Short tour," she said. She was examining me now. I liked the way she did that. That was no idle observation. She was demanding an explanation.

"I got time off for good behaviour," I said.

"Good thing they didn't apply a behaviour standard to nurses," she smiled. "I'd still be there."

I thought about that and about her abortion.

Mrs. Bromley buzzed to tell me I was late for my non-existent next patient. I was in no hurry to cut things short with Maureen Banting. But Maureen was already standing up, so I told her I'd be willing to hospitalize her as soon as we got a low blood sugar.

"Then you don't think there's much to all this?"

"I didn't say that."

"Not in so many words," she said. She did not look pleased. "You'd admit me right away if you thought it was anything real."

She hadn't been a nurse for nothing.

"I need some numbers."

"Can't argue with that," she said. "After all, you're the professor."

I thought that was an odd choice of words. Most people would have said, "You're the doctor," or "You're the expert." I could have bet she almost said, "the investigator," and I would also have bet it wasn't Jerry Finney's idea that she come to me. I would have bet she got my name from a better source: Saturday's newspaper.

"But something's happening to me," she said. "And I need someone to find out what."

There was a lot of hypoglycemia in town lately, and it seemed like most of it needed my special attention. In the case of Maureen Banting I could have been easily persuaded to lavish a little special attention. She was one good-looking woman. There was a kind of flash every time she smiled.

She stood up and shook my hand with her solid grip and she looked right into my eye with her grey and white beamers.

"Call me if . . ." I started to say, but she had already left the room.

9

The Head Nurse on Seven North had General Dhieu's nurse waiting outside her office, ready to meet me. Mrs. Bromley had arranged that. The Head Nurse was about forty and friendly enough, considering I was probing a foul-up on her floor. We drank coffee in her office before asking the nurse, Karen Sweeney, to come in.

"We don't really think Karen is likely to have given the wrong dose," said the Head Nurse. "She's worked here three years, and gives insulin all the time."

"How are meds given here?" I asked. "Do you have one nurse who gives out all the meds, or . . ."

"No, it's primary care nursing. Karen gave all the meds to her own patients. She knew Mr. Dhieu and his dose. In fact, it's a unit pharmacy system."

That was a relief. It meant I might be able to identify the bottle of insulin she had used. I asked the Head Nurse.

"That was the first thing we did," she said. "As soon as they came by and told us about the autopsy. Each patient has a drawer in the med cart his nurse uses, and all his meds are kept separately in that drawer."

"Then you had the bottle she got his insulin from?"

"The Director of Nursing has it."

I asked about the nurse, Karen Sweeney, accounting for every year since she got out of Saint George's nursing school. There wasn't much there: she'd graduated three years before, worked on Seven North since then, and had a clean record. She didn't have any brothers killed in Vietnam or any other obvious reason to have it in for General Dhieu.

"I know you have to ask about that," said the Head Nurse, "but I'm kind of getting sick of that kind of speculation."

"You been hearing much of it?"

"Evening news last night. They want to make a Robin Cook novel out of this thing. Nurses knocking off patients. You know the scenario: techno-horror. Hospital with psychotic nurses stalking the halls."

I didn't get much from Karen Sweeney, except some insight into what this kind of incident can do to a nurse. She was twenty-five, a pale-looking brown-haired thing, who would have been pretty except for the dark circles under her eyes. She'd been suspended with pay until the investigation was over. Standard procedure when a possible medication-related death was being investigated. It wasn't much comfort to Karen.

"I live with two other nurses. They go to work in the morning. What do I do? They've told me not to leave town. I don't even want to be in the house when my roommates get back from work," she said. "I mean, I'm under suspicion, aren't I?"

I didn't know what to say.

"How can I be sure?" she said. "I drew up insulin four times that shift, on four different patients. I mean, I'm always careful, but how can I really know? It's so automatic."

"I gather from the chart, General Dhieu wasn't too sick from his pneumonia."

"He had some pretty good rigors the night he came in." said Karen. "But he was holding up pretty well," she said. "He was a pretty tough old bird."

"I didn't see anything about shaking chills in the nurse's notes."

"Didn't Ginny put that in hers?" she asked. Ginny was the night nurse who took care of the General Thursday night and signed off to Karen the next morning. "She told me about it Friday morning at report. He was really shaking the bed. You could hear the rattling all the way down the hall in the med room, Ginny said. He kept telling her it was 'Maria,' Ginny said. She kept telling him, 'No, Mr. Dhieu, it's just pneumonia.' She finally figured out what he was trying to say: malaria."

"I'll have to talk to Ginny," I told the Head Nurse. "None of this was in her note."

"I'm sure it's right," said Karen Sweeney. "I remember because Ginny found him taking his own meds from his own bottle. There wasn't any order or anything. He was taking it on his own, meds from home."

"He was taking something the nurses didn't know about?"

"Quinine," said Karen. "It said so right on the bottle. He brought it from home."

"Do we have that bottle?" I asked the Head Nurse.

"The Director of Nursing has it. The night nurse locked it in Mr. Dhieu's drawer in the med cart. All his meds were impounded."

That was better. The nursing people ran a tight ship. Of course, nobody had thought to write any of this down. They were probably too busy trying to take care of patients. Besides, patients do that kind of thing all the time, take some medicine they brought from home without telling anybody.

I turned back to Karen. "I know it's easy for me to say," I said, "but don't worry. We'll find out what happened and you'll be back at work."

"Do you think it was the insulin? I mean, they said his blood sugar was like twenty or something. When I heard he died I thought he had an MI or something, until I heard about the sugar. I gave him the right dose."

"I don't know yet. But you've satisfied me for now."

"I can't understand the sugar," she said. "Do you think it could have been the insulin? I mean, like a bad batch?"

"I don't know. Whatever it was, I don't think you should blame yourself. Let me work on it. And don't jump to any conclusions."

We all sat there, shifting in our seats for a while, and Karen Sweeney started looking uncomfortable and the Head Nurse asked if I had any other questions.

"Just one," I said. "Do you remember whether or not the patient had an IV the next morning during your shift?"

"An IV?" she asked, confused. "I don't think so. I could be wrong. I just don't remember. Wasn't it in my note?"

"I looked for 'IV infusing well,' " I said. "But I couldn't find that anywhere, except the first day he was in, Thursday."

"I don't think he did. They must have D/C'd it on evenings."

"Wasn't there a note about discontinuing it in the nursing notes?" asked the Head Nurse.

"There was an order to D/C the IV, but nothing to confirm that it'd been done."

"Did the nurse sign off the order?" asked the Head Nurse.

"Yes."

"Then you can assume the IV was discontinued."

"I can't assume anything," I said, trying to say that nicely. It didn't come out nicely enough.

"Who was the nurse who signed off the order?" asked the Head Nurse.

"Just initials: V.S."

"Ginny – Virginia Smith," said Karen Sweeney.

"There were no nurses' notes about the IV after that?" asked the Head Nurse.

"None. But there was no 'IV discontinued' note either. I realize it's a small point, but . . ."

"No point is a small point. We'll have to speak with Ginny and be sure we know whether or not the IV was discontinued."

"I'm almost sure it was," Karen Sweeney blurted, but a look from the Head Nurse cut her off. It wasn't a question of being almost sure.

Karen looked at her hands in her lap.

"Anything else?" asked the Head Nurse.

I told her no.

She turned to Karen and asked her to wait outside.

I watched her stand up and try to smile in my direction. She wasn't having an easy time with the smile. Her heart wasn't in it. She said, "Thank you," to me, for some reason, and her shoulders sagged and she walked out the door.

"Well, what do you think now?" asked the Head Nurse, as soon as we were alone.

"Anyone can make a mistake," I said. "Get distracted. Pull up a few cc's more fluid and give a little more than you realize."

"But she's been doing this for years."

"We'll just have to see what else surfaces. Once we eliminate all the other possibilities we may have to come back to human error. But there's lots of other possibilities."

"Like what?"

"Like a bad batch," I said. "She mentioned that. I'll check the bottle. I'll tell you what I've discounted. He didn't have an insulinoma. The autopsy ruled that out. And he didn't have a blood sugar that liked to play roller coaster. His chart told me that. And he wasn't in renal failure. And ten units was his correct dose. He'd been on that for six weeks. It was in the attending's note."

"Then what?"

"The number of possibilities is finite," I said. "I'll just go through what's left, one by one. And we'll check that 'quinine,' too."

I walked out of the office, leaving the Head Nurse sitting there, looking after me. I looked at Karen Sweeney sitting next to the door, out of uniform in a plaid skirt and round-collared shirt, looking like a schoolgirl waiting outside the principal's office.

"Don't worry," I said. She tried to smile, but she wasn't happy. She thought she might have killed a man.

# 10

My next stop was the lab. The lab tech at the receiving window was reading the paper and I stood there in front of her clearing my throat and making noises, but she wouldn't look up. Finally, I said, "Excuse me," and she glanced up, but went right back to her paper.

"I'm here to see Dr. Potter," I said. Potter was the director of the lab. That didn't seem to impress her. She pointed to a door down the hall and went back to her paper.

Potter was only slightly more receptive. He said, "So you're the guy they roped into this Dhieu assassination thing." He inspected me briefly. He looked like the governor of Mississippi greeting James Meredith. He was short and fat and he breathed noisily, rocking in his desk chair, one paw on his computer terminal, the other wrapped around a coffee mug on his desk.

"Everybody but me seems to know this was an assassination," I said.

"Well, I mean, that's what the lawyers and the newspapers are all screaming," he said, with a rubbery smile.

"When did you start listening to lawyers and newspapers?"

"I don't, of course. But that's what you're going to have to answer to."

"I'll decide who I'll answer to," I said. "Right now, I'm doing the asking. And that begins with the lab."

He didn't push back from his desk more than a few inches, but it looked like he'd jumped a foot. He looked at me from the corners of his eyes. "Lab studies come under the heading of confidential medical information."

I handed him my letter signed by von Dernhoffer. He read it over about five times, chomping on an unlit cigar dredged up from a shirt pocket. Then he rubbed the skin behind his ear and said, "Looks like you've got carte blanche." He handed me back my letter as if it were on fire. "What do you need?"

I told him, not waiting for him to catch his breath as he scribbled it all on his pad with a felt pen. I told him to do insulin levels on the blood he had frozen from the autopsy and I listed a few other tests. He told me the insulin level had to be sent out to a reference lab and would take about nine or ten days.

"Just be sure it's Dhieu's blood that's sent," I said. "And we should ask them to check on the sugar on the sample they run the insulin on. And I'd like you to run his blood again here, for sugar, just to check that twenty-four level."

"We ran the sample four times," he said. "I have no objections to running it a fifth."

"As long as you're checking, run a quinine level on it."

"Quinine?" he said. "He a druggie? I thought he was some kind of big honcho."

Quinine's used to cut drugs like heroin and PCP, and the blood's often positive for quinine long after the other drugs are cleared.

"He may have been taking it for malaria."

"We can check haematology and see if they did thick and thins," he said. "But that's not something we can check on frozen specimens." Thick and thin smears detect malaria. Nobody had ordered one on the General. The autopsy might indicate if there was a chronic malarial infection or it might not. But we could still find out about the blood level of quinine.

He asked if I had any more questions. I said that would be all for now, and I'd get back to him with more later.

"Any time," he said. He was very cordial now, at my service. I think I had him properly intimidated, probably with von Dernhoffer's letter more than anything. I'd heard von

Dernhoffer swung a lot of weight and swung it often, but the letter trick demonstrated just how much. Potter walked around his desk and showed me the door and we stood there smiling at each other and I looked down the hall to the broader expanse of the laboratory. It was all white lab tops, stainless steel and glassware. It looked like a movie set for a spaceship movie. They ought to be able to give me a few answers, I thought.

We shook hands and I walked out, thinking about the things I knew, and the things I didn't know or had to confirm, and the things I had cooking. The key item was the blood insulin level in the blood sample from the autopsy with that vanishingly low blood sugar.

# 11

Mrs. Bromley paged me at eleven-fifteen. She wanted to know if I'd solved the case of General Dhieu yet.

I told her I hadn't. In fact, it was getting more complicated.

"I have faith," she said. "You'll do it."

"That makes me feel worlds better."

"Oh, it's a lovely case for you," she said. "And I've got the feeling this is just the beginning."

"The beginning of what?"

"Your rise to fame and fortune," she said. "Shall I make a note to call this Potter man about the insulin level in ten days?"

I told her I'd appreciate that – she really was very organized, Mrs. Bromley was.

"Can you measure insulin in a man taking insulin by needle?" she asked.

Now that was a very good question.

"Actually, Mrs. Bromley, there are some technical difficulties connected with that."

"Yes, I've been thinking about all this," she said. "After all, if the insulin level is high, you still don't know how it got there. It could be from the insulin the nurse injected, especially if she gave too much, in error, or it could be that someone else gave him a little more later on, or isn't it possible his own pancreas could have contributed some, especially if it had that tumour in it your CPC lady had in her pancreas?"

"First you have to find out whether or not it's high, Mrs. Bromley. Then you worry about how it got there."

"But it *is* a pity he was getting insulin injections, isn't it? If he weren't, and his insulin was high and his sugar low, you'd know he had a tumour, like your other lady."

"Or, as you said before, he got insulin from a needle we didn't know about."

"From someone who didn't like him? As the widow said?"

"Anything's possible."

"How exciting."

"What's even more exciting is that he may have made enough antibodies to insulin we won't even be able to measure his blood level accurately."

"That *would* be a kicker."

"But he'd only been on insulin a few weeks – we ought to be able to measure his levels. And if they're way up there – forty per m.l., say, that level didn't come from ten units the nurse gave him."

"I'll call the lab man in ten days," she said and we hung up.

Mrs. Bromley was right, as usual. It would have been a lot easier if the General wasn't getting insulin injections and his insulin levels measured out high and his sugar low. That's the way it was with that Mrs. Best in the CPC they gave me. But real life is never that neat.

# 12

I stood there by the phone for a moment and went over things one more time. One thing I couldn't shove out of mind was the insulin dose: ten units. Ten units was a low dose, a starter dose. Ten units dropping a sugar to twenty-four in a patient who'd had that dose for six weeks? Not likely. Even if Karen Sweeney had drawn up fifteen units, it didn't seem likely.

I walked to the lift, pushed the button and thought about the insulin, and was still thinking about it when the lift arrived and I stepped on. I was absorbed enough not to notice my fellow passenger for a few moments, and ordinarily I would have noticed her immediately and have had a hard time being subtle about it. She was holding an Igloo ice chest and she was a pretty cool number herself. Long black hair, fine-boned, you could see the delicate facial bones beneath the skin. She was definitely Vietnamese.

Look at me, months, *years* trying hard not to think of anything Vietnamese – now they hand me the case of General Dhieu, I pay a visit to Little Saigon, and every Oriental is automatically Vietnamese. But she had that exquisite angularity in her face – she had to be. She looked at me straight on for a moment, without fear or coyness or even much interest; then she watched the numbers change as the floors went by and she stepped off on the second floor. I watched her hips shifting under her knit dress as she walked away. It was a very fetching little dress: striped red, white and blue. She looked like an undulating flag, but with a lot more there to hold the eye.

I rode the lift up to the sixth floor, where the Director of Nursing had her office. I was still thinking about that Vietnamese beauty from the lift. Were there suddenly a lot of Vietnamese in town, or was I just noticing now? Were there suddenly a lot of stunning women around, or had I been sensitized by Maureen Banting? I was looking again. It was like a second puberty. All the wiring was there – someone had to turn on the current. And someone had.

I rode the crest of that surging hormone wave into the office of the Director of Nursing and crashed with it, right on her threshold. The Director of Nursing was a little old bird who must have weighed all of ninety pounds, but she had a two-hundred-pound sense of her office and her job. Everything about her was tight, from her hair in its bun to her mouth to her buttoned top collar button. She was a graduate of Saint George's School of Nursing, class of '34, and she sat straight as a broomstick behind her dark mahogany desk.

Her secretary had stopped me in the outer office and took my letter of introduction from the Chairman of Medicine. The secretary had been buzzed by the Director of Nursing, apparently directing a call to the Chairman of Medicine to check me out. Then I was invited in. She had shaken my hand firmly with her cold bony hand and ordered me to sit down in front of her desk. I sat.

"Karen Sweeney is a good nurse," said the Director. "But even good nurses are not immune to error."

The Director produced the bottle of insulin from which Karen Sweeney had drawn General Dhieu's dose. She had it sealed in an envelope and locked in her desk drawer.

"I am authorized to hand this over to you," she said. "I can verify that this was the bottle from which the dose was drawn."

As soon as I looked at it I knew I had something. Most insulin in the United States, until recent years, was made by Lilly or Squibb. This was made by a company called Biocon, and it was grown in bacteria by cloning techniques. Until the gene-splicing revolution, insulin had to be harvested from slaughterhouses, from the pancreases of pigs or cattle. Now they could grow it in bacteria. Biocon was a new company, and cloning a new technique. Any time patients are subjected to anything new in medicine, there's potential for things to go wrong.

I asked the Director about the insulin.

46

"It was the preparation ordered by the patient's attending physician," said the Director, letting me know quite clearly that it is not the nurse's role to choose the medicine, but simply to administer the proper dose according to doctor's orders.

"Do we have any other bottles of this insulin being used in the hospital now?" I asked.

"I'm sure I don't know," she said tonelessly. "That is a question for the head of Pharmacy."

"I think you have another bottle for me," I said.

She looked at me stonily.

"The quinine."

She reached into her drawer and handed over another bottle from another sealed envelope.

"Were there any other bottles in his med cart drawer?"

"Just the antibiotics, but those are discarded after they are used. And, of course, these."

She handed over a third envelope, with bottles of digoxin and nitroglycerin.

I thanked her and left for the pharmacy, wondering if there was anything I'd forgotten to ask her. If there was, she certainly was not going to volunteer it. Nursing was not happy about General Dhieu.

# 13

Mrs. Bromley paged as I was leaving the Director of Nursing's office.

"Sorry to interrupt the investigation," she said. "But Mrs. Simpson's called four times this morning and I simply have run out of insipid comments with which to fend her off."

"What is it?" I knew it wasn't Mrs. Bromley's fault, but I had still to see the Director of Pharmacy, the Chief of Pathology, the pathology resident who did the autopsy, the medical resident who took care of General Dhieu, and several others. "Sorry, didn't mean to be short," I said.

"I quite understand," she said. "I don't see how you can concentrate with all these frantic females calling incessantly. She's feeling very sorry for herself this morning. And two drugstores have called wanting renewals for patients they insist are actually waiting in the stores, bloody liars."

"What's Mrs. Simpson want?"

"A prescription for amphetamines. She's just read about them in *Glamour*. They are positively the only diet pills that work at all."

"Would you call Mrs. Simpson – I realize that's a painful task – and tell her I'll call her later? You might also mention that there's no way I'll give her amphetamines to lose weight. Tell her they'll send her blood pressure through the roof and kill her dead."

"I will do that."

"And tell the drugstores okay on both those prescriptions."

"Shall I simply hold all your calls, except for dire emergencies?"

"What's a dire emergency?"

"A call from the White House."

"Not dire enough."

"A call from Dr. von Dernhoffer?"

"By definition, that is a nonemergency call."

"A call from Stephanie Shaw? She did call. I told her you were investigating even as we spoke. She asked where. I refused to divulge your whereabouts."

"Good work."

"Keep at it," she said. "I'll hold them off."

"Don't know what I'd do without you."

"Starve, most likely," she said, and hung up.

I needed a reward for having dealt with Mrs. Simpson and the pharmacies, and found the vending machine room on the way to the pharmacy. I waited in line for the dollar bill changer, behind two Arabs in black and white burnooses. Got my change and plugged it in for a Coke, and stood there gulping the icy drink, listening to the conversation at the table nearest me. A woman was talking to her two kids in French.

48

The other tables had Orientals in blue jeans and knit shirts, a black man in a three-piece suit who had tribal markings in keloid scars on his face.

Walking down the hall to the pharmacy I kept the image of that vending machine room and its people in my mind. There probably weren't five other cities in America with vending machine rooms containing that kind of ethnic mix. In Washington, and at Saint George's in particular, English was just one of a cacophony of languages. After a while, you hardly noticed. It seemed natural. Washington was set up to handle the newcomer, the stranger.

But I knew about one stranger who hadn't been handled quite so smoothly. Or maybe he'd been handled too smoothly. There were traces of what had happened to him, bottles, initialled notes in hospital charts, but I still couldn't get a picture of the man.

In the hallway was a framed print of Raphael's version of Saint George dispatching the dragon. The hospital was very fond of that painting, and had it on many walls. I'd walked past it a thousand times, but now it held me. The dragon wasn't too overblown and no flames engulfed Saint George. But that big lizardlike thing was wrapped around the spear, and the outcome was by no means certain. The damsel in distress caught my eye. I could almost envy Saint George for her. But the forest setting was vaguely sinister and reminded me of the jungle around Saigon. The dragon looked like he just might win this time.

# 14

The pharmacy director was a tall gaunt man with hooded eyes and oily-looking hair that smelled of Wildroot. He spun the bottle of Biocon insulin I'd brought him on his desk-top, watching it come to a halt each time before spinning it again.

He listened to my story without apparent interest as he played spin-the-bottle, until I stopped talking. Then he swivelled in his chair to the computer terminal by his desk and punched a few keys and said, "No, Mr. Dhieu was the only patient in the house on Biocon long-acting insulin. In fact, he was the only patient we had on any form of Biocon insulin."

"Until we know more," I said, "we'd better not give any more Biocon NPH, or any Biocon anything to anyone."

"I'd better make out a drug report."

"I'm not sure we've got much until we've got the insulin level back."

"Better safe than . . ." he waved a hand. "Besides, I'd better notify the company. They'll want to talk to you."

"I've got nothing to say to them, until I have the insulin level results."

"Oh, but they'll have quite a lot to say to you," he said, eyes opening full circumference briefly. "Especially if you're going around putting all their products on ice. They're not going to like that. And they're going to like your questions even less."

"Right now, they're just questions."

"Questions about their quality control." He raised an eyebrow. "Those questions they don't like hearing."

"They're going to have to put up with them."

"Your life insurance is paid up?" he said, with a curl of his lips that might have been a smile.

"You think I'd better be paid up?"

He nodded.

"All I need is a beneficiary."

"Maybe that's why von Dernhoffer picked you for this job."

I looked at him, but his face was unreadable.

He said: "I hear Biocon spent eight million on advertising alone for their new insulin."

"How much they spend on quality control?"

"Ask them," he said. "They'll love you for it."

I asked him if he could analyse the pills in each of the bottles I had from the Director of Nursing. He knew the digoxin and nitroglycerin on sight and looked up the quinine in a book, but he couldn't tell me for sure that they were actually the pills they looked like. I thanked him and left his office wondering

50

where I could have the tablets analysed. If Dhieu's blood was full of quinine, I supposed I wouldn't have to bother, as long as the blood wasn't full of anything else.

I walked towards the car park, thinking about the people I'd talked to that morning, people for whom General Dhieu was simply another headache. So far I'd only seen one person who'd actually seen and touched Dhieu, Karen Sweeney. All the others dealt with his artifacts. They couldn't tell me enough. Their contact was too remote. But that's the way a hospital works. People like the lab director can tell you things that can be vital. I couldn't get impatient. The system had to be made to work for me.

Ducking into the doctor's lounge, I phoned the lab and told the receptionist who I was and asked for the lab director. She said: "Oh, Dr. Abrams, of course. He'll be right with you." I asked Potter to run a full drug screen on Dhieu's blood as long as he was running it for quinine. He said: "Of course."

Then I walked out to my car. The Oriental vixen in the red, white and blue was swinging along ahead of me, carrying her Igloo ice chest, headed towards the car park. She made those stripes curve and ripple in some very pleasant ways. She tossed the Igloo into a white Corvette, slid in and revved the motor and drove to the gate house, leaving me there in the wrong parking area, looking after her. I had followed her without really thinking about where I was going.

I headed for my own car park and car. Here I was, following the trail of Vietnamese all morning, winding up in the wrong car park.


# 15


At noon I made it to my car and was quickly onto Reservoir Road heading towards Foxhall. That's a stretch I dreaded. Somehow my answering service always knew when I was on that road, no matter what time of day I happened to hit it. They knew and they paged me.

There's only one phone on that road, at the Foxhall High's store, and parking is next to impossible, but I'm honour-bound to consider any page a dire emergency, since I gave the service clear and incontrovertible instructions never to page except for a life-and-death emergency. I also told them that if it's *that* urgent, they ought to tell whoever's calling not to waste time waiting for me to answer – just go straight to the nearest emergency room.

This day was no different – my beeper went off just before Foxhall Road. I considered not stopping, since I would have to park illegally, but as I said, I felt honour-bound. Besides, I had a strange feeling it might be about General Dhieu.

It wasn't about General Dhieu. It was Mrs. Simpson of the obesity and nonthyroid disease. I've since learned better about taking on patients like Mrs. Simpson. She was unwilling to accept the notion that I might not be able to wave a wand and make her instantly thin. "Can't you do anything, doctor?" she implored me.

"You're the one who has to do it," I said.

"But it would be such a help just to have you encourage me."

So I had agreed to see her once a week, to weigh her and to encourage her. It had been a quiet time in the office and Mrs. Bromley had been making noises about how slow things were. So Mrs. Simpson paid me thirty-five dollars a go to weigh her and to tell her to keep up the good work. That is, she paid thirty-five dollars for the office visits. She paid nothing for the dozen phone calls, usually timed to coincide with my drives on Reservoir Road.

Mrs. Simpson was on an eight-hundred-calorie diet, hating every minute of it. She got light-headed, had abdominal pains, diarrhoea, nausea, bad breath, hyperventilation and a hundred other things, and as soon as she noticed a new pain fibre firing off, she had her husband call. Mrs. Simpson never got on the phone at times like this. She was too sick to hold the phone and speak. She put her husband on and I'd have to ask her through him if she had any chest pain or whatever came into

52

my head to ask her about, until I got tired of that and demanded he put her on. Then she'd come on with a weak little voice to let me know how close to the brink she was and I'd tell her just what she didn't want to hear, that she wasn't sick enough to stop the diet.

I knew she'd love me to call it off. And I would have, long ago, but she annoyed me so thoroughly I persevered, just to see who'd crack first, me from all the phone calls, or her from the diet.

"I'm really a thin person in a fat body," she'd tell me. Could have fooled me, I thought.

Now it was Mr. Simpson, on the phone doing his wife's bidding. For once I wasn't totally unhappy to hear his voice. *Mr.* Simpson was retired State Department and he had spent a fair amount of time in the Far East Section.

"She's afraid she's got meningitis," he said.

"Not real likely, Mr. Simpson," I said. "Did you ever meet a General Nguyen Duc Dhieu, when you were at State?" I asked.

"Yes," he said, "I believe I did once." His voice changed, speaking of Dhieu. He wasn't hen-pecked Mr. Simpson any more. He was Simpson of State again, and he formed his words more carefully, voice alive and professional.

"Do you think anyone in the Vietnamese government would still care enough about him to want to knock him off?"

"I read that you'd been assigned that investigation," he said. "I might have something to offer. We might talk," he said coolly, "in person."

We weren't talking on a safe phone. Did he think the Vietnamese had bugged his phones?

"But why would a government that had *won* the war be interested in getting a general they'd beaten?"

"There are many examples of generals who lost wars being found dead in suspicious circumstances years after those wars. It wasn't always the winning side that had commissioned the deed."

"You mean the losers got after their own generals for losing?"

"Many cases of that, yes. But we should talk later."

53

The thought of having to sit around Mrs. Simpson's house overwhelmed my desire to know more.

"Thanks a lot, Mr. Simpson," I said. "I may have to take you up on that. Your opinion would be very useful."

"No trouble at all," he said. "Call again," and he hung up, no doubt with Mrs. Simpson looking on in great consternation.

I walked back to my car thinking about the angle. If it looked like the General had died of an overdose of insulin, I might have to call for help. There'd be no way to know if the Biocon insulin Karen Sweeney had given him had been added to, even if the next dose had been a totally different type insulin. All insulin looks the same to the assay. I could bring the case just so far. If there was an overdose, I could find out. Who was responsible for the overdose was a different question.

I drove down Foxhall to Canal Road and onto the White-hurst Freeway. It was a clear day and you could see the Kennedy Center and the Watergate complex at the bend of the river. It was a pretty drive and a pretty city. In places. But it had its dark side too. If this general had died in Altoona or Poughkeepsie or Baltimore I probably wouldn't have given foul play or stealthy foreign agents a second thought, but look at me now.

That thrilling little thought lasted about two minutes, until I reached the road along the river. The fact was, the most likely explanation was the same in Washington as it would have been in Baltimore – the nurse simply gave the wrong dose. Real life was the same all over. Real life was calls from the Mrs. Simpsons of the world, going to the office every day, going to the clinic every afternoon or no money to pay the rent.

I drove along adding up the pluses and minuses. I really liked having Mrs. Bromley for my secretary, and I liked my office and having a place to hang my duck prints and all the diplomas and things I'd kept in drawers for years thinking one day I'd hang them in my office.

And I liked my wood desk and the Persian carpet. There were days I worried about becoming a fat-cat doctor, all caught up in referrals and image of what kind of art to hang on my office walls – the kind of materialist for whom we all had such contempt in college, where we cut the alligators off our shirts as an antielitist statement. Worrying about becoming a fat cat happened less and less now. Since Vietnam, I'd worried less about the corrupting influence of money and more about not having enough. Scruffiness and doing without no longer felt morally superior.

Nothing felt morally superior any more.

Less and less felt tainted. I wouldn't have felt sullied if my practice made six figures. Of course, my practice placed me in no danger of making an unconscionable income. I made enough. And I liked not having to rush into work worrying about whether I'd beat the boss in, or whether I was working hard enough. And sometimes I'd lie in bed in the morning and thank my lucky stars I didn't have to face writing another grant application. But usually, if I stayed in bed long enough, the phone would ring and it would be the answering service.

# 16

Monday was the last time I went to Saint George's that week. There was nothing more to do until the lab results came back, except to talk to Ginny, the nurse Karen Sweeney had mentioned. I had her number from the Head Nurse so I called her at home and she confirmed all the important parts of Karen's statement: the General's IV had been removed Thursday night; he had had severe rigours during her shift. "If I didn't know better," she told me, "I would've thought he had malaria."

Von Dernhoffer called once, all honey-voiced, wanting to know how the investigation was going. He knew to whom I'd talked, but he asked questions as if he didn't. I didn't like that. In the end, he said how pleased he was that I was touching all the bases, which made me think about all the bases I hadn't touched, and it had me squirming about maybe touching a few more: the pathologist who did the autopsy (Mrs. Bromley had called for the report, but I hadn't spoken with him myself); the intern and resident who admitted the General; the private attending who took care of him and who prescribed the Biocon insulin; the people at Biocon itself. The more I thought about it, the more the list of possibilities exploded heavenward: political cronies and former brothers-in-arms of the General; the ambassador from Vietnam; Kissinger; Nixon.

Then I took firm hold and sat myself down for a rational consideration of the plan. The idea was not to be asking questions before I had some answers. If the Chairman wanted someone to chase around and touch all the bases willy-nilly, he could find someone else. It was such good press after all, somebody would want the job.

The next few days were like any other I'd had since coming to Washington, except I felt more alone. It dawned on me slowly that somehow the feeling was connected with Maureen Banting. At night I found myself turning on the TV just to hear a voice in the room. I'd watch the evening news and wonder if she watched "McNeil/Lehrer" or Dan Rather or who she watched, or if she watched the news at all. She sure read the paper, I was convinced of that now.

And I kept dreaming up scenarios about meeting her on the street, in Kramers bookstore, at the Kennedy Center, and what I'd say and what she'd say and how the night would progress. I hadn't done that in a long time, fantasized like that about a woman.

Maureen Banting was one good-looking woman. But it was more than that. I'd seen lots of good-looking women around Washington. I'd even met a few. There was something about her anger I liked. She had a certain appealing aggressiveness. I don't know what to call it. I just wanted to see her again.

Before she walked into my office I hadn't thought much beyond the next clinic, rounding up a few more patients to keep Mrs. Bromley happy and getting home to my porch. I hadn't done much thinking about whether or not answering phone calls from all the Mrs. Simpsons was a meaningful existence, whether I was doing the right thing with my life. I awakened in the morning, alive and with nobody shooting at me and that was enough. Now things were different, and I wasn't sure things were better.

There was a certain itchiness there.

It was Thursday and I had to do the Martin Luther King, Jr., Clinic. If life now looked drab, the Martin Luther King, Jr., Clinic was the drabbest thing of all. I never liked that clinic, and the thought of going down there that Thursday after Maureen Banting had glossed up my life briefly was downright unappetizing.

Mrs. Bromley called it my African Experience. "It's a safari," she said. Getting there was more like interplanetary travel – out of one world and into another: you drive down a pretty stretch of Massachusetts Avenue; past some elegant brick embassies; through Cleveland Park with all the wonderful Victorian homes with turrets and wraparound porches; along Calvert Street past all the fancy hotels; across Connecticut Avenue into no-man's-land, a transition zone called Adams Morgan; and beyond, to Sixteenth Street, to a part of Washington you don't see on the postcards.

It reminded me of the bleaker parts of Bedford-Stuyvesant, with all the burned out town houses and the flat terrain with nowhere to hide. Black Washington, black poor Washington, Washington with garbage in empty lots and drunks vomiting in the gutter, hookers on corners and drug sales in plain sight, and no police, except once in a while in a locked patrol car. It was the Washington the black middle classes had escaped, and it scared them as much as anyone. It was the part of town you drove through with your windows up, where you didn't stop for yellow lights.

The Martin Luther King, Jr., Clinic was in a brick building built around the time Lincoln was freeing the slaves, and repainted once during the Kennedy administration. A combination of government grants paid me and the patients paid nothing or next to nothing.

The waiting room was always packed. The nurses couldn't understand why I couldn't bring myself to walk out at three-thirty with the waiting room still half-full, and I couldn't understand it either, really.

"All the other doctors are out the door at three," the older nurse told me. "No call for you to do what you don't get paid for."

The nurses were black, and they went home at five, no matter how many patients were still left.

"They ain't paying for it, honey," said the old nurse. "They know what to expect."

I tried to say something, but the old nurse said, "I ain't getting caught in this neighbourhood after five o'clock, honey. And you'd best be even more careful, pale as you are."

I knew she probably had a point, but somewhere back in medical school during the rarefied sixties the notion had asserted itself that you can be a drunken bum derelict, stinking to high heaven, but once you presented yourself to the door of the clinic you were a patient, and that was the highest status of all. I couldn't shake that feeling. I don't know why. It had something to do with the anger that oozed up when other doctors just happened to mention the Supreme Court justice or senator they numbered among their patients. All that talk of glamour practices grated a little. A hangover attitude from the sixties, I guess.

Those hangover attitudes had got me into trouble entirely too often. I still get choked up when they play Martin Luther King, Jr., intoning "I have a dream." It was that speech that got me into doing the clinic. I would never have taken the job. They had me come down to the clinic to interview and to look around. I was depressed by the grime and ready to go right back to my office and call them to refuse the job. But on the way out the door I stopped to read the "I have a dream" speech. They had it painted on the wall with a picture of King above it. So I stood there reading it with tears in my eyes.

"When all God's children, black men and white men, Jews and Gentiles, Protestants and Catholics, will be able to join hands and sing in the words of the old Negro spiritual, 'Free at last, free at last, thank God Almighty, we are free at last.'" There were two little black kids playing under the mural and I was still choked up when I got home and called the clinic and told them I'd take the job. I'd regretted it ever since.

I parked in a fenced car park about three steps from the back door and wasted no time getting inside. There was a uniformed guard at the door and he said, "Good afternoon, Doc." I was glad to see him. He was always very pleasant. He was also very big and carried an intimidating black gun about the size of a small Howitzer. It made me feel better seeing him there.

As soon as I saw the nurses I announced I was walking out that clinic door by three-thirty, no matter what. I would get out and go to Kramers Bookstore at Dupont Circle and meet Maureen Banting and we would sail away.

There were fourteen patients and as soon as the nurses heard I wanted to try to get out by three-thirty, they took it as a personal challenge, and started moving them through the exam rooms like recruits at a processing centre.

"Most of 'em's just pressure," said the nurse. "You can do them in no time."

The first four went quickly, so quickly in fact that I started feeling guilty about it. No reason they should feel like cattle just so I could get out of the clinic early.

By one-thirty I'd seen eight patients with a modicum of pacing and pleasantness, when I stepped into an examining room to find Mr. Lucius Blackledge. Mr. Blackledge was the best thing about the Martin Luther King, Jr., Clinic. He had been a pilot with the 99th Army Air Corps, back when you had to die for your country in racially segregated battalions. When he got back home he discovered there wasn't much market among the airlines for a black pilot, so he drove a city bus for thirty years. His favourite topic was the Civil War. When he retired from the bus company he discovered Bruce Catton, and read everything Catton ever wrote. Then he read everything else he could find on the Civil War. Sherman, he assured me, was a lunatic. You could see it in his photographs.

"Madman's eyes," he said. "And that wild hair. The man was a maniac, a depressive, quite mad."

"Effective though," I said, and me from North Carolina, defending Sherman.

"No one ever said you couldn't be a madman and be a good

general," said Mr. Blackledge. "If my tour of duty was any guide, insanity might be a requirement of the rank."

I was trying to move along, so I steered things back to business and kept him answering questions about his diabetes and his angina. He had the same combination General Dhieu had had, and he happened to be on the same dose of insulin as the General. He seemed a little disappointed when I stood up to go.

"You're pressed for time today," he said.

"Yes," I said. "I've got to get to the hospital."

"I had wanted your opinion on Burnside at Fredricksburg," he said. "But it can wait. You've got more important things to attend to than talking about dead generals."

I looked at him for meaning, but he smiled an impenetrable smile and shook my hand. I was beginning to think everyone in Washington knew I was on the case.

After ten minutes with the next patient I realized I didn't have a chance of making it before five o'clock. She was the first of three new patients, and she was a patient in search of a problem. Her chief complaint was "Don't feel good," and all subsequent answers were "Dunno," or some variation thereof. She was five feet tall, 210 pounds, and she sat on the exam table looking sad.

My Martin Luther King, Jr., Clinic headache began pulsating behind my left eye. Her blood count and urine were normal. I examined her as well as 210 pounds will allow itself to be examined, getting no help from her. I told her she could get dressed and she said, "Can you gimme somethin'?"

"Something for what?"

"Well, sometimes I get this *feeling*," she said, pressing her temples with both hands.

"In your head?" I said eagerly, hoping she had at least enough synapsing neurons to complain of something that I could call a headache.

"Well, sort of. What's good fo' that?"

I wasted ten more minutes trying to drag a specific symptom out of her, but she didn't seem to have the vocabulary for it. All I got was shrugs and "dunno"s and head shakes. I knew how unfair it was, but I couldn't help comparing this sad lumpish thing with the nimble energy of Maureen Banting. Where Maureen detailed nightmares and sweats, this woman had "problems."

"Before I can give you medicine, I need a diagnosis," I said.

"A what?"

"To find out what's causing the problem."

"Oh," she said, heaving her shoulders in a sigh. She wasn't interested in diagnoses. She was interested in a prescription.

I was examining the next patient when the nurse came in with a paper in her hand.

"That Carmella Jones you just saw," she said, "wants you to sign this for her."

"What is it?" I asked, trying to visualize the optic nerve of the patient before me.

"Disability."

"What?" I asked, turning on the lights in the exam room. The nurse showed me the disability form.

"I'm supposed to put a diagnosis," I said.

"Put what you always put," she said.

So I wrote *Unbelievable* under "Diagnosis," and signed my name and the nurse went away. I had signed thirty or more forms that way in this clinic and never got a call from the disability office. And the patients kept coming back every six months so I could write *unbelievable* and sign my name, so apparently it satisfied the disability people quite nicely. One of the other doctors told me they always accepted a diagnosis if it had more than ten letters.

I saw the last patient at five-five. Maureen Banting would have to wait for another night. My headache was peaking and I was in acute need of a hot bath and a glass of Drambuie.

The guard held the back door open for the old nurse, who stepped through ahead of me, and he held it for me and said, "Good night, Doc. Thanks." And he smiled.

When six feet, seven inches, and 250 pounds of muscle smiles, I smile back. When we were outside and the door closed behind us I asked the old nurse why he said that.

"If the patients likes you, Big Bob likes you," she said. "Besides, he sees how you always stays late."

# 17

The last Friday of August began still and hot, the kind of Washington weather that leaves you gasping. Then the skies filled with inky storm clouds, moving fast, and thunderstorms followed, with big concussions you could feel inside the office, and with flashes like artillery in the night.

I was watching all this when Sumner Barrington III, MD, telephoned.

Sumner was a colonel in the Army Medical Corps, stationed at Walter Reed. I knew him from Vietnam. He was the first to tell me I was admirable and insane to ride the riverboats bringing science, penicillin and the American Way to the villages. He also told me every other Public Health Service doc on every other Coast Guard cutter hated my guts for doing it. I had violated the pact they all had made to refuse to leave the ships, where, after all, their first duty to the crew was unassailable.

Sumner heard I had gone upriver and made it his business to meet me and decide for himself whether I was a grandstander or just not too smart. We sat on cots in the sick bay of the *Yakatak*, drinking one bottle of Coca Cola each. Coke was something of a prized item on board. I had dipped into my personal ration in honour of this visit from the Army Medical Corps.

"What are you, gung ho or what?" Sumner began. "Volunteering. You had to volunteer for the riverboat rides. They can't make you do that you know."

I took a gulp of Coke, moved it around my mouth and swallowed it and said nothing. I watched Sumner scrutinize me.

"You're gung ho," said Sumner, shaking his head. "You

think you're some kind of patriot," he said, letting me know exactly what he thought of patriots by the way he said the word. "What'd'you think you're accomplishing, going upriver? Think you're gonna make those villagers love the U.S. of A.? Forget it. You're just a big white storm trooper to them. You're not a doc. You're an American and they hate you. Why'd you join up, anyway? Going to bring America to the villagers in your little black bag?"

"I was drafted."

"There's hope then. You didn't volunteer to come to this piss hole."

"I was trying to learn medicine, getting through my internship, and the day it ended I went to my mailbox and found my greetings."

"You should've got out of it."

"I tried. But if you're healthy enough to practice medicine, you're healthy enough to practice medicine in the army."

"Robert fucking McNamara probably thought that one up himself."

"The war was going to be over by the time I graduated. I repressed the whole thing."

"But what the fuck you going upriver for? They can't *make* you do that."

"Four years in medical school, year of internship, forty-eight days on this tub," I said. "Besides, I like the food in the villages."

"You're lucky they haven't poisoned it."

I shrugged. "I'm here. I don't want to be, but what am I going to do? Sit here on the ship?"

"Don't I fuckin' wish I could sit on a ship. No doc's ever been lost to enemy fire on a ship that I know of. You're just making the skipper look good. You're not going to get anything from putting your ass in a long boat."

"What're you doing here?"

"Berry plan. They had my ass all along," said Sumner, shaking his head at his own folly for signing up for a government programme that landed him in the army. "So you want some war stories for your grandchildren?" he said.

"I want some stories for me."

"Good. You want adventure 'cause you've been in school all your life and you want to see some action. That makes sense. But if you keep going upriver, don't plan on telling stories to the grandkids, 'cause unless you already got kids, you're not going to live long enough to have any."

Sumner did not think the riverboat trips a sound idea. He suggested I confine my study of the Southeast Asian culture to Saigon and he offered to act as my guide. Sumner suffered from the delusion that he was Hawkeye Pierce and that Vietnam was actually not happening. He believed it was a vast fabrication of the TV networks and that all the Viet Cong were in the employ of CBS News.

It didn't really matter what Sumner thought.

He'd done a medical internship and residency, so he wasn't assigned to the operating room, and since he was assigned to a Mobile Army Surgical Hospital, the 4044th MASH, that presented certain difficulties. They'd put him in charge of infection control, which gave him the status of a small town shamus. Nobody wanted Sumner nosing around for unsterile techniques in their operating rooms. Nurses got wet pants over surgeons, some even liked anaesthesiologists, but nobody even talked to Sumner, except when he felt compelled to make the required inspections of the operating rooms to point out all the unsterile places and practices.

Sumner was also ordered to control infection by injecting penicillin for gonorrhoea. He met nurses that way, but the wrong ones, and it wasn't all that gratifying treating gonorrhoea in Vietnam where there were so many resistant strains.

There was plenty for Sumner to do, given the rate of gonorrhoea and given the rate of sexual activity among enlisted personnel and officers. Sumner's personal sexual activity rate, unfortunately, did not match local norms, Sumner being just a shade over five feet tall, pretty nearly bald and somewhat flaccid. He compensated with a lot of aggressive talk. He remembered the war as the best time of his life.

He was on the phone now to invite me to the Washington Endocrine Society meeting at Walter Reed, where he was Chief of Endocrinology and Metabolism and current president of the society. I told him I'd be there.

"You're just saying that," said Sumner. "You won't show."

"Sumner, I said I would come. What do you want, a deposit?"

"You never show up. I don't know why I bother calling you every time. I don't call everybody. Just my buddies. And this is Chase Barnett – the new generation of hypoglycemics. You'd probably even find it interesting, if you came."

"I'll be there."

"What're you doing tonight?"

"Why?"

"I was thinking about doing some Liver Rounds."

"You think about doing Liver Rounds every night. You're getting a bit long in the tooth for that."

"Bite your tongue, I'm too old. When I'm too old, I want you to put a forty-five to my temple and pull the trigger. A loaded forty-five."

"Last time you were telling me about some red-headed lieutenant nurse all hot to trot, cooking you dinner every night. Why're you still hitting the bars?"

"Because you need outside business, big boy. That's axiomatic. You don't shit in your own backyard. I can't be screwing lieutenants. They'd all want it. Come on down to the Capitol Dome. We'll meet some senators' secretaries, bored and looking for real men to tell them their war stories."

"Don't know any. You want to come have a beer, sit on my porch, listen to the crickets, feed the mosquitoes, you're invited. I left my nightlife in Saigon."

"You've got it bad," said Sumner.

I refused to ask what I had bad because I knew what he would say and I knew he'd say it even if I didn't ask.

"Terminal mellow," said Sumner.

"I sleep nights. Only wake up five or ten times. No dreams so bad I have to fire my gun."

"You call that mental health? You need the ethanol cure. You are not a well man."

"We are none of us well men, Sumner," I said. "Which reminds me. I have a case you might be able to help me with."

"A patient, you mean? Don't talk to me about medicine. I

was talking to you about life, women and the pursuit of happiness."

"Where can I get some pills analysed? I'm not talking about identified. I know what they look like. I want to know what's really in them, for sure. And a bottle of insulin, too. I want to know how concentrated it really is, not just what it says on the label."

"Those are two different things, doctor. The first is mass spec or liquid chromatography and the second might be bioassay. What's this for?"

"A case I'm working on, you'd be bored. It's all death and disease."

"Not so fast, big boy. Tell Dr. Barrington all about it."

"It's this General Dhieu thing."

"General who?" Sumner was interested now. "A *general* and Dr. Sumner Barrington the Third, colonel, U.S. Army Medical Corps, does not know about it?"

"It's been in the paper. Don't you read the lay press?"

"Certainly not," huffed Sumner, who had not read a paper since the Tet offensive of '68.

He made me tell him all about General Dhieu, or what I knew of the case so far.

"What'd this pathologist say about the post?"

"Haven't talked to him yet. The Chief Medical Resident says it was inconclusive: a little pneumonia, a twist of hyperacute MI maybe, and a sugar of twenty-four."

"You've got to talk to the pathologist yourself, big boy."

"I'm waiting on the insulin level before I talk to him."

"Did he section the pancreas? Those insulinomas can be missed."

"I'll ask him," I said. "But I doubt they'd miss something like that, especially once they knew his sugar."

"Got to talk to the man, personally," said Sumner. "Had a case, actually several cases like this once myself, in Nam. Somebody decided to knock off some prisoners in an EVAC hospital with insulin in the IV lines. Nasty business. Couldn't prove squat. Couldn't do insulin levels at an EVAC hospital. But the sugars were twenty, twenty-two, that range."

"His IV was out after the first day," I said, "Anyone slipping him insulin would have to jab him in the skin, and he'd have bitched plenty about that."

"So you think the insulin was too concentrated? Not likely. More likely the nurse just fucked up."

"I'm just trying to cover all the bases. The nurse says she gave him ten units."

"You gonna believe nurses now? Nurses were who were knocking off those prisoners I was telling you about in Nam."

"This is Washington, Sumner. War's over."

"Maybe for you. Besides, this guy's a papa-san, ARVN."

"Sumner, I'm asking for names. Who can run this stuff for me? The insulin especially."

"Why not call the drug company? I'm sure they'd be just delighted to test that bottle out for you."

"I'm sure they would."

"If the insulin in this general's bottle was overconcentrated, then he wouldn't have been the only patient with hypoglycemia. There would have to be a bad batch, and probably hundreds of bottles of the stuff."

"Heard anything about cases like this?"

"Zilch, but you might have one of the first."

"I'll call the company. In fact, the Pharmacy chief sent in a report already. But where can I get an independent assay done?"

"You could send it to some other company, like Lilly or Squibb, and have them test it. But then Biocon might claim the other companies are competitors and have axes to grind, only too happy to tell the world that Biocon doesn't know how to make this new kind of insulin. Poor quality control. Oh, they'd love it. Biocon's not going to like you much."

"Names, Sumner. I need names. Not other drug companies. I need someone above the fray, someone who has nothing financially riding on the outcome. Someone pure. Some professor somewhere."

"How 'bout your friends at Hopkins?"

"No one there does that kind of thing."

"Would the National Institutes of Health be above the fray enough for you?"

"Now you're talking."

Sumner gave me the name of a PhD who ran the toxicology lab at NIH. He had known all the time exactly who I needed.

"But I tell you, big boy," said Sumner. "I think you're wasting Saint George's money. Chances are that insulin's okay. The nurses just fucked up. Some of these bimbos can't add two plus two."

"I just want to check it out."

"Lot of trouble," said Sumner. "It's probably just a dumb nurse gave too much insulin."

"I met her. She didn't strike me that way."

"Aha! She going to be real grateful if Dr. Abrams saves her ass? *Now* I see why you're going through the whole parade."

"Purest motives. I'm just a humble country doc trying to understand why this ex-general should crump for no apparent reason."

"Pure motives. Pure, unadulterated desire to get into nurse's pants. What's she look like? Blonde, I bet. Blonde and a nice little ass?"

"She's six-three and weighs four hundred pounds."

Sumner went on at length about the possibilities for hot times with the nurse if the insulin turned out to be overripe and the whole blame shifted to the drug company. Not just the nurse, but the entire nursing profession would be in my debt, and knocking down my doors. He wanted me to remember him, to footnote his contribution.

I was eager to get off the line and call the toxicology man at NIH.

"You'll get your reward," I told Sumner. "In heaven."

"That's not where I want it."

The NIH man asked only a few questions: What made me think the bottle might be overconcentrated? When did I need the answer? He agreed to do it.

"Probably a medication error," he said. "The nurse probably just pulled up too much."

"I just want to check for sure."

"No problem. If Biocon blew it, it'll be a case report. You can be second author."

I thanked him and hung up. I sat there wondering how long I could put off calling Biocon. It made no sense to call until the insulin level in the sample with the low blood sugar came back – if the blood level of insulin was not high, the Biocon insulin could not be incriminated. It was really premature to ask for the assay on the Biocon insulin, for that matter. But the NIH man had told me he'd need a week or two for his assay, so it was nice to have that cooking, just in case. At worst, it would waste some of Saint George's money. At best it would save time. And the Chairman of Medicine said time was of the essence.

Biocon was not wasting time, either. Their man was on the line, Mrs. Bromley said, calling from New Jersey. They had received the Saint George's Pharmacy Director's report and they had a few committee meetings and they were trying to track down all the bottles in the batch that General Dhieu's bottle came from.

"Those bottles went to fifteen different states and who knows how many drugstores and hospitals," said the Biocon man. "It's going to be expensive to catch them. You're sure this guy had too much insulin?"

"I don't know that yet," I averred. "We'll know when the insulin level comes back."

"When's that?"

"A few days now."

"What makes you think the nurse didn't just pull up too much in her syringe?"

"She might have, but she's been pulling up insulin for a long time."

"Three years isn't such a long time. She got a C-minus in pharmacology in nursing school."

I could believe it was going to be expensive for the drug company now, especially if the nurse did not make an error and the insulin turned out to be overeager. They had gone to the trouble of checking out Karen Sweeney's nursing school record. They were preparing their defence. Biocon was in for a big bucks lawsuit, if their insulin was misbehaving.

It would be wrongful death. That's what the lawyers would call it. General Dhieu gets the drug the way the company says

69

he should get it and his sugar falls through the floor and his brain dies and it's called wrongful death. I always liked that phrase. It made me wonder what kind of deaths fall into the other category.

"Of course we'd like the bottle," said the Biocon man. "So we can assay it." He paused and waited for me to say something and when I didn't he said, "I understand you have the bottle."

"Not anymore," I said. "I just dropped it off at the National Institutes of Health. I'm sure they'd be happy to give you the bottle, after they take out an aliquot."

He asked for the name and number of the PhD, and hung up. I called NIH back as soon as the Biocon man hung up.

"Sure, if he calls I'll tell him we have the stuff already," said the PhD. "But don't make me a liar. Bring it over today."

I thanked him, hung up and sat there behind my desk waiting for my heart to slow down. I didn't want to drive to Bethesda. Then I thought about Karen Sweeney and how she looked sitting in that chair outside the Head Nurse's office. And I thought about all those bottles of Biocon insulin from General Dhieu's batch.

And then I thought about the third possibility, the one the widow had raised, the one the newspapers were rooting for. It would make a spectacular story, the third man angle. GENERAL KILLED BY OLD ADVERSARIES OT FORMER COMRADES. I could see Stephanie Shaw's headline and lead sentence now: "For General Nguyen Duc Dhieu the war in Vietnam did not end in 1975, it ended in a hospital bed at Saint George's Hospital in Washington, D.C., this past August." It was a lovely opener and it made a good story. A nice story, but very difficult to prove. There's no way to tell Biocon insulin from any other insulin. There's no way to know if Karen Sweeney was the only one to give General Dhieu insulin that day.

I didn't like the way this case was developing. Any way you sliced it, someone was going to get hurt. Someone already had been.

# 18

Mrs. Bromley volunteered to drive the Biocon insulin bottle over to the National Institutes of Health.

"Driving's a pleasure, now that the weather's cooled off," she said. She then launched into her hardship-payment anecdote, as she did whenever Washington weather came up. When the British foreign service first shipped the Bromleys to Washington, they paid a wage supplement called a hardship allowance which was generally reserved for places like Addis Ababa. "Washington summers are just as bad as Ethiopia," she said. "This weather won't last."

At any rate, it was cool now, and I didn't even mind driving down to my moonlighting job. On hot sticky days, if you drive a beat-up Triumph without air conditioning, you have to roll down the windows or put down the top – then you get caught behind a bus with its exhaust pipe at eye level spewing right in your face every time the driver presses the accelerator. But on cool breezy days the drive down Independence Avenue is very pleasant.

The nice weather brought out the police, which made the drive less pleasant. In Washington there are more police than any other form of living creature: city police, park police, Metro police, military police, uniformed police from the Secret Service, embassy police, government building police. One of my patients told me the Navy has half its people in mufti, because if everyone wore his uniform the town would look like an armed camp. Now it only looks like a police state.

Nobody does twenty-five miles an hour on the stretch in front of the Kennedy Center. The police can pull over whomever they want. I slowed down, causing all kinds of problems for traffic. But we all got by the park police and I got to clinic on time.

The clinic was in a big government building with long bleak corridors and fluorescent lights. I got paid for doing physical exams on federal employees and for listening to them avow that their hypertension, bad breath, high cholesterol, you name it, were all job-related. Stress-on-the-job. Big diagnosis in government circles.

After the clinic it was especially important, for my own mental health, to walk through Georgetown, which still has a little eccentricity, and which keeps a little spiritual distance from the big buildings downtown. There's usually no place to park in Georgetown. But late Friday afternoon you've got a fighting chance, and I found a space on N Street. I stood there and read the parking sign all the way through. The city government can't seem to do much, but they can tow cars. In that department, they've got the Strategic Air Command beat for vigilance.

"It's legal," said a voice ahead of me.

It was a fine-boned Oriental woman, vaguely familiar, nice face.

"I've read it three times, and I'm still not sure," I said.

She just smiled and walked off down N Street towards Wisconsin Avenue. She was lithe and she walked wonderfully. Watching her, I told myself to calm down, to go on to Mr. Smith's, which was originally on the agenda, and to resist distractions.

But she was some distraction. And we had practically been introduced. She was ahead of me on N Street and I had her in my sights for half a block before I realized who she was: the girl from the lift at Saint George's. She had been carrying the Igloo ice chest.

I was struggling with myself to give up the chase when I noticed her pause by a street side stand and filch a Neil Young cassette tape. Now I was sure she was Vietnamese, with those quick street-sure Saigon fingers. I'd seen all that before. She was beautiful. She was trouble. I told myself to let her go, but we were headed in the same general direction, towards Foggy Bottom.

72

She swung into a bar, a dark place with much wood and brass and not too loud. I tried to be a good boy and hold myself to the plan: Mr. Smith's, look at the crowd, have a beer, go home. But she had the scent out and I followed.

She was sitting at the bar drinking a daiquiri, smoking a cigarette, listening to a fat man with a gold necklace and a hairy chest. She was smiling in a bored sort of way. I sat down on the other side of her, but she was looking towards the fat man.

I ordered a daiquiri. She turned, hearing my order, and said, "I drink daiquiris, too."

She wasn't Vietnamese. She was American.

"We've got a lot in common," I said. "I even like Neil Young."

Her smile faded, but returned quickly.

"Who do you work for?"

"Nobody. Myself." I knew it wasn't coming out smoothly. "I just follow pretty women."

"I wouldn't admit to that."

I swallowed and smiled idiotically, trying to think of something clever to say.

"Would you like to come to my place and listen to Neil Young?" she said.

"Very much." I was very proud of myself for getting that out without blinking more than a hundred times.

The fat man with all the hair and necklace leaned forward and looked me over.

"I was talking to the lady, buddy," he said, with a look that let me know very clearly that I had violated some important rule of barroom etiquette. He was talking to her first.

"What am I?" asked the lady, with a short barking laugh and eyes that said that she didn't like what she had heard. "Branded cattle? I talk to whom I like," she said, and she turned very slowly towards me and said very slowly, deep-voiced, "And I like you."

The fat man rolled his shoulders away and started talking with someone on the other side of his stool.

My Neil Young fan looked me over with rich brown eyes and an amused smile. "Do we share a fondness for other

pleasures?" she asked. "Besides Neil Young and daiquiris?"

"We could probably find something," I said, and being
nervous added to my eternal mortification, "I like Camus."
God alone knows where that came from.

"Camus?" she laughed. "The existentialist or the liquor?"

I don't know what I said, but she said we ought to get out of
that bar, and I agreed and we wandered off down M Street,
and she asked where we should go and I couldn't think of any
name except Mr. Smith's. So we went there.

We sat at the mahogany bar with the chrome rim and
ordered daiquiris. I was squirming trying to think of what to
say while she looked at me, reaching into her purse and
removing a gold cigarette case without ever taking her eyes
from my face. I was thinking of a hundred things a second,
discarding them all, completely tongue-tied.

Just then my beeper went off and I considered how to ignore
it.

"You bugged?" she said.

"Harassed. It's just a beeper. Be right back," I said. "I'm
buying daiquiris."

I struggled back through the crowd towards the phone in the
rear, and stumbled over a little table behind which sat a very
good-looking Asian lady in red silk and a solemn old boy, also
Asian, in a grey suit. I had noticed her in the other bar, and
now here she was again. She looked up and smiled. He just
steadied his glass and kept talking to a man next to him.
Crossing paths bar-hopping was not unusual, but it made me
feel followed. I wondered about my Neil Young fan. Did I pick
her up or she me?"

The phone was next to the bathroom door. I was talking to
my answering service when a big-busted woman came up and
tried to yank it open. I was glad it was locked, because she
would have put me into the wall with it. The answering service
said Mrs. Simpson had called.

I called her back. Mrs. Simpson had a headache and it made
her stomach queasy.

Just as I hung up, the door to the bathroom flew open,
missing me by almost a full inch, and catching the big lady

74

in the bosom. Coming out of the bathroom was Maureen Banting.

"This must be my lucky day," she said. "Here I blow lunch and several fine martinis, and who do I meet but my doctor?"

She caught me by the bicep and leaned forward to steady herself. I could smell the martinis on her breath and feel her breast pressing my arm. I looked down the bar to find my Neil Young fan. She was gone.

## 19

I should have been happy, of course. Lose one, win one. Here I was with Maureen Banting. But it was a Maureen Banting smelling of martinis, good-looking but sexually abstinent by her own declaration, and swaying like a reed in the wind. Maureen Banting, drunk, nonhypoglycemic.

She followed me as I moved along the bar towards the front, bumping the table with the red dress woman and her male friends. This time they all looked up. We kept going to an empty table near the door. There was a cool breeze and Maureen leaned her head back against the wall, letting the air wash over her face.

"Play me music," said Maureen. "I trust your taste implicitly."

I walked over to the jukebox. Three for a quarter: "Positively 4th Street," "Sympathy for the Devil," and "It's All Over Now, Baby Blue." Then I went back to Maureen.

There was a man sitting in what had been my chair, talking to her. He had high cheekbones, clear skin, golden hair straight and neatly parted, and a blue three-piece suit. Maureen had her chin in her hand, elbow on the table, and would have looked very absorbed in what he was saying except that her silly smile gave her away. I was thankful for that smile – it was the only thing that kept me from going right out the door.

"Oh," she said, when I reached their table, then to the fair-haired boy. "Meet my doctor."

"Your doctor?"

"Yes. I keep him around when I'm drinking. See, he has a beeper. He's the genuine article, all right."

He stood up and shook my hand and said some name. He didn't look comfortable. He was trying to figure out who I really was.

"Don't you just love his suit?" Maureen said to me. He smiled, not sure yet which direction things were going. Maureen put his doubts to rest. "That is a marvellous suit," she said. "But it's a little *old* for you. When did you get out of college? You *are* out of college?"

He gave the year. He wasn't long out.

"But you're just a baby," laughed Maureen. "Who told you you could wear a suit like that?"

"Well it's kind of a uniform," he said. "On the Hill."

"The *Hill*?" said Maureen, sounding impressed, looking at me, then back to him. "*Which* hill is that?"

"Capitol Hill," he said grimly, to his drink. He knew with which end he was being stirred now.

"For a senator?"

"I work for a congressman."

"Oh, you're on somebody's *staff*," said Maureen. "On the *Hill*. You're one of those people who give the city colour. All the secretaries come to places like this trying to meet men in suits, just like you."

He said nothing, and the smile was long gone. I tried to think of how to end his misery. He didn't seem to have enough sense to get up and leave.

"What do you *do* for the congressman?" Maureen was asking. "Buy his suits?"

"I'm sorry," he said. "I didn't realize I was interupting." He left.

Maureen looked at me.

"What a nice boy. Works on the *Hill*."

"You really unloaded on him."

76

"Did I?"

"Both barrels."

"Well, he had it coming, wearing a suit like that," said Maureen. "Dressing for success. Probably thinks My Lai's the name of a cocktail."

"That's not his fault."

"Well who's fault is it?" She looked around for him. "Maybe you're right. But he thought he was Mr. Glamour and that entitled him to get into my pants and I'd just finished getting drunk and sick."

"Were you really sick?"

"Was I ever."

For a recently sick lady, she looked very unruffled and unsplattered.

"The highway is for gamblers, better use your sins," sang Dylan.

"I like Dylan," said Maureen, listening with a dreamy look. "Certain songs can flash me right back to certain times. Do you ever flash back?"

"Sometimes."

"It's not always pleasant," she said. "I'm okay now. Will you get me some coffee? Then you can take me home to your place."

I felt old. Old because in all my scenarios it hadn't come so easily and somehow I was disappointed. I could have been anyone.

"Or don't you fraternize with your patients?"

"I'll get your coffee."

When I got back she said, "You knew I liked you that time, in your office, didn't you?"

"You left angry."

"I do that a lot. No, I liked you . . . a lot. I thought you knew that."

"I miss a lot. I'm not real perceptive."

"*Au contraire*, Dr. Abrams. Smooth you are not. You are most perceptive. And considerate. You didn't push me about the personal stuff. You were careful not to make me uncomfortable. And you tried not to make me feel like a crock, even though you thought there's nothing to all this."

77

"I try to keep an open mind."

"And I liked the picture of the peasant in the rice paddy."

I tried not to look too surprised.

"You liked my picture?"

"It made up for the rest of the office."

"What's wrong with the rest of the office?"

"It's just too much, too overcompensated, intensely imitation WASP – the Audubon prints, all the wood and leather, and the secretary with the British accent, and all your academic merit badges on the wall, framed and mounted: Swarthmore, University of Virginia Med School, Columbia internship, Hopkins fellowship."

"You know my whole academic pedigree by heart."

"That's the point, isn't it? The point of the wall. It's very impressive, if that sort of thing impresses you."

"But that sort of thing doesn't impress Maureen Banting?"

"It doesn't disqualify you, in my book, unless you take it too seriously," she smiled. "But I get the feeling you don't."

"What gives you that feeling?"

"For one thing, that certificate behind your door: Hebrew Sons of the Confederacy. I was glad to see that, even if you put it behind your door."

"It *is* a very nice certificate."

"And the peasant's photo, of course. You took it yourself, didn't you?"

I said I had.

"I could just see you standing knee deep in that rice paddy with that old peasant smiling up into your camera, kind of shy and sweet. You could not possibly be a jerk and take that picture and hang it on your wall. There wasn't a single picture of guys with guns or any of that."

I looked at her as steadily as I could, trying not to drop my eyes to her knees and shuffle my feet and say, "Aw, shucks."

She held me with those grey and white sparklers of hers and said in a very controlled, almost neutral tone, as if she were talking about someone else, "I liked this Benjamin Abrams, MD, even before he set foot in the room."

That was said very straightforward, and with enough feeling to make me like her again. I sat there watching her watch me.

She looked me over, an amused smile playing at the corners of her mouth, and she said, "So I'm not just a drunk floozy going home on the shoulder of a convenient sailor."

I tried to think of something clever to say, and failed miserably.

"How'd you get out of Nam early?" she asked. "Wounded?"

She knew I had to have been wounded because they sent me home before my year was up. She had added it up and stowed it away.

"Just a little. Sick mostly."

"Wasn't everyone? Wasn't the whole thing just sick?"

"I got malaria."

"Didn't you take your pills? Naughty. And a doctor yet." She drank more coffee. "How'd you get malaria on a ship?"

"I didn't get it on the ship."

"Let's get out of here," she said. "Where's your car?"

We stood up and I watched her walk ahead of me. She was fine now, walking with that dancer's grace in high heels, her heart-shaped ass outlined in her cotton dress. Just drop her off at her front door and sail on home. That was the thing to do. But then my night would end as all the other nights since I'd come to Washington. Something about her started the juices flowing. And it wasn't just her good looks. There was something there that made me think she just might be the genuine article. We shared it, and it wasn't just Vietnam. Whatever it was, she had me going and it was a nice feeling.

# 20

"Can you put the top down on this thing?" Maureen asked, when we got to the car. "Night air might clear my head."

It was a fight getting the top down on that old car. She put her head back as we drove down M Street. We stopped at the busy Wisconsin Avenue intersection for the eternal red light. There was horn-blowing and shouting behind me and I glanced at my rearview mirror. Two figures in a black Mercedes behind me were also turning round. The angry voice was behind the Mercedes.

"How could anyone argue on a night like this?" asked Maureen, as the light turned green and we started forward. "Lord, look at those stars."

The honking and shouting grew louder and a dark van roared past the Mercedes and swerved in front of it behind me. Brakes slammed, tyres squealed, and someone leaned out of the van gesticulating at the Mercedes. At Canal Road there was more screeching of tyres, angry shouting, and the Mercedes roared past us followed by the van very close behind.

"It's a dogfight," said Maureen, watching their tail lights disappear into the distance. "You'd think they'd be more careful, in a Mercedes."

"Hard to be sure," I said. "But it looked like the Mercedes was just trying to shake that van and get away."

There weren't many cars on Canal Road at that hour and in the night air sound carried well. We could hear a great crash, ahead of us.

The van had apparently attempted to separate the front half from the back of the Mercedes. The tail lights of the van were still lighted, and I could see a figure open the van door and limp away from the wreckage. They had collided right above Fletcher's Boat House, and the van driver was moving up the hill on foot, following Reservoir Road, correctly concluding that the law would not look kindly on his attempts at remodelling the Mercedes.

We had almost reached the scene when Maureen said, "Better stop."

The Mercedes looked compacted. If there was anyone alive in there, they weren't healthy.

"What can I do?" I said. "Give 'em last rites?"

"That'd be a first," she said. "An ordained Hebrew Son of the Confederacy. Stop the car."

I slowed and pulled over.

"What are you going to be able to do?" I asked.

"I may not be sober," she said, "but I can still mouth to mouth."

"And get TB or sued for your trouble."

I stopped on the grassy shoulder and put my blinkers on. We got out, went over and peered into the Mercedes. It was the lady in the red dress from Mr. Smith's, and one of her gentleman friends. He was sitting in the driver's seat with a lap full of vomit, looking pretty dazed. But he was still breathing and conscious.

We got in from the passenger's side. The lady in the red dress said she was okay.

"But my belly is hurting," she said. Her accent was familiar. Vietnamese, I was sure.

I asked her if she had hit the gear shift. She said she might have. We helped them out of the car and had them lie down on the grass. I wasn't happy about moving them, but there was the insidious odour of gasoline, so I thought we'd better get clear of the wreck. The woman's friend came to and started talking to her in Vietnamese. I was checking her belly through her dress. Every time I pressed her left upper quadrant, she flinched.

"There's some houses up on Reservoir Road," I told Maureen. "Why don't you go up there and have them call an ambulance?"

"Don't go anywhere," she said, and took off at a good pace. She was back by the time the police arrived. They came with lots of noise and lights and Maureen explained what had happened while I went over the man, who was looking better, but smelled bad from the vomit. His belly was nontender and his pulse under a hundred and he kept talking to the woman who was smiling and pale and insisting she was fine.

I could hear Maureen talking to one of the cops. She kept saying, "I wasn't driving the van. I'm too drunk to drive. My doctor was driving that Triumph."

The cop looked unamused, and said something I couldn't hear from my post next to the lady. I could hear Maureen, though. She was getting loud.

"Why don't you guys go direct traffic or something, if you're not going to help the people who got hurt?"

The cop with Maureen wasn't getting anywhere.

His partner had been on the radio and came over to me while I examined the lady.

"You call an ambulance?"

"On the way."

"This lady's got to go to the hospital," I said.

"I want to go home," she said.

"I'm a doctor, lady." I had told her that about ten times, and she was letting me poke all over so I figured she believed me.

"You a doctor?" asked the cop. He was a grey-haired black cop with a very patient air. He knew people were infantile and hostile and unhelpful by nature and he was in no hurry to figure everything out at once. His partner was a younger white cop with a Pete Rose haircut and he was getting nowhere with Maureen.

She was not doing a lot to endear herself.

"Who the hell made you guardian of the public morality?" she was shouting.

He was going for his citation book when I reached them.

"What's the problem, officer?" I asked, stepping between him and Maureen. His face was set and his eyes narrowed and he was ready to exert some authority in Maureen's direction.

"This lady's drunk and disorderly," he said.

"Let me have a word with her," I said. I turned Maureen by her elbow and walked her over to the grass away from the cop.

"You better get nice in a hurry," I said.

"The hell I will," she said. "He's acting like I drove the car that hit them."

"He's about to run you in for disorderly conduct," I said. "You want to be strip-searched, have some police matron with her grimy fingers up your vagina?"

Maureen looked suddenly a lot more sober.

"What?"

"If he books you and throws you in the slammer, they'll search you, for the protection of other prisoners. You might knife someone with the switchblade you always carry in your vagina."

"They can do that?"

"Can and will."

"Land of the free, home of the brave," she said. "No, I don't want to be arrested."

"Then we will have to make amends."

We walked back to the cop.

"My friend was upset," I said. "She wanted to stop to help the people in this wreck, not to make trouble. But the blood and all – she's upset. She didn't know what she was saying. A little hysterical."

The cop looked less than completely placated. He wasn't sure he had exerted enough authority yet. He was still trying to make up his mind when Maureen said, "I'm sorry," and smiled him a dimpled smile. "Didn't mean to take it out on you," she added.

The cop's honour was now fully intact. He hitched up his pants by the heavy black belt that held his holstered gun and said, "I'll let you go this time," and he tried to look as stern as a twenty-year-old face could look and he said, "But you'd better be careful about how you talk to people. I could run you in for that kind of abusive trash."

When the ambulance arrived, the young cop offered to drive Maureen to the Emergency Room in my car.

"You be nice," I told her as she turned to follow him.

"Oh, I'll charm the socks off him."

The older cop followed the ambulance in the patrol car and Maureen and the young one took up the rear and I went in the ambulance with the lady and her companion, who turned out to be her husband.

The whole way to the Emergency Room, he kept looking me up and down, so I stopped examining his wife and told him I thought it was possible she had ruptured her spleen on the gear shift and she'd probably have to stay the night in the hospital. He looked not at all happy to hear that, but he didn't say anything.

Finally he said, "You saw the accident?"

"I came up just afterwards. Didn't see him hit you."

83

"Then you didn't see the man in the other car?"

"Just his backside."

"Then you couldn't identify him?"

"I'd know that backside anywhere," I said. "But I don't imagine they'll have a line-up of backsides."

He didn't smile. "So you were just happening along?"

I didn't like the way he said that, but he had just been decelerated rudely against a steering wheel, lost a pretty Mercedes, and had his wife injured, so I took pity on him and answered.

"It's called the Good Samaritan," I said. "We're supposed to stop and lend a hand in this country."

He raised an eyebrow. "Do you know what country I'm from?"

"No," I lied. "And I don't really care."

"You were very kind to stop," said the wife. Her red dress had risen well above midthigh and we had got very chummy during the trip. I had kept my hand on her pulse, after I finished going over her belly, and she had grasped my forearm with her free hand to steady herself during the ride. It must not have looked good to her husband, but I had the feeling she didn't care. She was a very good-looking lady.

"What was it you were saying about my spleen?"

"You may have ruptured it. It's common in accidents like this."

"What happens if that spleen is ruptured?"

"They have to decide if it really is ruptured first."

"And if it is?"

"They'll have to take it out."

"Surgery?"

"Only if you need it."

"What if I don't have the surgery?"

"You could bleed to death."

"I see."

"The first thing they'll do is something called a four-quadrant tap, to find out if it's ruptured. They won't miss it."

I felt very proud to have remembered about a four-quadrant tap from medical school, which is the last place I'd heard of it. Endocrinologists don't handle a lot of spleens.

84

We arrived at the Emergency Room and they wheeled her off and I went to talk with the ER doctor who was going to see my spleen lady.

I didn't catch his name, but I noticed he didn't speak English real well and he didn't seem to understand me much better than I did him.

Maureen and the young cop walked by me, on their way to the waiting room.

She winked. "We're getting on famously," she said. "Just you watch."

I talked to the husband before I left. "I'll be glad to have you as my patients. If you'd like."

"That's very kind," he said. "But I will call our own doctor."

"Will he come to see you tonight?"

"I expect so."

"Fine then. But if they don't admit your wife, be sure you call me or your doctor."

The husband smiled, but I didn't feel very reassured. She was his wife, though. Couldn't really blame him. I must have looked like a real ambulance chaser. Or worse.

I wrote a note in the ER, making it very clear I thought she had a ruptured spleen in case the ER doctor thought otherwise. If he let her go, and if anything happened to her, it wasn't going to be because I didn't tell him. I felt a little bad, though. She was a nice lady.

From where I was writing I could see Maureen talking to the young cop. They were standing on the other side of glass doors. They were best friends now. She was smiling. He was grinning and he had his hat off, his face close to hers. He looked like a young stud at a Friday night happy hour. His older partner was on the phone, next to me.

Just as I handed my note to the ER nurse, I saw Maureen connect with a stinging right-hand slap across the face of the young cop. I was through the door before the red impression of her hand had faded from his cheek.

Maureen was screaming, "What kind of a girl do you think I am?"

The waiting room was filled with the usual Friday night

crowd, and all eyes were now on the red-faced cop, who looked totally bewildered.

"I'd like to report this officer to his superiors," Maureen said as I reached her.

The cop said, "No offence," not to Maureen and not to me, but to the waiting room in general. By now the older cop was with us and he nodded to the door and the young cop flew out into the night.

The older cop smiled at me and said, "Good evening," and looked to Maureen without smiling, but amused and knowing, and followed his partner out to the car park.

"You ought to be ashamed of yourself," I said.

"Me?" said Maureen, all innocence.

"You set him up for that," I said. "Feel better now?"

"Immensely," she smiled. "Did you see him scamper out of here?"

"And he didn't even have his pants down."

"So sweet," she said. "How's the lady?"

"Might have a ruptured spleen."

"Now don't you feel better we stopped?"

"She's a nice lady. Can't say as much for the husband. He acted like I was driving the car that hit him."

"He must have been pretty shaken. Don't suppose he'd have any way of knowing for sure who hit him. Then we show up."

"No excuse for all that hostility," I said. "Wish they'd taken us to Saint George's, though."

"What's wrong with Memorial?"

"Community hospital."

"Oh," she said, laughing. "I *beg* your pardon. We do not truck with nonacademic centres."

I started to say that I wasn't that kind of snob, but it would have been protesting too much so I kept it to myself. But I knew the docs in the Saint George's ER all spoke English.

"Well," she said, "I'm glad you stopped."

"I would have gone right by, if you hadn't . . ."

"No, you wouldn't have. You just talk like that. You'd have stopped, even if I weren't there."

86

I looked to see if she meant that, and I could see she did. She wanted to believe I actually would have stopped.

"Why was it so important to stop?" I asked. "They would have got to the hospital without us, just the same."

"It's not so important for *them*," she said. "It's important for me, and for you. People like us can't just look the other way."

"But we do it all the time. Every time you pass a bum on the street. You can't take in all the stray dogs."

"You do what you can," she said.

We were sitting in my car with the top down, looking at the sky, and I was beginning to wonder what was going to happen. I was trying to decide about taking her to my place. I was going back and forth in my mind as we pulled out of the car park.

On one side, she was a boozer, a professed hypoglycemic, and very likely a Catholic schoolgirl neurotic tease – the worst kind because they think it virtuous. But she was very good-looking and she hadn't abused her body with alcohol so badly you could see it.

What you could see looked very healthy and began to win out over everything else. And it was a fine cool Washington night with a blanket of stars spread out against the sky and the sound of crickets all around.

She held more cards than she cared to show. And she had pieced things together about my being wounded. It had been a while since anyone had shown that much interest. She probably did that with all the boys.


21


My beeper went off on the way home and all I could think was that it would be someone with chest pain or something I'd have to treat in the Emergency Room and I could kiss goodbye to the rest of the night with Maureen. I got on the phone as soon as we got home and watched Maureen wander around looking for the bathroom.

It was a patient of Tim Doolan's, one of the docs I cover for. The patient was a forty-year-old engineer for the Department of Transportation. (He told me that right away and I kept trying to fit that in with what he was calling about, but never could.) He was calling because he had stuck his arm in one of those blood-pressure-for-fifty-cents machines in a shopping mall and it read 160/90 and a little sign lighted up – SEE YOUR DOCTOR. That had happened at ten that morning. It was now midnight and he had decided he better call the doctor.

"But you say this happened this morning? I'm trying to figure out why you're calling now. Do you have a headache, anything happening that got you concerned, just now?"

"Well, no. But I thought I'd better check it out. I mean, should I take anything for it? Should I cut down on my salt, or change my activity?"

I considered really scaring hell out of him and ordering him to call an ambulance and get to the Saint George's ER immediately. But then I thought, Be a doctor, and said, "No, I think you ought to have your blood pressure checked several times over the next week and then see Dr. Doolan with a record of those readings. One high reading does not a hypertensive make."

He thanked me and hung up, one relieved engineer.

Maureen was standing next to me now. "He called you at midnight to ask about his blood pressure?"

"He thought he might have to change his diet. That can worry you at midnight. Thinking about cutting out all that salt."

"I can't believe it."

"He's just an engineer. Probably only had four years of college. What can you expect him to know about hypertension? He probably had two biology courses his whole life. Taught him all about DNA. No one learns squat about anything they need to know."

Then Maureen said, "Do I get a tour, or do we go straight to bed?"

Even with that, she still sounded a little tentative and ironic, so I gave her the tour and didn't push things. She liked the place. "It's called a bungalow," I told her. It wasn't real expansive, but the living room had a fireplace and built-in floor-to-ceiling oak bookshelves. It was the only place I'd seen that could hold all my books.

"This is the way doctors should live," she said. "The Cadillac in the driveway, the pool and all that makes me sick."

She looked around the bedroom and my study. She took up the old framed picture of my high school swimming team and examined it.

"You keep that body up?" she asked.

"I just keep the picture."

She laughed and said she wanted me to get a fire going and asked me if she could use the phone.

"It's midnight," I said.

"My roommate will be worried." She called from the living room phone, while I stood there looking at the fireplace. It was almost cool enough for a fire but I hadn't put in a supply of wood. All I had was some kindling, so I stacked that while she talked on the phone. I guess she wanted me to hear what she was saying, to prove she was really talking to her roommate. I made a great show of unconcern and tried to look engrossed with the kindling, but listened.

"Yes, I'm okay. I'll be home in the morning."

She told her roommate about the accident and sounded very innocent, so I couldn't tell whether it was a man or woman she was talking to. She didn't say much about whom she was with or how she had met me, except right before she hung up she said, "I'm fine. I'll be perfectly fine." She hesitated just enough before *fine* – I knew she had almost said *safe*. She could have been talking with her mother.

The kindling went up with a great roar and she stretched out on her belly in front of the fire. The curve of her back and her round little bottom looked very pretty in the light. I stretched out beside her and she started rubbing the back of my neck.

I was determined to go slowly, expecting things to collapse momentarily, working her dress up her legs. I hadn't had a good look at her legs and was very impressed with what I was finding. Up to her hips, it was a very nice view and I was about to investigate further when the phone rang.

Answering service. Call Memorial Hospital ER. It was the lady from the car accident. They were letting her go. They hadn't done the four-quadrant tap and she was afraid to go home. I told her to go to Saint George's Emergency Room and that I'd call ahead.

Her husband got on the phone. "I'm sorry to bother you at this hour," he said, sweetly enough. "But we could not reach our doctor and my wife is worried. She is still having pain. We thought perhaps you might be kind enough . . ."

Kind enough to leave Maureen and tend to the lady's belly. They were in a tight spot, though, and if I thought it'd do any good to talk to those clowns who were discharging her from the ER I would have. But, instead, I told him to meet me in the ER at Saint George's.

I called the surgical resident there and he said he'd see her and hold down the fort until I could get in.

Maureen by now was wrapped around me, listening to my side of the conversation. When I hung up, she pulled her dress back into place and said, "Drop me off, on your way."

"I'll be back before sunrise."

"I'd better go."

I did not want her to leave. She was one of those women who look better when you get their clothes off than you could imagine looking at them dressed. But she seemed excited that I had been called back into the fray. Maybe it was just rationalization, but I had the distinct impression it titillated her that I was leaving her for the sake of being an important player in the little drama down at Saint George's. Somehow, I thought I'd better live up to her expectations and not look too crushed about having to leave her.

I dropped her off at her place. She kissed me very actively before she ran up the stairs to her porch. I sat there looking after her with the distinct feeling that she actually would complete the bargain next time, that this interruption had the effect of arousing her. She was one hell of a lot less tentative in the car in front of her place than she had been back at my house. But some part of me said she had her escape planned all along.


# 22


The surgical resident in the Saint George's ER had asked the full-time ER doctor to evaluate my spleen lady with him. They had done the four-quadrant tap before I arrived, and the lady was already on her way to the operating room. She had a belly full of blood.

Her husband was busy with the admitting officer, so I just stuck my head into the room and shook the husband's hand. He smiled and said, "You have heard about the spleen?"

"Yes."

"I have now reached our own doctor for recommendation for a surgeon."

"Fine."

"He says the surgeon they have called is very excellent."

"I agree."

"You will assist at the operation?"

"I'd just get in the way."

"Then you will leave now?"

"Yes. I will call in the morning on your wife." He did something to my syntax. Just listening to him, I could hear myself invert phrases.

"We thank you for your troubles tonight."

I waved good-bye and drove home to my smouldering empty hearth.

# 23

The sun was rising on Sunday when I reached the gates of the doctor's car park at Saint George's. I inserted my special plastic card and watched the wooded plank rise in front of my car. I drove into the car park feeling a little sensation of special privilege, having got past the wooden plank and been admitted to the castle. Of course, it was one of those bonuses so typical of the perks given doctors, letting you park in the hospital parking space so you could round on your patients at an hour when most sane people were at home in a warm bed.

I could see my breath in the car park air and I stopped for a moment to look at the light changing on the leaves across Reservoir Road. Autumn was teasing its way into Washington. The weather had been alternating between sultry and frigid for days and nobody would know how to dress until November. In New England the leaves flame out and temperatures drop slam, bang over three weeks, and then it's winter. In Washington, autumn flirts first with summer, then with winter and back again for months. I thought about the ebbing-flowing seasons for a minute, then I walked upstairs to the main building.

Nurses were streaming out as the shifts changed. A very fat nurse was talking to a priest in the hall. I noticed her because she wore white stockings as the older nurses still did, but she was a young one. She would have been pretty, eighty pounds lighter. She had the false gaiety some fat people have, smiling about the mouth, but angry in the eyes.

"Good morning, Father," she was saying.

"Good morning," he said. He had a clean pink face. "It's lovely weather we've been having, so cool and crisp."

"Have you seen the leaves along the canal?" she asked with a very bright little smile.

"They're just beginning to turn," said the priest.

He did not say anything about the leaves being a wonder of God's creation, for which I was profoundly grateful, especially at that hour, and he continued walking into the hospital while she walked past me out the door.

I rode the lift up to see the lady from the accident, thinking about what a perfectly superficial conversation those two had just had and how much pleasure they both seemed to take in it.

The lady's name was Le Van Que. I read her chart outside her room. The spleen was ruptured all right, and they had had to give her four units of blood during surgery.

The fact sheet said her husband's name was Kam Din Que, and he was "self-employed." His business address was "Khuyen Imports," Arlington, Virginia. She was forty-four, and was listed as a housewife. She was awake, watching TV when I stepped in. She looked happy to see me.

"You were right about the spleen," she said. She spoke of the spleen as if it had no connection to her, which in fact was now true.

She turned down the volume on the TV as soon as I walked in. I always appreciate that. Nothing more annoying than a patient who can't seem to tear herself away. She reached out for my hand and held it in a way which made me glad her husband wasn't around.

She wanted to know if she would miss her spleen and I said no, she would get along fine without it – as long as you don't get pneumonia, I thought, but didn't say. She asked what function the spleen served, and I told her it helped defend against infectious disease, arming the white blood cells to fight off bacteria, which is as close to the truth as you can get in one sentence. I told her she'd need a Pneumovax vaccination yearly, to protect her against pneumonia. I wondered whether or not General Dhieu's doctor had taken care of that, and decided it was about time to call that doctor.

"But now I will have a scar," she said. "And I never even had so much as a stretch mark. I am disfigured."

"It'd take a lot more than that to disfigure you." I don't

know how that slipped out; it just did. But I meant it. Even the morning after, in a hospital gown, she was a stunner.

She patted my hand. "You're a nice man."

"I'm glad you called last night."

"My husband will have our doctor come this morning," she said. "But I would like to have you for my doctor. My Kind Samaritan."

"Good Samaritan. I'll be happy to see you." I fished in my wallet for a business card. I'd never gotten accustomed to being a grown-up and having cards to pass out.

She looked at the address and said, "Oh, you're right across the street from our house. How very convenient."

For a moment she sounded like her husband had sounded the night before: *How convenient, what a charming coincidence*, but she looked happy and nonironic, so I guessed she meant it.

"You sure your husband won't mind your coming to see me?"

"I can take care of my husband," she said, with only the barest flicker of a smile. I believed she could at that. "But he is very suspicious."

"You mean he's a jealous husband?"

"Jealous?" She rolled that word around a little. "No. Vietnamese men are protective of their women. Too much, I think. No, I mean he is suspicious. That is the right word."

"He acted like he thought I was driving the car that hit you."

"We have learned to be, what is the word? Too suspicious? Too much."

"Paranoid."

"Paranoid, yes. He thinks all the time of the CIA and FBI."

"He thinks I work for the CIA?"

"He thinks everyone does," she laughed. "Sometimes even me."

"Has he cause," I asked, "in your case?"

"To be suspicious? Not of the CIA." She smiled then, a very fetching smile. "I am a woman though, with a woman's appetites."

I smiled back, at her appetites, the day after surgery yet.

"You will come back to see me, when I am looking more presentable."

# 24

Monday morning the helicopters woke me at seven. They fly over on their way to the CIA campus across the river in Virginia. I don't know where they come from, or who they carry. My head was full of General Dhieu and his possibly absent spleen and all the people I had to call. I must have been dreaming about him. Usually the helicopters don't wake me up, but this time they knocked me right out of bed and onto the floor. Must have been the combination of dreaming about Dhieu and that Vietnam echo, the helicopter noise, put me right on the floor.

I thought about stopping at Saint George's to see Mrs. Que before going to my office, but by the time I got back from my morning run it was too late and I had to push it just to make it to the office by nine. Mrs. Bromley was looking at her watch when I charged in.

"Another thirty seconds and I would have had to scold you," she said. "You know you have a nine-o'clock."

I made contrite noises and asked her to call the resident who did General Dhieu's autopsy and to call the General's private physician.

"We are hot on the trail," she said. "Will they be in now?"

I told her to start trying.

"And should I interrupt you?"

I told her to put them through. I didn't think she'd get either one on the first try.

"I called the laboratory about that insulin level," she said. "They put me on hold for ten minutes and told me they'd get back to me. Do you know how maddening it is to be left on hold for ten minutes?"

95

"Don't tell me, I can imagine."

"Nice weekend?" asked Mrs. Bromley.

"Quite nice. Oh, I almost forgot. We have a hospitalized patient to bill." I handed her an index card with Mrs. Que's name and address.

"New consultation?"

"Just a hospital visit. Auto accident. She had some surgery."

"Exciting. And what did you do? Read her EKG?"

"I held her hand."

"Nice work, if you can get it," she said. "Was she grateful?"

"We'll find out when she gets the bill."

I took the chart Mrs. Bromley had prepared on the new patient and went out to see her in the waiting room.

The patient, Mrs. Waterhouse, was forty-seven and a deputy assistant something with the Department of the Interior. She was a neighbour of Mrs. Simpson's. I was about to think kind thoughts, for once, about Mrs. Simpson, for referring me a patient, when I noticed that Mrs. Waterhouse had printed in a tight little hand on her form under "Problem": "*Hypoglycemia.*" When it rains it pours.

I considered trying to drive her away with a few questions about whether she had licensed any oil drilling in coastal spawning grounds lately, but decided to give her a chance to hang herself.

The deputy assistant title came out when I asked her if she worked. Funny thing about people in Washington, they'll tell you right away where they fit in. For people in this town, all the world's a hierarchy, and all the men and women merely rank-holders. People here will tell you with minimal prompting their neighbourhood status (Potomac, Georgetown, McLean or Chevy Chase), their job title, where their kids go to college, or if their kids aren't in yet, what their SAT scores were and where they are applying.

This particular deputy secretary lived in Potomac and had one kid at Dartmouth and one at the Sidwell Friends School.

"He's talking about MIT, but I think he'll wind up at Harvard."

"Well," I said, "he'll be in Cambridge, in any case."

"He'd be more well-rounded at Harvard."

"I guess he might."

"Although there are more National Merit Scholars at MIT."

"Well, now, that is a factor."

"But Harvard would open more doors."

"Probably so."

Mrs. Waterhouse had consulted her local doctor because she'd been "all washed out." She got up in the morning feeling relatively energetic but was ready to go to bed by noon. Lately, she'd had a constant low-grade nausea, abdominal pains and she'd been crying for no good reason.

Her own doctor had drawn a few blood tests, put her on Elavil and sent her on her way. She just got more and more tired, lost weight and felt worse. Extensive research with *Glamour* and *Redbook* had suggested the diagnosis of hypoglycemia.

I sat there trying to think of a have-you-ever-considered-a-psychiatrist buildup when she produced a photocopy of the lab tests her doctor had done. It's hard for me to kick a patient out of my office once she's gone to the trouble of getting her lab reports from another doctor, so I read them.

Her blood sugar was on the low side, but that meant nothing. Her local doctor had done what local doctors often do to cover themselves – he had ordered a screening series. Her blood count was loaded with eosinophils, which apparently had not impressed her local doctor, but those eosinophils cried out for an explanation.

Having seen the numbers, I looked at Mrs. Waterhouse with new interest. She was sitting there in her neat green tweed suit, twisting her handkerchief with dirty-looking hands, like a true crazy. Her knuckles looked dark and I asked her about that.

"I can't seem to get my hands clean," she said, holding them up.

Her hands weren't dirty. They were pigmented. Her palmar creases were dark.

"I think I'd better examine you," I said.

While she was undressing in the examination room, Mrs. Bromley buzzed to say she had the pathology resident from Saint George's on the phone. I explained who I was, and asked him about the pneumonia in General Dhieu's lungs.

"Just one lobe," he said. "The rest of the lungs looked pretty decent. I can't say for sure he didn't die from what he had, but I'd be surprised if he died from that pneumonia alone. The rest of the lungs looked pretty decent. There had to be something else."

I asked about the spleen.

"Surgically absent," he said. "Scar on the belly. He had had some abdominal surgery, and it had to have been a splenectomy."

"He was supposed to have had malaria."

"There were some changes on gross," said the resident. "But we have to wait for the slides."

I thanked him and started to hang up when he said, "You know about the sugar?"

"Doesn't everybody?"

There was a long silence, uncomfortable enough that I was sure he was the one who'd talked to the reporter.

"We checked his pancreas. I mean we did micro sections. There's nothing there on gross. I can't believe we'll see anything on micro."

I remembered now: this was the same pathology resident who had presented the findings on Mrs. Best, the lady with the insulinoma from the CPC. He was having a regular run on patients with low blood sugars.

"Anything else you think I ought to know?" I asked.

"Not right at this moment," he said. "But I'll call just as soon as the slides are ready."

"Make me first on your list," I said. "I hate reading about these things second-hand."

"That's kind of a dirty crack," he said

I had to agree with him.

I went in to see Mrs. Waterhouse. Her nipples were darkly pigmented, as were her gums. She was freckled with dark little moles which she said she'd had all her life, but which had lately looked darker. That was all I needed to admit her.

Once she was dressed and back in my office, I broke the news, trying not to sound too excited.

"We're going to have to admit you to the hospital. But I think there's a good chance I can make you feel considerably better."

She started to cry. She didn't look like a Deputy Assistant Secretary of the Interior then; she just looked like a woman who couldn't keep that controlled exterior in place any more.

"The hospital?"

"We could probably do it as an outpatient, but I think it'd be better to do the definitive test in the hospital."

"For what?"

"Addison's disease."

"Addison's disease?"

"Adrenal gland failure."

"Kennedy had that," she said. She had a president's disease.

"Right."

"Is it serious?"

"Only if you miss the diagnosis."

"How'd I get it?"

"Let's be sure you have it, first. But if you do, there probably won't be any explanation. Some people are just unlucky."

"If you're right, I'm not so unlucky."

"How's that?"

"I found a doctor who knew what he was doing."

I buzzed Mrs. Bromley on the intercom and asked her to arrange admission for Mrs. Waterhouse to Saint George's.

I felt very pleased with myself, catching that diagnosis, but then I considered how very close I'd come to missing it. She sounded like a classic neurotic, and the bad-breath self-diagnosis of hypoglycemia had almost sealed her fate with me. It was only those eosinophils that saved me – and her. Eosinophils are a type of white blood cell, and they increase in Addison's disease. Asthmatics get eosinophils. So do people with trichinosis and other parasites. But she didn't have any of that. You had to explain the eosinophils. After the physical exam got done, the diagnosis seemed pretty apparent. But her own doctor hadn't examined her. And I came close to making the same mistake. It wasn't as though I was just too compulsive and methodical to miss it. I'd lucked out.

I sat at my desk and wrote my note in her chart and dictated an admitting note for Mrs. Bromley to type so I could put it in the chart at Saint George's. Mrs. Bromley hated typing long technical things like that, but this time I knew she wouldn't object. We had discovered someone with big-time disease. Mrs. Bromley felt very fulfilled whenever that happened. It was what doctors and their offices were all about.

A case like that could wake you up. Lately, I'd realized I could use a little waking up. I don't know exactly when or how it happened, but some vital parts of me had numbed. I'd gone to Vietnam alive and tingling, out of school, my first real job, going to war, exotic places, not thinking about politics or morality or right or wrong. All the preparation was over. I was going to meet life with a silver bar on my collar. But life wasn't what happened. It wasn't what I saw. I just saw what the napalm did, and the looks in dark eyes who saw me not as Ben Abrams, adventuring doc, but as just another American, another enemy, another baby killer.

After a while, maybe I saw myself the way they saw me.

Then there was the blow out on the river, and the long run home and the medevac and Walter Reed. Surgery. Anaesthesia. And I never really woke up. Started medical practice somnambulant and kept on going. It seemed like an appropriate response, drifting through the Martin Luther King, Jr., Clinic, the government stress-on-the-job clinic, the midnight phone calls about hypertension.

But lately things had begun to happen. The CPC, General Dhieu, and then Maureen, most of all Maureen. She started it. She got me into this Mrs. Que case. And she had me looking at every patient with a little more interest.

It was an uncomfortable feeling: like when your arm falls asleep and then starts to wake up, all pins and needles. You want it to wake up but you wish the pins and needles would stop.

But I wasn't sure how much I wanted to wake up.

I wanted to recapture that drive I had in medical school and internship. Leave no stone unturned. List every possibility and work your way through them. Get that anal sphincter tone jacked up: be obsessive-compulsive overachieving migrainous four-plus aggressive and don't miss a thing. But somehow all that heel-clicking self-discipline was connected to what came later. Change that white uniform for khakis; it was all just spit and polish. And what good was it?

It takes more that a smile and a white coat to be a doctor.

The trouble is, the world's a noisy place when you're practising medicine. The noise inside my head hadn't quieted, and the phone kept ringing and patients kept talking. There were too many Mrs. Simpsons in the world, too many midnight callers with high blood pressure, too many sure-I've-got-hypoglycemias.

It was tough to pick out the insulinomas, the Addison's diseases, even the ruptured spleens from among all the walking worried.

But you have to be compulsive if you want to avoid missing things. Even if a given possibility seemed remote, you had to check it out. You had to touch all the bases, like calling the pathology resident. I buzzed Mrs. Bromley and asked her to get me General Dhieu's private doctor.

"His secretary said he'd call back," she said. "Teach me to trust a secretary. The lab said the insulin level isn't ready yet. They said they'd call when it is. Famous last words." She hung up, then buzzed back.

General Dhieu's doctor was on the line. He had a very thick Vietnamese accent. I asked him why he had put the General on Biocon insulin.

"Very good stuff," he said. "Very strong."

He didn't think the General had had any hypoglycemic reactions to the insulin, but he didn't sound as if he would have known. I asked him whether or not he had given the General any Pneumovax, but he didn't seem to have heard of it.

"Dumobax?" he said. "Give him how?"

He didn't want to say much about the quinine, but he did know the General had malaria, although he couldn't say which species. He got tired of my questions and hung up.

Mrs. Bromley buzzed with Mrs. Simpson on the line. Mrs.

Simpson said she had a twinge in her gall bladder and wanted to know whether or not that could mean she had Hodgkin's Disease.

I hung up and thought about the General's doctor. I knew there were docs like him in the world, and had stopped wondering long ago how they ever got licensed and what they did to their patients. Now I had something more important to worry about – how different was I? They tell you in medical school there are no average doctors, only good ones and bad ones. Either you plug all the leaks or you let the boat go down. I hadn't been running such a tight ship lately, myself.

There weren't any other patients that morning and I drove down to the government clinic thinking about Mrs. Waterhouse and thinking about Maureen and her hypoglycemia. I hadn't even examined Maureen, at least not in my office. She didn't seem to require it. In her case, the history told the story. Or so it seemed.

# 25

Wednesday was exactly nine days since I formally began examining General Dhieu's death, and it was the day Dr. Potter, the lab director, had said the insulin level might be ready. It wasn't. At eight A.M. I stood in the middle of that vast gleaming lab while a lab tech punched General Dhieu's name into his computer terminal and saw PENDING flash onto the screen in the space next to INSULIN LEVEL. *Pending* meant it wasn't back from the reference lab. No result yet. They did have the drug screen ready. The terminal glowed with the names of twenty drugs, all negative and then QUININE: POSITIVE.

From a lab phone I paged the intern who had admitted the General.

"We got fifteen admissions that day and night," he said. "I could hardly remember who he was, when they told me he'd coded."

"I presume he wasn't too sick," I said. "Or you would have put him in the ICU."

"I guess," he said. "As I said, I really don't remember the guy too well. I remember I had some trouble getting a history from his doc, who didn't speak English much better than the patient. And I remember he was on that special insulin."

"The nurses tell me he had rigours his first night."

"Wouldn't be surprised."

"You didn't get called to see him?"

"Fifteen admissions. Seven different floors, two different buildings. No, they didn't call me. If they had, I probably wouldn't have come."

Saint George's was not the place to be if you looked good when you were admitted and then turned sour. The interns were spread thin.

"I wish I could be more help," he said. "But I'd just be bullshitting you. I hardly saw the guy. You know who you might try? Ask his med student. They spend hours with the new admissions. I don't remember who had him. It'll be in the chart."

The med student hadn't known the patient was a general and his chart note hadn't impressed me. I didn't think the medical student deserved a top spot on my list of important players.

Mrs. Bromley looked up when I charged through the door. "Ah," she shouted. "The very man everyone's been trying to reach."

"I'll call them later."

"Dr. von Dernhoffer," she said, ignoring my protests, following me back to my office with a wad of telephone message slips in her hands, "would like you to call him. Nothing urgent, you understand. Just call the instant you walk through the door."

It wasn't anything urgent. He was just keeping the heat on.

"I thought we might have your report by now," he said. If you can hear a smirk over the phone, I was hearing one. He was really enjoying this. Even with the newspapers putting pressure on him, I think he'd have liked to see me give up. Doctor Smug brought down in flames – got nowhere on the Dhieu case.

"Well, well. I've been hearing from everyone. You've been pressing this case very aggressively."

Tell it to the newspapers, I thought. "I've been trying to stay on top of it," I said.

"Any news?"

"The big thing is the insulin level. That's still not ready."

"Does Dave Potter know? Can he speed things up?"

"Insulins are a send-out. There's not much he can do to hurry Federal City Lab."

"Oh, I don't know. Dave might be able to light a few fires under them. Touch base with him," said von Dernhoffer. Having discharged his executive responsibilities, he felt better and hung up. I wondered what it would be like having a job which consisted of phoning people and telling them to call other people.

I thought about the General, and tried to visualize his admission from the moment he walked through the front door of the admissions office to the lift ride up to Seven North to the nurse meeting him and taking him to his room to the exams by the med student, intern and resident. There were big lapses I couldn't account for. At least three nurses, two doctors and one student had been with him, but nobody spent much time, and for all that contact, nobody remembered him very well.

He must have looked like a lot of other patients at Saint George's, small, wanly smiling and nodding, humbled by the handicap of not being able to speak in a language anyone around him could understand. Here was a man who'd been shot at, mortared, pirated and survived. He comes into a hospital where five people try to do something for him and he quietly dies, without so much as a pull on the nurse's call cord. It just didn't seem right.

# 26

Friday, I saw five patients at the government workers' clinic: two forty-five-year-old men who hated their jobs and were just holding on to get in their twenty-five years for retirement, a black woman for a Pap smear, and a woman with an earache who thought she had a brain tumour. One of the men had trouble satisfying his wife. He was sure it was all the stress at work. I wasn't so sure. His breasts were a little plump and he didn't need to shave much any more because his beard growth had slowed. That was a lot to explain from stress on the job.

Just after the last Pap exam, Maureen telephoned.

"You do move around," she said. She had called the office and Mrs. Bromley gave her my number at the clinic.

"Moonlighting pays the rent," I said.

"I hope you pay that sweet lady who answers your phones."

"Regularly, but not nearly enough."

"Why not enough? You have to pay people what they're worth."

"Can't do that with Mrs. Bromley."

"Why not?"

"She's worth too much."

"Had some symptoms this morning."

"Did you get a blood sugar drawn?"

"I tried. But the health unit had this sign up, 'Nurse Does Not Come in Until Nine.' This was eight-fifteen. By nine I'd be out cold. So I ate."

"You felt better?"

"Later I did. I probably should have gone ahead and had it drawn anyway. I just kept eating all morning. The feeling kept coming back."

"Get a blood sugar."

"Okay, Doc. Now, tell me, what happened with the slinky lady in the red dress? She have a spleen or what?"

"She had one, once."

"No kidding?"

"Was your roommate happy to see you get home early, safe and sound?"

"Oh, she wasn't even home. Works nights. We saw each other at breakfast: her coming home, me going."

"She works nights?"

"Nurse."

"You say you ate breakfast this morning?"

"My roommate insists on breakfast."

"So you ate before you went to work?"

"Yes, doctor. I am a good girl now. Between you and my roommate, I'm getting to be very good and very fat."

"From what I've seen, you're not fat."

"I'll take that for what it's worth," she said, and paused, dropping her voice. "Until you've seen more."

"When will that be?"

"Soon, I hope."

"No, you're not the kind to show too much."

"I guess you'd know about that."

I waited to hear why she was calling.

"Do you realize what today is?" she asked.

"I give up."

"Friday. And as a special bonus, I'm going to let you take me out."

"What a break."

"I can withdraw the offer."

"So I've seen."

"What's that supposed to mean?"

"Nothing."

"It wasn't my fault your honey in the red dress called you out at all hours."

"I know."

"Well, I was going to let you buy me dinner, but now I'm not so sure."

"I'd love to."

She told me to pick her up at seven. She lived in Glover Park, just off Tunlaw Road, not far from the Russian compound, in a row house with a front porch. I like Glover Park. It's tree-lined and has lots of little parks where people play softball in the summer and it has neighbourhoods where people sit on porches and drink beer and talk to each other.

I was a little early, so I sat outside in the car and read the newspaper, something I scrupulously avoid, until I get caught someplace where I have to kill time. Two congressmen had been caught screwing eighteen-year-old congressional pages, which delighted all the congressmen who hadn't been caught because it gave them a wonderful opportunity to make speeches for the folks back home, condemning immorality and strongly supporting Basic American Values. The speeches were also welcome items for the editors of the paper, it being early September and there not being much real news.

They printed the speeches right next to a story about a congressman who had presented himself to a publicly funded clinic in his own district in Brooklyn, posing as a patient with chest pain. His photograph was centred above the article. He was shown with arms outstretched, bruises where they had drawn his blood. The congressman was outraged at the blatant waste of government money and the affront to human dignity he had uncovered at the clinic, where he had been subjected to an electrocardiogram, blood drawing, a physical exam and a chest X ray, all at a cost of seventy-five dollars, which I thought was a great bargain, since it would have cost him a hundred dollars in my office. He had had the standard workup for a suspected heart attack. He had them coming and going. If they'd done any less he could have experts testify they didn't care enough to do the right workup in that public clinic. But he was outraged they had done all that to him, spent all that money, and then discovered that there was nothing wrong with him.

When I couldn't read any further, I balled the paper and threw it into the gutter and walked up the stairs to Maureen's place and rang the bell.

Maureen's roommate answered the door. She was the fat nurse I'd seen in earnest and banal conversation with the priest at Saint George's on Sunday morning.

She stood behind the louvred glass door and said, "You're Benjamin Abrams?" She made that sound like something very good to be and let me in.

I followed her to the living room.

"Maureen will be right down. Why don't you have a seat?" She sat down on a couch across from my chair. I felt as if I were sitting with my date's mother. I hadn't felt like that in a long, long time.

Her name was Helen and she had baby white skin and there were no chairs in the living room that could hold her, which was why she was sitting on the couch. Her neck passed from chin to chest in a straight line and when she moved great undulating waves were set in motion under her cotton dress. She sat with her legs crossed at the ankles because she could not possibly have crossed them any higher up, and she breathed with little gasps because her abdomen compressed her lungs when she sat.

I kept thinking how pretty she'd be if she were only a hundred pounds lighter. She had a lovely voice and a too urgent laugh and I had the impression she was bursting to tell me something.

"You're a doc, and you left Nam before Maureen got there," she said. "That's all I know, except Maureen's smiling again so you must be something special."

"I'm not so special."

Helen glanced furtively at the door to the hallway and said, "She hasn't smiled too awfully much since we've been back."

"Back?"

"From Nam."

"But that's been years."

"Don't I know it."

"Well, we don't know each other all that well," I said. "I doubt I have much to do with it, if she's brightened up."

"I think I know Maureen," she said. "All I can say is I'm happy to meet you. She actually seemed excited to be going out tonight."

I sat there looking at Helen's bright, approving face and tried not to feel too encouraged. Maureen never seemed too depressed to me.

I was happy when Maureen bounced in. She was wearing some kind of sweet perfume and sheer white slacks you could see her panties through and a green knit shirt with a pink sweater tied around her shoulders. She looked wonderful.

"Come on, I'll show you around," she said.

She had her own room, all bright greens and blues and light-coloured woods and framed Smithsonian posters on the walls. We went by Helen's room and I looked in. It had a traffic sign that said SOFT SHOULDERS and a shelf full of stuffed animals.

We went back down to the kitchen and Maureen went straight for the refrigerator.

"Jesus, I'm parched," she said. She poured us each some orange juice.

Helen came in.

"Oh, don't drink that old juice," she clucked. "Let me make you a drink."

"This is fine," I said.

"I meant to throw it out," said Helen, taking my glass. "It's spoiled. I just had some when I got home. Things just sit in there and rot when we don't get home nights," she said with an attempt at a real smile. I wasn't sure if that was a complaint or a little joke, but Maureen smiled and I guessed it was all right.

"Oh, don't bother with the drinks," said Maureen. "I'll make Ben buy me a pitcher of sangria. Want to come?"

I couldn't believe that she had just invited Helen on our date. But she had. To my great relief Helen said, "Oh, no. You two don't need a third wheel." Helen was quite right about that and I didn't give Maureen a chance to respond but guided her out the front door by the elbow.

"Don't worry," said Maureen when we got to the car. "She wouldn't have come. She can't fit into the chairs at most restaurants. Besides, she wants us to have a nice romantic evening."

"Why's that?"

"She thinks you're good for me," Maureen said. "Poor deluded thing."

"I'm not good for you?"

"You are wonderful for me," she said. "Just don't let it give you any ideas."

We drove down Thirty-seventh Street and headed for Enriquetta's. Maureen asked me about my clinic and I told her about the man who couldn't please his wife.

"What do you think's wrong with him?"

"Sounds like he's hypogonadal, for whatever reason: pituitary, testicular burnout, whatever – he's just not making enough testosterone. I'd bet dollars to doughnuts if he came to see me and I got a testo level, it'd be low."

"Will he see you?"

"I gave him my card. I've got a fair number of patients that way from the clinic."

"So what would you do for him?"

"Testosterone shots every three weeks. Make a new man out of him."

"Sounds like vitamin $B_{12}$ shots for old ladies."

"Not at all. If the level's low, they really respond to replacement. Course, if he's got enough testosterone and he's just bored with his wife, he's not going to get better with a shot of hormone he's already got plenty of."

"How likely is it he doesn't have enough?"

"It's a fairly common deficiency, when you look for it carefully."

"But you have to do things systematically, and get the numbers," smiled Maureen. "Like getting blood sugars."

"You have to be sure what you're dealing with," I said.

"I might send you a friend of mine who's got some problems in that department," said Maureen. "Maybe you could work him up."

I looked over at her but she was looking out her window. I mean, what was that supposed to mean? She's sending me a boyfriend for me to fix up for her? Suddenly I had the distinct premonition that this night was not going to end any differently than the last time had.

My mother always told me to stay away from Catholic schoolgirls. I guess that's one reason I never could.

110

## 27

There was no place to park. We wound around the back streets, bumping over the streetcar tracks and over cobblestone sections, watching for cars pulling out of spaces, listening to street sounds and to the dull drone of a radio talk show. A United States senator was telling us about the importance of prayer in his life.

"Can you believe this?" said Maureen, turning down the volume on the radio.

"This is, after all, one nation under God," said the senator.

"Amen," said Maureen.

The senator was for putting God back into the classroom. "This is a Christian nation," he said.

"Hear that, infidel?" Maureen said to me.

The senator then informed us of the congressional prayer breakfast. We also heard about the role Jesus played in his life, and I learned things I never knew about Godless Communism, and about misguided liberals. Maureen finally switched stations to one playing Billy Joel doing "Only the Good Die Young."

"God, it makes me feel better, just knowing there's a man like that writing our nation's laws," said Maureen. "It explains a lot, don't you think?"

Just as we got to Twenty-eighth Street, my beeper went off and I had to find a place to park quickly. That's an exercise in the absurd in Georgetown on a Friday night, but I tried Olive Street and it came through. Olive Street is where all the Georgetown dowagers walk and water their toy poodles and Chihuahuas. Its pavements are fairly pungent and slippery, and it's one of the last blocks to fill up on a Friday night.

I used the pay phone outside the Corcoran School while Maureen huddled close to listen.

"It's the man with the frustrated wife," she said. "He wants his shot."

Actually, she wasn't that far off. It was Rapur Shamur, a patient to whom I was giving monthly testosterone injections. Burglars had walked off with half his apartment, including his shaving kit containing all his cortisone and thyroid pills.

"I'm sorry to bother you, doctor. Very sorry. But you see, you told me to always take my pills and I have no pills. All gone."

"That's quite all right, Mr. Shamur. You were quite right to call. Give me the number of your pharmacy and go by tonight and pick up the prescriptions. Do you have money?"

"Yes, yes," said Mr. Shamur in his fast breathless accent. "Besides, the druggist will let me have without money."

I was out of change but Maureen had some and I called in the prescriptions.

We walked to Enriquetta's. She wrapped her arms around my arm.

"You like Mr. Shamur, don't you?"

"Poor bastard. Lebanese Jew, if you can imagine. Noticed his breasts were swelling and milk was staining his shirts. Big prolactinoma."

"I'm just a poor dumb ex-scrub nurse."

"Pituitary tumour makes the hormone that helps you lactate. His tumour was about the size of a baseball. Fortunately for Lebanon, it's not far from Israel, and they took out what they could at Haddassah Hospital."

"But he still has some left?"

"Oh, yes. But it's under control with bromocriptine. Of course he needs cortisone to stay alive, thyroid to function and testosterone to want to."

"What is he, a diplomat?"

"Sure. The Jewish ambassador from Lebanon," I said. "No, he's a student. Studying business administration at George Mason or some damn place. Works all day, goes to school – for all the good that place'll do him – at night."

"He pay his bills?"

112

"How's he going to pay his bills? He's lucky to afford his medicines."

"And you still see him? I thought it was cash on the line in your office."

"What made you think that?"

"Mrs. Bromley – just about tackled me before I could get out the door."

"Don't know what I'd do without her," I said. "But, no. We have a special arrangement for Mr. Shamur. He says a special prayer in Hebrew for my practice every Friday night, and we let his bill ride."

"Many more of those arrangements, your practice'll need a prayer."

"That's exactly what Mrs. Bromley said."

"Great minds think alike," said Maureen. "I do like that kind of arrangement, though, in principle. Payment in kind. That's the way the world should work. I even like the idea of pay *back* in kind. Guy steps on your toe, you step on his."

"Eye for an eye. Very Old Testament sense of justice you have there."

"I like justice that has symmetry," she said, holding my eye. I had the feeling she was telling me something important and I was too obtuse to understand. "It bothered me that LBJ died of a heart attack; he should have been napalmed," she said with a smile her lips had discarded by the time it reached her eyes.

We were standing in front of the Biograph movie theatre, across M Street from two Vietnamese restaurants. There was a line in front of one of them, ten people deep.

"Ever try them?" asked Maureen.

"I left all that behind."

"No, you didn't," she said. "No one does."

She dragged me across the street and into the quieter of the two. I hadn't had Vietnamese food since I was there. It felt strange, sitting there in safety and coolness, with the food smells carrying me back, but with Americans in tweeds at the surrounding tables. It felt as authentic as a stage prop.

A Vietnamese waiter stood silently in front of us. Maureen ordered a Manhattan for herself and a beer for me and the

113

waiter went away. I looked after him, not realizing Maureen was watching me.

"What were you thinking, just now?" she said. "About him."

"Nothing."

"Yes, you were. You were feeling sorry for him."

"I was thinking I'd better have him taste the drinks before we drink them."

"Why?"

"If he falls over dead, I don't think I'll drink mine."

"They wouldn't stay in business long if they poisoned the customers. Even if they poisoned just a few."

"Couldn't blame them, if they did."

Maureen raised an eyebrow. Then smiled. It was a warm smile and she reached across the table and covered my hand with her own.

"I was thinking," I said. "In Saigon, that guy took orders from Americans. Now he's still taking orders from Americans. He must love it by now."

"He was probably an ARVN colonel and black marketeer. Now he owns a condo on Kalorama Road and drives a Porsche."

"Not likely. He's a little guy. He's spent his life just trying to stay out of the line of fire. Now he lives in a two-room apartment in Little Saigon, with his mother and the one kid we didn't incinerate."

Maureen looked me over carefully. She said, "You really left it all behind, didn't you, soldier?"

"I wasn't a soldier. I was a conscript."

"Ever see any incinerated kids?" she asked quietly.

My throat by this time was dry. I could feel the sweat coursing down under my arms and I reached for the ice water and gulped it down. "Just once," I said.

The waiter came with the drinks. He set them down and stood there silently, pen in hand, waiting. Maureen picked up her menus and ordered for both of us, in Vietnamese.

Unless you'd been in Vietnam, I don't think you could have noticed how the waiter smiled when she started chattering away in his language. It was the rare and ultimate compliment

114

from a Westerner, and an American at that, speaking his language. He didn't smile with his lips or even with his eyes. He smiled with his shoulders and his back, and he replied, briefly, softly, but directly to her. I knew the smile was in there. Then he took our menus and slipped away. I figured I could eat the food without having to test it first.

"You got pretty fluent," I said. "How long were you there?"

"Just the one year. Learned it when I got back, mostly. I tried to learn when I was there, but you know, you really couldn't. No, I speak Berlitz Vietnamese. Enough to order in restaurants. No big deal."

Funny how people can change right before your eyes. I realized she got me into this place in part to show off her Vietnamese, but it didn't matter.

"What happened with the kids?" she asked.

"They got snuffed."

"Don't say 'snuffed'," she said. "You don't feel that way. Don't try to go tough on me, with 'snuffed' and 'wasted'."

"It was part of our pacification programme," I continued. "Or was it our Vietnamization programme? I forget. Vietnam for the Vietnamese, I always said."

"But what happened?"

"Why ask? You must've seen the same thing plenty of times."

"But I want to know what you saw. I thought you were on the boat."

"They took me off, once in a while," I said. "That's when we were still winning the hearts and minds of the people."

"Before people started saying, 'If you've got them by the balls, their hearts and minds will follow'," said Maureen.

"They flew me over Quang Ngai province to a land-based hospital. Ever see Quang Ngai province from the air?"

"No."

"It looked like the surface of the moon. Mud, craters. Burned-out *villes*. No people. I read later they killed seventy percent of the population in Quang Ngai with the B-52s. Looked more like a hundred percent to me. Didn't win over a lot of hearts and minds in Quang Ngai. Anyway, they were taking me to some hospital, and when we got there it was dusk."

Maureen sipped her drink and looked at me over the rim of her glass. I had to swallow some more ice water.

"They're showing me around and we're in the radio room and some helicopter pilot calls in saying he's bringing in some civilian evacs. Kids. He says – I can still hear his voice – he says, 'Good Christ, they're *glowing*.' I couldn't figure out what the hell he was trying to say. He said something about Willie Peter. Know what Willie Peter is?"

"Phosphorus."

"You must have seen it, then. The kids came in. Twenty-three kids. Burned, some of them crying, but most of them just listless and quiet the way kids get when they're really hurt. Floppy little kids with singed-off hair and white phosphorus splashed all over. Smell of burnt flesh. They all died."

"How'd it happen?"

"You know that stuff was used to mark targets. Some steely-eyed killer from the blue decided their *ville* was hostile. He 'knew' they had VC hidden in this *ville*, you understand. He knew that from a thousand feet, at two hundred miles an hour. He knew those kids had to be taught a lesson, the American way."

Maureen looked down at her empty glass.

"They all died," I said.

Maureen looked up at me, with a strange, appraising look.

"Want to hear some more war stories?" I said. "I've got some'll melt your heart. But then, I guess you've got plenty of your own. Why talk about it?"

"Oh, yes," she said, with an irony even I couldn't miss. "Why even think about it? It's all behind us now."

"Why did you learn Vietnamese after you got back?"

"Because I hadn't learned it when I was there."

"You know what I mean. Why'd you go to Berlitz and spend the time and money?"

"Oh, I don't know. Maybe I'll go back someday. It's a damn pretty country. Ought to be lovely now the fighting's over."

I didn't say anything.

"Wouldn't you want to go back? Did you ever see the beaches?"

"Probably put your blanket down on a land mine. Sit down right on – what did they call those things? A Bouncing Betty?"

"I think it'd be a lovely trip."

I looked at her. I think she really meant it.

The food arrived. I had never learned the names of those dishes, not like Maureen. I'd just eaten and enjoyed it while I was there. Tonight I didn't have much of an appetite.

Maureen went through two more Manhattans with the meal, along with the wine. When we'd finished, she said something about going somewhere for a drink and I wondered how I was going to get her there. Another drink and she'd have to be wheeled out in a cart.

But she walked out of the restaurant under her own steam and pretty steadily and by the time we got to the car, you never would have guessed she had had a drink, except for a vagueness about her eyes.

We drove down M Street, past the busy pavements and the street musicians, past the bagpiper with his hat on the pavement, full of coins. We got to Canal Road and there were blue flashing lights. A policeman pointed at me and we pulled over. It was a "sobriety checkpoint," a roadblock. The cop was very polite and smiling and had me blow into a breath analyser. My one beer passed inspection and they let us go.

"Fucking vermin," Maureen said, as we pulled away.

I glanced over. Her face was dark and hateful.

"What's wrong?"

"That's just this town all over," she said. "Friend of mine was stopped walking across Twenty-third Street. She'd *jaywalked*, for Chrissake."

"I didn't know you could be stopped for that."

"You can in this town," she said.

"There is a lot of law here," I agreed.

The phone was ringing when we got home. Answering service. For some reason I was sure it was going to be about Mrs. Que, but it was only Mrs. Simpson, who had a pain in her neck. I told her I'd meet her in the emergency room at Saint George's, sure she wouldn't want to go that far at that hour unless it was really hurting. She said she thought it could wait until Monday.

Maureen meanwhile had poured herself a fair-sized Kahlúa and one for me and was curled up on the couch in front of the fireplace. I sat down on the floor beside her.

"I've decided," she said. "You're not such a bad guy."

"Now how'd you figure that out?"

"For one thing you're nice to Mr. Shamur, and you're even civil to Mrs. Simpson, when anyone else would bawl hell out of her for calling at all hours."

"My practice isn't so big I can afford to lose even Mrs. Simpson."

"For another, you always wait to be told, when it comes to personal things."

"You'll tell me what you want to tell me," I said. "What you don't want me to know, you won't tell me."

"What makes you think there are things I don't want you to know?"

"Just guessing."

"There are things I want you to know, and I'm counting on you to find out."

I waited for her to say something more but she just drank her Kahlúa and asked me to start up a fire.

It must have been fifty degrees, but that time of year it felt cool and the lady wanted a fire.

We sat on the floor in the warmth as the kindling and newspaper went up. She said, "Tell me how you got shot up."

"It wasn't too difficult."

"But you were on a boat. What happened? Viet Cong navy torpedo your ship?"

"Their navy was not a big factor. We had no fear of their naval might," I said. "They caught us in a riverboat."

"I thought you were on a cutter."

"We used to make goodwill visits upriver. Great white doctor from Uncle Sam."

"You volunteer for that?"

"They cooked these great village feasts every time the great white doctor arrived. I got sucked in by the cuisine."

"But the Cong didn't like your goodwill trips?"

118

"Apparently not. Never said anything about it to me personally. Never would have done it if I'd thought they'd be displeased. Made it a point not to offend the Cong. But one day they shot up our boat."

"They were not warmed by your goodwill?"

"Shot up the boat. Killed everyone but me, and the boat went down. I got swept along downriver and washed up on the bank. Ran all the way home. Took ten days."

"They chased you for *ten days*?"

"Off and on." I was beginning to sweat. Nobody had asked me about this for a long time and it made me a little queasy to talk about it.

"Lovely," she said, looking at me seriously. She put a hand behind my neck and pulled me towards her. She must have liked the story, judging from her kiss.

"So why'd they send you home early?"

"I was pretty beat up."

"Shot up?"

"That too. Lost some blood. What blood I had left was host to malaria."

"And you left it all behind."

"I remember the good times."

"And your friends the villagers. Pictures on your office wall."

"You did like that picture, didn't you?"

"I liked what it said about the guy who hung it up there."

If I'd known how much mileage I'd get out of that photo, I'd have worn a copy in a locket around my neck.

"They chased you for ten days. You had a bad time. But you put a picture of a guy in black pyjamas on your wall."

"He wasn't one of the guys who chased me. Not as far as I know, anyway. Couldn't have blamed him if he had."

"Why not?"

"It was *his* rice paddy. His country, for that matter."

"You say that as if it's so obvious," said Maureen. She leaned over and kissed me again. I felt like a trained seal who'd done the right thing.

"It sure as hell wasn't my rice paddy. I don't know anybody who had any doubts on that score."

"I knew plenty."

"Who thought what? That it was our country we were blowing away?"

"Listen to Helen sometime. You'd think the war was in San Francisco and they'd attacked us."

Her face was tight now, startling in the swiftness of its change.

"Helen?" I said, trying to understand how Helen came into consideration. "You two are something of an odd couple," I said. I don't know how that slipped out.

"We go back a long way."

"Helen was labouring under the misapprehension we were actually invited?" I asked.

"She still wants to heave a brick through the window of that Vietnamese restaurant in Georgetown. I always steer her away from that street."

"Some people take longer to forgive and forget."

Maureen laughed a dry, biting little laugh. She turned on me with a couple of arched eyebrows you could have hung curtains from. " 'Forgiveness to the *injur'd* does belong,' " she said. "Dryden," she added. "Conquest of Grenada."

"Grenada," I said. "Now there was a nice little war."

She smiled, but I couldn't read anything into it.

"Helen was prety gung ho, I take it," I said after a silence.

"Helen still thinks we could have won, *would* have except for the bleeding-heart peaceniks and a few South Vietnamese Benedict Arnolds."

I suddenly remembered what Mr. Simpson of State had said about General Dhieu's assassin coming from the ranks of his former comrades-in-arms. And I focused back on Maureen, whose eyes were searching my face.

"What do you think?" I asked her. "Did you go over to win the war?"

"I went," said Maureen, pausing to phrase things properly, "I went for the adventure. I went because I hated college and all those fleshy, glabrous, poor-excuse-for-a-man wimps I was meeting at Amherst. I went because the real men were the Vets who hung around the Student Union at U Mass, and I was inflamed by their stories."

120

"But you weren't wearing an American flag on your lapel?"

"Christ, no. I was . . . drawn. I wanted to do hands-on work with the suffering third world people."

"But you were nursing for the capitalist army."

"It got me there."

"And you had your adventure."

"I saw America for what it really was," she said. Her eyes drew down to narrow cracks and her chin tucked in. She had seen something all right.

"Bad things happen in war," I said, profoundly. "The VC weren't such nice fellows. But they got away with what they did."

"Not all of them."

"Who didn't?"

"The ones we managed to get our hands on. They paid. The avenging angels got them."

"How do you mean?"

"We really worked them over," she said, looking me in the eye. "Even in the hospital."

" 'We' meaning you? Or 'we' meaning the U.S. of A.?"

"Not me, no. No, the angels of mercy and wrath with the American flag emblems in their lapels."

"They were tough on the Cong patients?"

"Tough?" Maureen's face tightened. "Lovely word that. Tough. Yeah, they were tough on them. I worked on what they called the gook ward."

"As I said, bad things happen."

"Did you kill any Cong?" she asked suddenly.

"No."

"No, I don't think you could have. It's too cruel. And you're too kind. And you have a sense of what's right."

We talked a little more about Nam, but I didn't get much about what happened to her. She kept to pretty nonspecific comments about the heat, the whores in Saigon and the booze at the officers' club. Somehow I thought her hypoglycemia symptoms might be tied up with what happened to her there, but that was just a semiformed idea.

We drank some more Kahlúa and about two A.M. she decided it was time for a shower.

Now, I've enjoyed showers before, but this was one memorable shower. Towelling each other off afterwards, I was glad I hadn't examined her in the office, even if it was the compulsive thing to do. Her body was such a wonderful surprise, and seeing it in the office would have been a sorry, analytical way to have been introduced.

"It's been a long time since I've done anything like this," she said. "You'll have to write me a prescription for a morning-after pill."

I said I would.

The sheets were cold, but they warmed up quickly and she seemed very intent on consoling me for all the bad times I'd had. "Poor baby, they chased you all through the woods." She woke me up once or twice after that for more. I hadn't had so much consolation since I moved to Washington and I wasn't sure I could take much more, me pushing forty and all. She made me promise I'd let her console me again in the morning.

# 28

When I awoke, I was the only one in bed. I could smell bacon and coffee. Maureen was in the kitchen, wearing my bathrobe.

"Did you ever call your roommate last night?"

"Aren't you considerate? Thinking of Helen. No. She knew I wouldn't be coming home."

"How's that?"

"I told her before I left."

"Pretty sure of yourself, aren't you?"

"There's no penalty for being wrong," she said smiling. I had my arm around her waist. "But I was hoping I'd be right." She started kissing me again and she had nothing on under the robe, but the bacon was burning and we ate breakfast.

Maureen read the paper and ignored me. She was laughing quietly to herself.

I leaned over to see what she was reading. She lifted her shoulder to block my view and then read aloud, " 'Widow Says Husband Died from Agent Orange.' " She laughed. "I love those 'Widow Says' stories. 'Widow Says Husband Died from Asbestos Exposure'; 'Widow Says Husband Died from Filling Out Income Tax Forms.' Those are the best articles."

I thought of another "Widow Says" article, the one about General Dhieu, and tried to catch her eye. Maureen had never admitted having seen that one. I thought she might open up about it now, but she ignored me.

She finished the paper and started washing dishes. She looked almost domestic washing dishes in my bathrobe.

A raucous squawking and honking came through the window over the sink, audible over the sound of the water and clinking dishes. Maureen looked skyward but couldn't see anything.

"Where are they?" she said, looking.

"You can't see them through the kitchen window," I said. "Try the bedroom window."

She ran out of the kitchen and into the bedroom. The sound of the geese was superseded by a low thumping motor sound, distant but then suddenly loud and shaking the windows. I could hear Maureen cry out: "Assholes! Flaming assholes!" from the bedroom, and I continued washing dishes. She came back into the kitchen, face grey and as unhappy as I'd ever seen it. She had her hands on her ears. The noise was impressive now. We had to raise our voices to hear each other.

"We're on the helicopter flight path, too," I said. I looked out the kitchen window. I could see them now, five or six of them, and I knew there were more I couldn't see.

"It sounds like Nam!" Maureen shouted. "There must be a hundred of them."

"More like a dozen," I shouted back. "Probably the presidential flotilla, on their way to Camp David."

"He wakes up the whole neighbourhood," she said. We could hear each other again.

"Local colour," I said.

"What a country," Maureen said. "It's like those cops with their roadblock last night. Like the generals in Nam. They

123

do just what they want and all the little people just have to take it."

She was truly angry. Her face was all red, and her eyes were as big as spotlights. Then she seemed to get over it. The insult to the republic passed and she started putting dishes away in all the wrong places.

I didn't want her to leave.

"Are you on call today?" she asked, seeing me hook my beeper onto my belt.

I was on call the whole weekend, for myself and for two other docs.

"Do you have to go to the hospital now, or can we play?"

"I can go in a little later. Got to see Mrs. Que."

"The spleenless lady?"

"That's her."

"She adores you."

"She just likes holding my hand."

"Better watch that one."

"Why don't we go fishing for an hour or two?"

"Fishing? Where?" She went to the window and looked out. She had never seen my place in daylight. "There's fishing around here? Where the hell are we?"

"Cabin John. We can walk down to the river."

She was looking across my lawn – or what should have been a lawn – to the neighbour's place across the street. Their front yard was strewn with automobile parts and they had a car on blocks in the driveway.

"Christ, Abrams, you live in the suburbs."

"Hardly. Suburbs is split-levels and sunlit lawns."

"This is the 'burbs. Probably a few Volvos and station wagons down the block. Shopping malls. Kids in strollers. Why do you live here?"

"It's close to the river."

She rummaged in my cupboard and came out wearing blue jeans and a flannel shirt and her own shoes and we walked outside past the renovated houses the architect and lawyer owned, down to MacArthur Boulevard.

"They've done some nice things with some of those old

124

wrecks," said Maureen. "Looks like the North Shore of Long Island."

I was glad she liked Cabin John. Not everyone does – it's a case of charm over trimness. She could see the meat between the bones and I liked her for it.

We crossed MacArthur and continued on down to the canal. We walked along the towpath about a mile towards Great Falls, Maureen carrying the tackle bag and me with the poles. There weren't many people out at that hour. Just a couple of fishermen about twenty yards behind us on the canal. We took a path through the woods down to the river. She had a hard time keeping up in her heeled shoes.

"You really learned how to run along river banks," she laughed. "Those Cong taught you well."

And I had learned how to look over my shoulder. The two fishermen were still with us. Even from that distance, I was sure at least one of them had been at the Vietnamese restaurant the night before. His hair was flat over the side of his head, where there should have been an ear, but wasn't. I was sure about the ear because the one he had stuck out of his fine hair and there wasn't even a bump where the other should have been.

Since Nam I'd always noticed Orientals lacking ears. Lopping off ears was a favourite U.S. marine interrogation technique. They started with the ears and worked down. I knew all about missing parts. The fisherman lacked an ear, which made him Vietnamese, until proven otherwise. So many Vietnamese in my life lately. There was probably something to that, but at the time I wasn't sure what.

"I wasn't wearing high heels when the Cong were after me," I said.

"These aren't high heels," she said. Then she slapped her forehead and said, "Oh, shit! Is this the second or third Saturday of the month?"

"Second."

"I'm all right then," she said, looking relieved.

"What happens on the third Saturday?"

"I'm supposed to be somewhere."

She didn't elaborate and I waited until I got tired of it and said, "A job?"

"Yes."

I shrugged. She was determined to be mysterious about it, and I decided to be uninterested.

"Planned Parenthood Clinic," she said suddenly, seeing the game.

"What do you do there?"

"Hold hands – little twelve-year-old girls mostly. Getting abortions."

"You're some Catholic."

"I've changed my mind on that issue less often than the Church has," she said, sitting down on a fallen tree trunk, next to the river, pulling off her shoes. "First few centuries, they were all for it."

I was trying to think of what to say without bringing up her own abortion.

"It's just men talking," I said, finally. "They change their minds."

"You weren't raised Catholic," she said. "Priests in uniform speaking from God."

We advanced rock-to-log along the riverbank. In the shallows, between big boulders, you could see fish burrowing and darting. Some were so big and slow you could have reached down and grabbed them.

"Should have brought spears," I said. "Hell with the poles and tackle."

"Why'd you come to Washington?" Maureen asked suddenly.

"Seemed like a good idea, at the time, as they say. Got tired of taking care of the poor and ignorant in Bedford Stuyvesant. That's where the PHS sent me for my last year, after Nam."

"So now you take care of the rich and educated?"

She was so serious I had the feeling I better consider what I said. Here was a woman who worked for whatever small change Planned Parenthood paid to help twelve-year-olds get abortions. I started to say the right thing, but then I figured, why am I being so careful?

"I take care of some poor and ignorant, more than I like to think about."

"Why do you say that?" she said. "Tough isn't all that

126

becoming on you. Besides, you take care of Mr. What's-his-face, the Lebanese Jew."

"He's not poor and ignorant. He's just poor. Poor doesn't bother me as much."

"Why?"

"It's not fun taking care of people who don't know what their liver is, who want prescriptions, not diagnosis."

"It's them that needs it." She smiled when she said that, but she didn't like me now.

"So you're a burnt-out liberal," said Maureen. "Congratulations."

I was too angry to say anything. And I was confused and wondering why I'd flown off the handle. I didn't think I could get that mad any more. She should know better. She was there, where the best and brightest told us we could do anything, and she denied what everyone had learned. I looked at her. She was smiling. She liked me again, though I couldn't say why.

"Why do you do it?" I asked. "Work at Planned Parenthood?"

"Because I know that compassion is a fire in the soul," she laughed. "And I like those poor little black girls who look so lost and pregnant and have nowhere else to go."

We had to cross the streams the river made and work our way to the big rocks that ran out to midriver.

The one-eared fisherman and his partner were still behind us.

We jumped onto the first big rocks that formed the start of a natural boulder jetty, surprising two big Canadian geese who took off full speed, honking and fussing. They were gorgeous taking flight out of the low mist on the river. A few more hops and leaps got us out from shore.

Maureen stopped short. She had gone a little ahead and come face to face with a big beaver, sitting squarely on the next boulder. He looked like he was not going to give an inch. He thought better of it when he saw me coming up and he dived in and swam away.

Maureen couldn't believe the beaver.

"That was a beaver. A bona fide beaver!" She was grabbing me and pointing to where it had slipped into the water.

"He didn't look nearly as impressed with you as you did with him."

"What the hell's a beaver doing on the Potomac River?"

"He was probably wondering the same thing about you, for better reason."

Then my beeper went off. We had to leap and splash back to shore and I saw our one-eared friend a few hundred yards downstream.

It took us twenty-seven minutes to get back home and for me to get to the phone. I know the time because it was Mr. Simpson paging and the first thing he said was, "It took you twenty-seven minutes to answer. I'm not going to sue you but you're walking a very risky line there."

That's real kind of you, Mr. Simpson, I thought.

"What's the problem, Mr. Simpson?"

"My wife has been stung by bees and is getting very allergic."

"How do you mean, allergic? Is she having trouble breathing?"

"No. She's all red and swelling up. And I had to get through to your answering service that this was an emergency and then it took you twenty-seven minutes to respond."

"Mr. Simpson, does she have hives?"

"You mean like welts?"

"Like that, yes."

"Yes, where she was stung."

"Nowhere else?"

"I'll have to ask her."

She said no, she had them nowhere else. I asked if they had any antihistamines in the house and they did. I told him to tell her to take one, not that I thought it would do any good, but they wanted the doctor to tell them to do something.

"And Mr. Simpson . . ."

"Yes?"

"If your wife is ever stung by a bee again and you're afraid she's having a serious reaction, don't waste time on the phone. Take her to the Emergency Room and they'll give her a shot of adrenalin. You live, what? Five or six blocks from Saint George's?"

"That's fine for you. Saves you the trouble. But then we have to wait around that zoo."

"If your wife really did have a bad reaction, I mean so that her trachea swelled shut, she could asphyxiate in five minutes. Don't waste time hanging on to the phone. I could be driving to my office or taking care of someone else. It could take me twenty minutes to get to a phone."

Mr. Simpson said a few words about my glibness and about my professional attitude and about my inaccessibility, and hung up.

I came out to the living room to Maureen, passing a few windows on the way, and noticed the Asian fishermen, down the block, putting their tackle away in the trunk of a car. It wasn't a common place for fishermen to park, my block. Too far from the river.

## 29

"He thinks his wife's anaphylaxing and he doesn't have enough sense to get her to an emergency room?" Maureen was saying. "The man and his wife are not playing with a full deck between them?" She was changing back into her own clothes in my bedroom.

"He was some sort of high mucky-muck in the State Department, before he retired," I said. "Not that that really answers your question."

"I'm glad you realize that. All that says is that he was a highly placed moron."

"If he really thought she was in trouble, he'd have taken her to the ER."

"Then why'd he page you, all hot and bothered?"

"He wants service!"

"So what are you? Call-for-action?"

"People who pay my fees like to feel they can abuse me."

Maureen laughed.

"You laugh. It's true, though. Had a woman who told my answering service it's a dire emergency. Paged me out of a ballet at the Kennedy Center."

"Who was dancing?"

"Baryshnikov."

"She should be shot."

"Wait, you haven't heard her emergency."

"She should be shot, no matter."

"Stubbed her toe."

"No!"

"Unvarnished truth. The lady stubbed her toe. She was having a dinner party – the Austrian ambassador was in attendance, you understand – and she walked into her dining room table with her little toe. Thought she might have broken it. A seriously maimed little toe."

"She should be taken out and shot."

"I told her to go straight to the ER, I was so outraged. I was just hoping she didn't have enough neurons to form a synapse, so she'd show up and I could put her in a full leg cast."

"She didn't fall for it?"

"Nope. Said she knew you don't treat little toes."

"Then what the hell she call for?"

"Same reason Mr. Simpson called: to talk to the doctor."

"How can you stand it?"

"It's private practice. I love it."

"But people like *that*."

"Most people are like that. People are no great bargain."

"Especially poor people," she said, smiling.

"Poor people are no better. It's all people."

"They just don't know."

"Half my patients hold themselves in reasonable control most of the time; the other half suffer from acute and chronic interrogatory incontinence."

"Must be hard to practise medicine when you hold such a high opinion of humanity."

"Money eases the pain."

"How?"

"Simple sequence: stubbed toe, call doctor, pained doctor, patient better, doctor bills patient, doctor better."

"Money won't help the pain you've got," said Maureen.

I waited for her to start the little speech. It was a very nice little speech: the loss of belief in America, motherhood and apple pie. The unwillingness to believe in anything. The hollow men. The burnt-out case. The lost generation. I thought Maureen could have delivered a swell version. But she didn't say that.

"Last night was nice," she said. "But I broke my own rule."

I looked at her determined not to ask.

She said: "Always leave before sunrise."

She smiled when she said that and the rational centres of my brain screamed, "Take her home!" But I didn't want to. If she had wanted to stay the whole weekend, I would've been all for it. Don't ask me why.


# 30


But Maureen didn't want to stay.

"I need some fresh clothes," she said.

I drove her home and watched her run up the stairs to her town house, hair bouncing, everything bouncing.

I had to round on Mrs. Que and Mrs. Waterhouse at Saint George's, which was only four blocks away, so while Maureen changed, I ran over there.

Mrs. Que was looking much better. I asked her if she had any questions.

"What about the sex?" she said.

"What about it?"

"When will it be safe?"

"When is it ever safe?" I asked, but I could see she didn't follow my little joke. "Nothing's been done to that part of you.

You can let comfort be your guide. You're ready, as soon as you feel like it."

"Feeling like it depends on my company," she said. And she smiled.

I may be pushing forty, but looking at her with her chocolate-coloured gown open to the breast and those wonderful legs crossing and uncrossing themselves, I felt suddenly a lot younger.

"You better be careful," I said. "Your husband may have bugged this room."

"Of *me* he is not suspicious," she said.

I waited for her to say of whom her husband was suspicious. She said nothing and her smile made me uncomfortable.

"You said that as if he *is* suspicious of someone."

"Of you."

"I can sign off your case, any time," I said. "You have another doctor already."

"I would like you for my own," she said. I wasn't sure how she meant that.

"What's bothering your husband?"

"He reads the papers."

"The papers?"

"He is a businessman. He worries about everything. He has friends in many places – embassies, government. I think he had some questions asked, and you are investigating General Dhieu."

"I see."

"My husband did business with General Dhieu. The General had many . . ." she searched for the word, "enemies. It was not always . . . comfortable to be associated with him."

"This is all very interesting," I said. "But I don't see what it has to do with my being your doctor."

"As you once said, my husband is paranoid. Our car is wrecked and you appear. You are investigating Dhieu. My husband thinks perhaps it is all arranged."

"Arranged?"

"The accident."

"And who do I work for? The CIA?"

"Perhaps."

132

"Your husband reads too many Washington novels," I said. "But I'll sign off your case."

"You will not," she said. She was a lady who was obviously accustomed to giving orders. "Our doctor does not come to see me in this hospital. He doesn't have any rights here."

"Privileges," I said.

"Yes, the privileges," she said. "And I want you."

She had a very provocative way of saying that. She asked a few more questions about when she could go home, how soon she could ride horses. I told her to ask her surgeons about it, since they were calling the shots now. I was just an interested bystander.

"But you will take care of me later?" she said. "To give me the vaccination?"

"The Pneumovax," I said. "Sure, I'd be glad to see you for that."

"You are so kind," she said, and took my hand again and squeezed and looked me in the eye with her hot look. That particular morning I was feeling particularly receptive to hot looks. I said good-bye and went to see Mrs. Waterhouse.

How I found her room, I don't know. I wasn't thinking about Mrs. Waterhouse a single step of the way. I was thinking about the Asian fishermen who I was now sure had been following Maureen and me that morning: Mr. Que's hessians, I'd give odds.

Mrs. Waterhouse was very glad to see me. She had been examined by a medical student, an intern, a resident, and then a large herd of white coats came around and did teaching rounds on her. She had never seen so many doctors, and their interest and their questions unnerved her. She had decided she was going to die.

"This is a teaching hospital," I told her. "And you, heaven help you, are an interesting case."

She was almost through with her ACTH infusion, which would nail down the diagnosis, and she was being discharged Monday, after she was started on her cortisone. I kept edging towards the door, pursued by her questions, and finally said, "Once you're on the cortisone, you'll have most of your answers."

133

In the hallway, I narrowly avoided being levelled by Helen, Maureen's roommate. She was moving like a fullback in open field and served to avoid me, spilling some of her coffee down the front of her white nurse's dress.

"Well, look what the cat dragged in," she said. She didn't look at all unhappy about her dress.

"I'm sorry," I said, looking at her name tag: HELEN SLIGO, HEAD NURSE, CRC.

"What's CRC?"

"Clinical Research Center."

"Where's that?"

"You're standing right in the middle of it."

"I thought this was the metabolic ward."

"Twenty metabolic beds. Twenty CRC beds. That outpatient suite is the CRC's," she said, nodding to a carpeted area at the end of the hall.

I asked her what the research centr, did.

"Mostly cancer stuff. That's where all the money is nowadays. All the congressmen love voting for cancer money."

"I remember," I said, "when I was a fellow, trying to get grant money for diabetes. Everyone told me to figure out some way to convince Congress diabetes is a malignant disease, and there'd be no trouble getting funded."

"Oh, we've got a few diabetes protocols," said Helen. "But it's true, most of the bucks are in cancer. Seen Maureen?"

I had a little trouble making the transition from diabetes and cancer to Maureen, but finally said, "She's back at your place."

"I'm rooting for you," said Helen.

I was wondering how she meant that and what to say. Was she rooting for me and against someone else or what?

"Why's that?" I asked.

"Because you're good for her."

I waited for her this time. She definitely wanted to tell me something.

"She went through a bad time, when we first got back. I was really worried about her. The wrong kind of guys. One in particular who's just poison for her."

Peculiar choice of words, I thought, poison.

"What's so bad about him?"

"Oh, he's a wonderful guy," Helen said. "But you know how sometimes two super people can be just awful for each other when they're together."

I never could get used to people who used the word *super*. I said, "I know."

"Well, I guess I'm being a busybody."

I smiled and decided not to say no. I hadn't had to deal with roommates since I was in college.

She smiled back at me and I wondered why Helen and Maureen were roommates. If they were coeds I could see it: the fat girl living in the reflected glory of the beauty, and the beauty reigning centre stage. But they were too old for that. I just couldn't see it.

While we were standing there smiling uneasily at each other I heard footsteps coming and an intern appeared and asked me if I would come see a patient with him. Helen winked and waved good-bye. She was impressed that the intern considered my opinion so valuable. I stopped at the nurses' station to call Maureen and to tell her I'd be delayed.

"Trouble with the spleen lady?"

"No. Intern asked me to see a patient."

"Good. That's good for business."

The patient was a sixty-one-year-old alcoholic diplomat who had destroyed his pancreas with years of alcohol mixed in a variety of concoctions, mostly imbibed between Samoa and Djakarta between the years 1943 and 1983.

"Margaret Mead's territory," I said.

"Margaret Mead didn't know her ass from her elbow," said the diplomat. "She could have written that stuff from an armchair in Morningside Heights."

He had been getting gradually weaker and noticing more muscular irritability over the past three weeks, and woke up that morning with his hands flexed hard at the wrists, in total body pain.

"Have you had any diarrhoea?"

"I'm telling you about my hands," said the diplomat. "The arms, too. They hurt."

"Greasy, smelly diarrhoea?"

135

"Yes, for about three months. What's that got to do with all this?"

"Was it difficult to wipe up after?"

"You some kind of nut? Yes, damn it to hell, it was difficult to wipe up after."

"We'll be able to get you better," I said. "May take forty-eight hours. But often quicker. I don't like to promise more than I can deliver."

"Then you're a damn-sight smarter than the guys who run the State Department."

I pulled the intern out into the hall and told him to pump magnesium into the patient and he said, "Magnesium? We've been giving him calcium."

"Measure his serum magnesium," I said. "What's his calcium done, after you pumped in your IV calcium?"

"Absolutely squat."

"That's because he needs magnesium. He's malabsorbing 'cause he doesn't have much pancreas left. No pancreas, no lipase, no fat absorption. And what vitamin do we know that needs fat to be absorbed?"

"Vitamin D."

"And when you malabsorb Vitamin D, you often also malabsorb magnesium. He's had lots of greasy diarrhoea – fatty stools – so he's going to have lost fat, magnesium and maybe Vitamin D, too. I'd give him both. But measure the levels first, just to be sure. You won't get his calcium to budge if you don't replace his magnesium." The intern looked at me with a look which could have been wonder, reverence or simply the look of a man trying to placate a maniac. I didn't care. I was right and he'd find out if he'd do what I told him. I had bigger things on my mind.

Maureen had a boyfriend. A wonderful guy, Helen had said, but poison for her. Couldn't have guessed Maureen had a boyfriend from our night last night. I kept telling myself to be grown-up and take the ride for what it was worth, that I had no right to be jealous or possessive or to expect anything, but the whole walk over to her place it gnawed on me.

People are like that, I know. You can think you know all

about them but they have their little secrets and intrigues and you'll never know unless they want you to, or you can catch them. But it bothered me. There was that one crack about her hypogonadal friend. Maybe that was meant to warn me. But there was all that abstinence talk. Unless her boyfriend wasn't able to perform. A comforting thought.

I made myself think about other things: Mrs. Que. I hadn't wanted to think about her because it seemed somehow disloyal to Maureen, not to mention dangerous, given Mr. Que's paranoia. But now I decided I'd better think about Mrs. Que, often and at length. She had lovely phrasing and a very expensive manner. Who was I kidding? It wasn't her cultivated phrasing. She was the kind of woman who could do things for a silk dress that would stampede a businessman's lunch. She could help me keep some perspective on Maureen Banting.

# 31

Maureen was sitting on her front porch drinking beer. It was only one o'clock. She was wearing shorts and a bright green and blue rugby shirt.

"How was the spleenless lady?" she asked. She held up a bottle of beer, but I declined. "She still holding your hand?"

"Whenever she can." I liked that. She sounded jealous. "You can too, whenever you want."

"Christ help me."

"I appeal to older women."

"What was the one they asked you to see?"

"A little tetany."

"Tetany? Why'd they ask you to see that?

"Low calcium."

"You figure out why?"

"Would I disappoint the fans? Left 'em cheering," I said. She frowned. "Actually, I'm not sure the intern believed a word I said."

"Why not?"

"Don't know. Maybe I was too glib."

"Yes, that's a problem for you."

"Not really. It helps."

"What's it help?"

"Eases the pain. Dealing with all the undersecretaries, special assistants to the president who want a ten-second response for bee stings."

"Don't forget the poor and ignorant."

"Who could forget them?"

On the way downtown we were stopped by a motorcycle cop. He stood in the road and held up all traffic coming along the Drive, below the Lincoln Memorial. He kept looking towards E Street, waiting.

"What's he doing here, on a weekend?" asked Maureen. We sat watching him peer down the road, standing in front of my car in his black uniform which made him look like nobody to tangle with, with the sun glinting off his blue helmet.

"What's he waiting for?"

"I think we're going to find out now," I said.

You could hear them before you could see them. Motorcycles. The first four passed by a few seconds later, moving fast down the Drive like a fighter squadron. Then another set of motorcycles, then two city police cars, lights flashing, no sirens. Then a black car with federal government plates.

"What is this?" asked Maureen.

Then came a long black limousine. That was the decoy. Another motorcycle. Then the real long black limo, with dark windows you couldn't see through, followed by a black flatbed truck carrying four black-uniformed agents in SWAT hats with automatic weapons, black and lethal-looking, on their laps. Then some more police cars and a motorcycle.

"Christ," said Maureen. "Looks like Darth Vader's motorcade."

"That was your President," I said. "Somewhere in all that."

"He's coming later, in an old grey Volkswagen," she said.

"No."

"Looked like Chile, after the coup," said Maureen.

The cop got back on his motorcycle and nodded at me and we continued on to Independence Avenue. I could see the long line of traffic behind me. Maureen was looking back at all the cars.

"He really brings everything to a halt," she said.

We reached Independence and I could see the motorcade far off, swirling around the Jefferson Memorial.

"Jefferson would puke," said Maureen.

It was a pretty day, bright and breezy. The leaves were green, but some were turning at the edge and they were moving in the wind. We drove down to the Lincoln Memorial and parked along Ohio Drive. I kept an eye out for public phones. I was on call for two other docs and my beeper had been improbably silent for almost three hours.

There were games on the fields all along Independence Avenue. We walked to the first field and watched a polo game.

"Those ponies are definitely brighter than the riders," said Maureen. "Look, they go after the ball way before the riders have any idea where it is." We watched them race up and down until Maureen got sick of seeing the horses get hit with mallets and balls and we walked over to watch the cricket players on the next field.

Cricket is an impossible game for anyone not raised in a Commonwealth country to understand. You have to learn it young, like a language. Not that you'd want to. Nothing much happens.

A few fields away, a rugby game was going full steam. We approached the line of spectators on the sidelines. We were walking slowly, shoulders touching, when I saw Mrs. Bromley watching the rugby and I moved a little away from Maureen.

"What a messy game," I said to Mrs. Bromley's back. She turned around.

"Good heavens, they let just anyone watch these games in this country," she said. Then she looked over and saw Maureen and really began to smile. I could feel my face go hot.

"You know Basil," she said. I shook her husband's hand.

He squeezed off the proper smile, but was far more interested in keeping his eye on the game, until he noticed Maureen.

"I like your jersey," he said to her. "You could almost play for Olney," he said, nodding to the team on the field whose players wore green and blue rugby shirts like Maureen's.

"This is Miss Banting," said Mrs. Bromley, with a look to me. I knew I'd have explaining to do Monday. He was being very British and proper now, but Monday I'd get the knife.

"I'd rather play for the black team," said Maureen. "They look so sinister."

Basil Bromley turned his full attention away from the game and to Maureen and looked at her to be sure she was smiling. She was, and he laughed approvingly. He was rooting for the guys in black, too.

He spent the rest of the game explaining rugby to Maureen, who was an enthusiastic student and seemed to please him more and more with each question.

"Why does he run out ahead of his friends?" she asked, pointing to the scrum half who had just caught a kick and was sprinting forward. "He's fast but he's not too bright, exposing himself like that."

"He has to put them on side."

"What a game!"

We walked down to the Tidal Basin after the game, Maureen and Basil Bromley ahead of Mrs. Bromley and me.

"She's a lovely girl," said Mrs. Bromley. "Figured her out yet?"

"You mean, medically?"

"Either way."

"No."

"Well, I'm glad you're taking a keen interest in your patient."

"She pays her bill, she tells me."

We bought hot dogs and Cokes from a vendor at the Tidal Basin and ate them under a cherry tree.

Mrs. Bromley said, "I tried Saint George's again, Friday afternoon; they've still not got that bloody insulin level ready."

This, of course, was said to me. Basil Bromley looked out

over the water, oblivious to the office chatter. Maureen, however, was alert and looking back and forth between Mrs. Bromley and me.

"I'll call and harass them again, Monday," Mrs. Bromley was saying. "The technicians they have answering the phones in the laboratory sound as if they've all had frontal lobotomies."

"Keep after them," I said. "They'll break down eventually and give us a level."

"Why won't they give you the level?" asked Maureen.

"Oh, he's just saying that," Mrs. Bromley told her. "They'd give us the level, if they were organized enough to find it."

"They don't do the test in the Saint George's lab. They're waiting for the results from some other lab," I said.

"You'd think they might have enough interest to call the other lab and inquire. It's been, what? *almost* two weeks. I tried calling the lab Saint George's sent it to, but I didn't know the requisition number from Saint George's and they couldn't help me."

"Just keep on Saint George's lab," I said.

"Is a patient waiting for the result?" asked Maureen.

Mrs. Bromley looked to me, a little sheepishly. "I suppose I shouldn't be talking about all this. Confidentiality and all that rot."

"Oh, you can tell me," said Maureen eagerly, pushing me away, stepping between Mrs. Bromley and me. "I'm a nurse, or was. It's all in the family."

Mrs. Bromley looked to me for a sign.

"It's been in all the papers," Mrs. Bromley told me, apologetically. "I suppose it's a matter of public record."

"Of course it is," said Maureen. I couldn't believe how eager she was, eager as a coed at a fraternity house, trying to find out who's upstairs with whom.

"Dr. Abrams is a recently proclaimed celebrity," said Mrs. Bromley. "We've even had reporters in."

"Reporters!" said Maureen. "What on earth for?"

"It's about that general who died," said Mrs. Bromley, looking over to me for a head shake or a nod. I just watched Maureen.

"And is that whose insulin level it is?"

141

"Yes," said Mrs. Bromley. "And Saint George's just won't produce. We've been calling since Wednesday."

"You've got a lot more out of Mrs. Bromley than the reporter did," I said.

"Oh, so what?" said Maureen. "What's the big deal? It's in the paper. General gets knocked off in Saint George's."

"Oh, he wasn't necessarily knocked off," said Mrs. Bromley. "The cause of death hasn't been determined. That's what the insulin level . . ." she caught my eye and stopped.

"Oh, he was knocked off all right," said Maureen.

"You've been reading too many newspapers," I said.

"Haven't read a thing," said Maureen quickly. "I just heard 'general' and drew the logical conclusion. Generals never die natural deaths. They live such unnatural lives. It wouldn't be just."

Mrs. Bromley laughed. "Careful now," she said. "Basil was a Commodore in the Royal Navy."

"Is that a general?" Maureen asked him.

"Not quite," he said. "But I rather agree with your assessment. Generals ought not to be *allowed* natural deaths, on principle."

"I'm quite sure Dr. Abrams will get to the bottom of it," said Maureen. "If there's foul play and unnatural causes, he'll find out."

Mrs. Bromley said something like "Hear, hear," to I don't know what.

Maureen added, "You'll keep me posted, Mrs. Bromley. I'll never get it out of him."

Mrs. Bromley smiled a little uncomfortably, and Basil said it was time to be off. We walked with them a short way and they waved good-bye.

"You made quite a hit with Basil," I said.

"He's so *English*."

"Didn't you like him?"

"Never got past the English."

"I'm not sure I follow."

"After you've been to Eton and Cambridge, what can anyone tell you?"

"Is he like that?"

"I'm not sure, but I think so."

"I've always enjoyed him."

"Oh, he's enjoyable."

"But you don't like him?"

"I get the feeling he's filtering all new experience through his Cambridge lenses. Happens to people who go to big-name schools, Swarthmore, places like that."

"Oh, really?" Not a clever reply, but I was taken off guard. "Am I like that?"

"Haven't decided about you yet."

"But I'm under suspicion."

"It's a syndrome I look out for."

"Why were you so interested in the General?" I asked.

"I was not so interested in the General," she said hotly. I couldn't be sure why she was so suddenly annoyed.

"Yes, you were. You acted like a gossip columnist on a hot lead."

"For Chrissake," said Maureen. She was really angry. At the time, I couldn't understand it.

We walked along Independence Avenue in silence. Finally, she said, "It was just because you were so determined to be all secretive about the whole thing. Playing Mr. Inspector Hound, very cagey, Hercule Poirot incarnate. Like it made you more important not to be able to talk about it."

We crossed the avenue and she suddenly took my hand and smiled at me. "I've got a bad temper, sometimes," she said.

We walked along the reflecting pool, heading back towards the car. We were enjoying the colours on the water and I was worrying about my beeper which had been so uncommonly silent all afternoon. I knew it would shatter the spell any moment and I'd have to leave her.

"Come to Clydes with Helen and me tonight," said Maureen suddenly.

"Sure."

I would rather have had Maureen all to myself, at my place, but she probably had this date set up with Helen, and my place could come later. Besides, Helen was my big booster. She was rooting for me.

We walked back to the car watching tourists trying to

143

control their kids around the steps of the Lincoln Memorial. I noticed an Oriental man taking a picture of a dark-haired woman, catching Maureen and me in the background. I couldn't be sure, but I thought he was one of the fishermen from that morning.

# 32

There was a crowd off to the Constitution Avenue side of the Lincoln Memorial, tourists with shorts and baseball caps and big bellies poking out under garish T-shirts, and unruly kids running around pushing each other down.

"You know what this is?" asked Maureen, nodding in their direction. I said I did. "Ever seen it?" she asked.

"No," I said.

"Want to?"

"No."

"Come on," she said, and she took my hand. We walked past the reflecting pool, towards the long, low sloping black marble that had all the names.

"Why haven't you gone to see it?" asked Maureen.

"I thought I might see a name I knew."

"But that's the idea."

"That's why I didn't go."

We started at the beginning and walked down the slope. I read the names under some safe years years, I wasn't there. There were all kinds of names, every nationality you could think of, every sort of background: Joe Bob Evans – you knew what kind of folks he came from, and what he must have sounded like, saying his name. Leroy Jones, Jesus Garcia, Patrick Michael Flynn, Phillip Wentworth III. You went along looking for some class, some ethnic group not represented, and you couldn't find it. Ira Goldfarb, 1967. Dominic Pettrucci,

1969. I couldn't take my eyes off the names. I tried to distract myself, tried looking at the three fat men with American Legion hats posing for photos in front of the names. I tried to think about their big bulbous red-veined noses on their sixty-year-old faces, faces that never saw Vietnam firsthand. But it didn't work. My eyes kept going back to the black marble. All those names from all those places, everyone in every little town touched.

And for what?

"Had enough?" I asked Maureen.

"It kind of shakes you up a little, doesn't it?"

I said: "Let's get a Coke and go sit under an American flag or something. Enjoy the way of life all these suckers died for."

"Is that what they died for?"

"Fuck if I know what they died for."

"Is that what it was for?" said Maureen. "So all those little people in the black pyjamas could sit around their village wells and drink Coke and eat hot dogs? And all this time I thought it was to stem the tide of communism."

We were in line at the hot dog stand. She was speaking softly, fortunately. We were surrounded by patriots in baseball caps.

"It *was* to stop communism," I whispered. "You don't see any commies around here, do you?"

"They're all in Ho Chi Minh City."

A big man holding a little girl was standing ahead of us on line. He was wearing a plastic baseball batting helmet with an American flag sticker on the back. Under the flag were the words THESE COLOURS DON'T RUN. I nodded at the helmet. "We showed *them*," I said softly. "What we were made of."

"What we were made of spilled out all over the operating room tables where I was," said Maureen.

"Keep your voice down," I told her.

We reached the window and I bought two Cokes. We sat under a tree and I looked around for more Asian surveillance experts.

"I thought a little trip to the memorial might motivate you," said Maureen.

"Motivate me? To do what?"

"To remember. To get angry again."

"Maureen," I said. "Time passes."

"You want me to leave it all behind?" said Maureen. "Like you did?"

"I'm not telling you what to do."

"Forgive and forget."

"Haven't you heard? All the hippies are into computers now. Kent State's just a place in Ohio."

"For you, maybe."

"Why are you so interested in General Dhieu?"

That caught her neatly between the eyes. Her surprise looked real enough to be believed. She was having trouble coming up with a reply. Finally she said, "Because you wanted me to be."

"No, it had nothing to do with me. You were grilling Mrs. Bromley before I said anything."

"It's front-page news. Why shouldn't I be interested?"

"It's old news. It's Vietnam news."

"That's no news, according to you."

"That's why I'm wondering what had you so interested?"

"You can be a real pill. You know that?" She was really angry now. She stood up and brushed off her slacks.

"Let's go," she said.

"Touchy about that, aren't you?"

"Better touchy than anaesthetized."

"What's that supposed to mean?"

"Who gave you the Nembutal?" she asked. "Nothing bothers you. Nothing matters. Something might stir you, you avoid it. You're not mellow, you're dead."

"No."

"No? Then what's this bullshit about Vietnam not meaning anything any more? It's all behind us. You don't want to even walk past the memorial, it's so irrelevant."

"That's not true," I said. "I wouldn't have even taken on the Dhieu case if I'd felt that way."

"Oh?" she said. She was smiling now, eyebrow up. She was moving in for a quick score. "I thought it was just an interesting case. A little free publicity."

"That wasn't it."

"What was it then? I thought you were through with Nam and everything Vietnamese."

"It's like jungle rot. You never really get rid of it."

"They must feel the same way about us."

"How's that?"

"You don't think all the burn scars melted away as soon as we pulled out."

"No," I said. "They're probably still paying for the war."

"They must have their hands full in the hospitals in Saigon."

"Ho Chi Minh City," I corrected.

She smiled one of her dark smiles and rubbed my neck. Occasionally, I got the feeling that something I had said or done had pleased her for secret reasons known only to Maureen. This was one of those times. It wasn't a bad feeling. In fact, it felt very nice, like being a kid and your mother smiles at you for just being her kid. Later, I could think back and understand most of these moments, but at the time I just knew she was happy with me and that was enough.

## 33

On the way back to Maureen's place my beeper went off. I was on the phone in the kitchen when Helen walked in, carrying a bag of groceries. She grinned and opened a bag of doughnuts, eating one after another as she emptied the grocery bag, putting things away. While I watched her I tried to deal with a Mr. Hughes, who was a seventy-year-old former deputy director of some agency, now a consultant-cum-lobbyist for people who felt more influential after paying Mr. Hughes large sums of money to place phone calls to Highly Placed People. Mr. Hughes maintained it was the stress of making all those calls that caused his high blood pressure.

I had run through almost the entire antihypertensive

armamentarium with Mr. Hughes, but every time I prescribed a new drug, he'd run right home and look it up in his *Physicians' Desk Reference* and promptly be stricken by every adverse effect listed. Usually, he'd start with impotence, if that was listed. Mr. Hughes feared impotence almost but not quite as much as he feared stroke, because he was a very hot item on the Washington over-sixties scene ever since he'd retired from the government, divorced, and become a consultant with an impressive office and a big desk he once described for me in soporific detail.

Now Mr. Hughes was calling because he had swallowed two of my latest pills before looking them up and realizing they were sure to make him impotent. He would have called me immediately but he had a date with his ex-wife, who snared him into bed, having heard what a stud he'd become since beginning his new life.

Mr. Hughes could not demonstrate his new prowess to his eager ex-wife. In fact, his business end was totally limp.

He drove home, raging, at two A.M. Saturday morning, intending to call me as soon as he arrived. But his newest girlfriend (a mere child of fifty) was waiting on his doorstep, and he spent the rest of the wee hours and all the morning and afternoon in the sack with her, making love like a teenager. She had just left and now, Saturday evening, he was calling to castigate me for making him a pharmacologic eunuch – totally impotent, at least with his wife.

"Mr. Hughes, you know at least half of sex takes place above the nose."

Helen paused in her unloading ever so slightly, but I knew she was taking this in.

"You mean it was psychological with my wife?" said Mr. Hughes. By the time I finished dealing with him, Maureen was finished changing and appeared, sparkling, in the kitchen. Helen finished putting away the groceries and said she didn't need to change, so we were ready to go.

Helen offered Maureen a doughnut but Maureen shook her head and all that shiny hair moved and fell back into place. Helen wore a fat girl's version of Maureen's style: blue wool sport coat and tartan pleated skirt. It should have looked neat and prim but on Helen it looked too young and tight. Maureen was all lustre in her khaki slacks, Fair Isle sweater, and blue blazer.

Clydes was mobbed and they told us it would be an hour's wait, so we walked down a few blocks to Mr. Smith's, where we were seated immediately, in the garden. They gave us a table for four.

We ordered daiquiris and watched the bartender make them up with real strawberries and bananas. We asked for a plate of fried zucchini, and ate that while we waited for the drinks. Or rather, Helen ate it and Maureen and I watched. Helen had initially announced she wasn't interested in "little stuff" and Maureen ordered it, but when it arrived, Helen went to work.

Maureen looked around the garden but she kept an eye on Helen.

Helen said, "Well, zucchini's got almost no calories."

Maureen said, "If you eat one or two, Helen."

"Well, have some," said Helen. She pushed the plate towards Maureen. I'd been waiting to see Helen erupt. She was always so smiley, too smiley, smiling when she really shouldn't be, as if she hoisted up that smile in the morning and was determined to keep it there. But you had the feeling she was real angry underneath.

She was angry she was fat and angry she couldn't eat the whole plate of zucchini, and angry that Maureen could and not gain a pound. I sat there thinking about what it would be like to be that fat, to have to think about something as ordinary as eating or sitting in a chair that might break under your weight. And I thought about all the isolation and rejection being that fat must bring.

Helen tried to recover and looked to me with a fresh smile. "Maureen's trying to save me from myself. I wish I had her metabolism. I can eat a carrot and gain five pounds."

"Oh, Helen, you know better. Tell her that's not true, Abe," Maureen looked at me. I sat there, in the middle, mouth open, not enjoying it. Maureen looked back to Helen before I could think of what to say. "You don't have to be like this. You weren't always."

Helen looked at me, determined to avoid looking at Maureen. She composed herself and said, "We go way back. She thinks I can weigh what I did when I was eight years old."

"When you were twenty," said Maureen to the tabletop. Then she looked at me and said, "She was a knockout. She had all the marine corpsmen trying to get in her pants at Binh Thuy."

"Holy Redeemer," said Helen, as if she hadn't heard a word of this. "Third grade. Sister Angelica."

"Knee socks and plaid skirts," said Maureen, laughing suddenly, clearing the tension. She plucked a big strawberry out of her daiquiri and popped it into her mouth. "Then Sacred Heart. Then Vietnam."

I asked what unit they were with and Helen said, "The dear ol' Forty-forty-fourth." Sumner's unit. "Hadn't seen Maureen since she went off to college. Didn't even know she'd gone to nursing school. Then one day the new nurses step off the bus and there's Maureen. I could have croaked."

Maureen was looking for a waiter to refill her drink.

"You were wounded, Maureen said."

"Never had the pleasure of being run through the Forty-forty-fourth," I said. "They medevaced me to one of those hospital ships offshore."

"Were you hit badly?"

"I had some lovely wounds," I said. "They got me home."

I was beginning to sweat and my well-healed wounds began to ache but I was saved by the arrival of dinner. Maureen and I had spinach salads. Helen had spaghetti and clam sauce.

"Look at you two eating salad," said Helen. "As if you needed to diet."

I looked at the spaghetti and said nothing.

"Oh Helen," said Maureen.

"I wish I liked rabbit food," said Helen.

"You could if you tried," said Maureen.

I was beginning to wish my beeper would go off for once when I needed it. Helen ignored the remark.

We ate in silence and I can't say I enjoyed it. The salad was probably good enough, but food had lost its appeal. Maureen finished her daiquiri and ordered a third.

"Salad's good," said Maureen. This was thrown in Helen's direction. "You ought to try it some time. Maybe even acquire a taste for it."

"You're happier with me this way," snapped Helen. "Less competition."

I slid back away from the table a little, in case bottles started to fly.

"As long as it's not for Tim," said Helen softly, to her plate. This name, Tim, was not for my consumption, and I wondered at the time who Tim might be.

Maureen's mouth tried to smile but was getting no cooperation from her eyes. "We're not talking about me. I bring the whole thing up because I care about you. The easiest thing would be for me to just let it ride."

"It's something metabolic," Helen said to me. I had been trying to play invisible, but Helen's comment brought me back into all this. "I can eat a carrot and gain two pounds. But nobody'll give me thyroid."

I made a sympathetic face.

"Why won't anybody give me thyroid?"

"It usually doesn't work," I said.

"But thyroid speeds up the metabolism," she said. "And hyperthyroid people lose weight. Isn't that right?"

"But thyroid pills can't make you lose weight."

"They'd just increase your appetite, Helen," Maureen interjected. "You've got to do it by willpower."

My beeper went off, and for once I was a little grateful to hear its intrusive voice. I hurried off to the phone near the bathroom, away from the ugliness rising at the table. It was a patient who never called unless she had to, a self-reliant nineteen-year-old woman who studied accounting nights at Howard U and worked days as a bank teller. She had come to me a year ago because she was gaining weight, hadn't menstruated and was nauseated in the mornings. She was pregnant, of course, and if that wasn't enough trouble, she had a vaginal discharge which was positive for gonorrhoea. A very nice boyfriend she had.

She stiff-upper-lipped it and decided to have an abortion, to save her college degree and her career, but I could see it tore her up and she got a roaring post-D & C infection and nearly died one night in sepsis, not wanting to bother me. Her friends dragged her to the Emergency Room, shocky and going rapidly down the tubes. So hearing her voice now I gave her all my attention.

"I'm real sorry to bother you and all," she said.

"That's all right, Georgene. I'd rather hear sooner than later, especially in your case."

"I know it could've waited 'til morning . . ."

I thought of how she'd looked in the ER, burning with a fever of 104, blood pressure dropping like a rock. "That's okay. I told you to call me any time."

"But I've been going crazy worrying. Have you heard anything about my . . . test?"

It hit me like a knee in the back – she'd come in for another pregnancy test a few days ago, looking worried – and I'd forgotten to call her. I just hadn't been keeping my mind on things lately. I told her the test was negative, and apologized for not calling her sooner. She thanked me effusively, which made me feel even worse for not calling her sooner, and I hung up. That's always the way: the ones who should thank you don't and sometimes the ones who should ream you out heap on the gratitude.

When I got back to the table Helen and Maureen were friends again. Maureen had a new daiquiri and was halfway through it.

Helen asked if the call was anything urgent and did I have to leave? I said no. I was beginning to wonder how we were going to work the going home. We had walked to the restaurant because there was no hope of Helen fitting in the Triumph, but would we all walk home together and Helen go up the stairs into the house and Maureen and I hop in the car and drive away?

Maureen looked at her watch and said, "We'd better get the bill." Then to me, "Why don't you get us a cab? I've got to be up at the crack of dawn, and that means this little girl's got to be in bed quickly."

"You're coming home?" asked Helen, surprised.

"Yes, Helen. I'm coming home."

"Are you . . . ?" Helen asked, but left it there.

"I've got to be up real early tomorrow," said Maureen, trying to speak to Helen and not watch me out of the corner of her eye. "I've got to give old Ben here a break. I've been leaning pretty heavily on his hospitality."

"I see," said Helen.

And I think Helen did see, although what it was she saw I didn't understand at the time.


# 34


I drove home that night along the Parkway in the dark, wondering what Maureen had planned for Sunday morning. She could have told me anything, any sort of lie about it and I wouldn't have given it a second thought, but all the mystery and silence had me wondering, which is what it was meant to do I suppose.

She didn't owe me an accounting of her social schedule. But she had me thinking. What could be so torrid about an early morning tryst? Romance over steak and eggs? Or maybe she wasn't planning to wait until morning. Maybe she was going out again tonight.

Whatever. She owed me no explanations.

I knew when I pulled up in my driveway there was no way I was going to get right to sleep. I sat on my car hood a while, looking at the hard cold moon, thinking about Maureen and who she was with and what they might be doing. That made me feel tight and squirmy and I knew I couldn't sleep, so I fetched my Levi jacket and a flashlight and my big hunting knife and started for the door when the phone rang.

I told myself not to be disappointed if it wasn't Maureen. It wasn't, and I was disappointed. It was Sumner. There was a lot of noise in the background.

"Lieutenant Commander Abrams? This is the opportunity you've been waiting for. It's definitely the best thing that's going to come your way tonight."

Sumner waited for me to say something.

"Still there?"

"Yep."

"Thought you might have fainted dead away. Look, got these two summer interns for Senator . . . what's your senator's name, honey? Whatever. And they want to go for a swim out at Dickerson's Quarry with two bona fide war heroes."

"Don't know any war heroes."

"Modesty, modesty. We're at the Crème de la Crème, off Dupont Circle. How long it take you to get down here?"

"Not tonight, big boy."

"Abe, you're going to just waste away on that porch."

"Sumner, you still there?"

"Change your mind?"

"You ever know a nurse named Maureen Banting in the Forty-forty-fourth?"

"Not nearly as well as I wanted to."

"You did?"

"She was some piece of work."

"She's a patient of mine."

"Well, that's a start."

"She a good nurse?"

"Think she was. There was some badness with some nurses when she was there, but she wasn't mixed up in it. She was balling some priest, though. Wouldn't give anyone else a tumble."

"Priest?"

"You know. Army chaplain. Even in Nam they had those. They blessed all the people we murdered and they blessed all the murderers. Did a real good job, most of 'em. Made everyone feel better."

"Priest . . ."

"Rumour had it he knocked her up. She disappeared for a week. They missed scrub nurses in Nam when they just took off for a week. Most people thought she was getting a D & C."

I don't know why but I felt like I'd been slapped across the

154

face. I managed to say something bright like, "Yeah, well, thanks," and went to hang up.

"I'll forgive you for tonight," I heard Sumner say. "But you got to get out the door. Got to get back into life."

He waited for me to say something, and when I didn't, he said, "Find out anything about that dead general?"

I had to think for a moment whom he meant. I told him things were cooking.

"Talk to the toxicology guy at NIH?"

I told him the toxicology man was running the Biocon insulin in his lab.

"You ought to go over there," said Sumner. "Personally. To the lab, I mean. I hear he's got a lab tech working for him knock your eyes out."

I told him I'd be sure and do that and hung up.

I walked outside and looked at the stars for a while, thinking about what Sumner had said and thinking about Maureen, wondering who she went home to see tonight.

Since I'd got out of uniform and moved to Washington, I'd been satisfied to wake up in the morning and find me alive. That was until Maureen. Now I was restless, alone at my bungalow. It felt empty.

I walked down to the canal.

It was cool by the canal, but despite the unseasonable chill and the days of subnormal temperatures the September algae on the water smelled dreadful, so I wound up taking a path to the river. That was not a smart move on two counts: there had been warnings about rabid raccoons and raccoons are nocturnal, and I hadn't walked by a river at night since Mekong. It was a stupid thing to do, and I knew it with each step towards the rushing sound the fast currents made. But it was one of those nights for masochism.

The moonlight was playing off the Potomac just the way it plays off rivers all around the planet. I'd seen light moving like that half a world away. And being there by the river at night brought it all back.

Right after the boat went down and I realized I was still alive and being swept downriver, away from the rifle fire, it was

155

pure euphoria. It was a damn fast river and things were rushing past me: logs, pieces of boat, and it dawned on me that I might be knocked unconscious and drown.

I tried swimming towards shore and realized I couldn't do that for long, not against that current. But the river made a big bend and the current carried me straight for the bank that jutted out and with five minutes of hard swimming I made it to land. Or rather to mud.

I clambered up to the grass line above the muddy riverbank and lay on my back breathing, happy to be alive and thinking I'd escaped. It didn't last, of course. They caught up to me. I could hear them before I could see them, coming along the path by the river. They were supposed to be as quiet as cats, but they were making plenty of noise. This was their country and if anyone had to be quiet, it was me.

I stayed just long enough to be sure they were Cong and not just some villagers. They were carrying assault rifles. I didn't stop to count how many they were.

At first I ran along the path by the river. That way I could always dive back into the water if they started shooting. But then it struck me that they might just split up and some of them get in a boat. Then they could get me easily.

And it was definitely me they were after. They had been looking out at the river pointing and looking at the path ahead of them. And they were laughing. They were enjoying the hunt. And me the fox.

I cut away from the riverbank, running bent low at the waist, following the natural paths between the branches until the forest got too thick and there were no paths. Then I found a little streambed with water still coursing down the middle, but muddy in most places and with clouds of insects. I ran along the water leaving no tracks.

They didn't need tracks: they knew where I was. They followed. The first night I didn't sleep, just rested crouching, and listened for them, and let the bugs eat me up alive, afraid to slap and make a sound.

The next day I didn't see or hear them all day, but I knew they were behind me, and the fever began and the bugs kept biting. That night I stopped and decided I had to chance curling up for some sleep. It was only then that it occurred to me I was wearing a gun. The bullets were soaked, of course, but I had a clip in my dry-pouch with the good wooden matches the ship's petty officer had made me take. And he gave me the clip to put in the dry-pouch. I had felt ridiculous carrying a .45. Even with the dry clip, I wasn't sure the gun would work, and didn't dare risk a test shot. But it made me feel better just having a gun, even if it wasn't much good from more than fifteen yards.

The third day they got close enough to shoot and it was then that I wanted very badly to kill someone. Anyone. Even a villager, but especially those guys with the guns. I wanted to stop running and ducking and weaving through the forest and wait for them and open up on one or two.

But I kept moving and moving and never stopping and always trying to go faster and to put more distance between us.

Now it was the Potomac and I was leaping and bounding in a cold sweat, flying along by the riverbank. But this time there was no one behind me. I caught myself and stood still, breathing, listening to my heart pound in my ears, listening to the night sounds. There was no one. I walked back to the canal and back up to MacArthur Boulevard. For an instant I sensed someone behind me, and whirled around. There might have been someone at the mouth of the path from the canal.

I stood on the road and waited for him to emerge. A small wiry man walked out onto the road. It could have been the king of Persia, but I was betting heavy odds it was a certain one-eared fisherman. I couldn't see well enough in the darkness. He turned off and walked down the road away from me.

Watching him fade off into the shadows, I found myself reaching reflexively for my .45. Not that it would have helped this time, any more than it would have helped when I did carry one. The important thing now was knowing for whom these followers were working.

So many new people in my life since the cloudy case of General Dhieu got tossed into my lap. Never knew there were so many Vietnamese in Washington. I might meet them all

157

before it ended: some who follow me, and others who just flit by, like the lady who liked Neil Young. Of course, not all the new people were Oriental. Too many years of trying to fit all the findings to one diagnosis maybe, but I couldn't shake the idea that somehow Maureen and her crowd were connected to the same tether, and that tether tied my follower to General Dhieu.

# 35

Sunday morning, I drove to see Mrs. Que and Mrs. Waterhouse at Saint George's. I hadn't really planned on rounding on them Sunday, but I woke up and felt like seeing Mrs. Que. And I wanted to tell Maureen about her. Then Maureen could be silent about the other man in her life.

Mrs. Waterhouse was asleep, so I went to see Mrs. Que. She looked wonderful. She was standing by her window in a red velvet robe and she had on her red lipstick. She looked very exciting in red.

"You are here quite early," she said.

"Not so early," I said. "Early for a Sunday maybe."

"Oh, you just want to come when my husband is not yet here." She smiled when she said that, and I, typically cool and in control, blushed down to my roots.

"I did not mean to make you embarrassed," she laughed.

I wouldn't have been, of course, had she not been right.

"You are a nice young man," she laughed. "But maybe too young for me."

I began to see the wisdom in Sumner's analysis of my situation. I hadn't been living dangerously enough. Why that thought popped into view with Mrs. Que standing there with that red robe hugging her contours escaped me at the time. But I had had lots of vague questions and discomfort the past few days and Mrs. Que looked like a lot of the answers.

"I'm old enough," I said.

"Old enough for what?"

"For whatever you have in mind," I said. Not one of your classic lines. But it had the proper effect.

"And I am healing like a young girl," said Mrs. Que. "The surgeons have told me."

"It's hard to believe you just had surgery."

"I will be like new in no time flat," she said. I loved her American expressions. "And you say I am ready for recreation whenever I feel like it."

Recreation. I liked that. And English her second language.

"When are they letting you go home?"

"Soon. Tomorrow maybe even."

She moved away from the window and sat on the foot of her bed, crossing her legs and looking up at me. "I think you are a fisherman, you said. Perhaps you can take me fishing once I am ready to let comfort be my guide."

I didn't remember ever having told her about fishing, but I remembered a one-eared fisherman who might have told her husband, if he worked for her husband. Or maybe he worked for her.

"Whenever you're ready," I said. It was one of those lines to leave on, and I turned to go.

"We will keep in touch. Me and my Kind Samaritan."

"Good Samaritan," I said.

"Yes, that's it."

My beeper went off, for once just when I needed it, and I thanked her and retreated to the nurses' station.

"There's a Miss Banting calling. She says it's an emergency," said the answering service operator. She gave me the number.

A man answered.

"Dr. Abrams? Maureen asked me to call."

"Yes?"

"We were having brunch and she turned bright red and fainted."

"She's unconscious?"

"Well, nearly."

159

"Where are you?"

"At Houlihans. Georgetown Park."

"Bring her to the Emergency Room at Saint George's. Know where that is?"

"Yes. We're not far."

"You have a car?"

"Yes. Do you think we'd better get an ambulance?"

"Don't waste the time. Bring her in."

I started down for the ER when my beeper went off again. One of the interns on the metabolic ward had an Addisonian in adrenal crisis, and I thought he must have meant Mrs. Waterhouse. He said she had no blood pressure and very little pulse and he wanted me immediately.

I called down to ER and told the resident to draw a blood sugar, an insulin level and a C-peptide on Maureen when she arrived, then to blast her with IV glucose.

"C-peptide?" said the resident. "Think she's taking some insulin on the sly?"

"I don't think. I just cover the bases."

I ran over to the ICU wondering how Mrs. Waterhouse had gotten into trouble so quickly. Then I realized I hadn't tried to wake her. She might have been comatose when I looked in on her earlier. Great doctor, Dr. Abrams. Through all that self-castigation the C-peptide thing stayed with me. C-peptides can catch a psycho who self-injects insulin. But Maureen didn't seem that frantic to prove to me that she really did have hypoglycemia. On the other hand, she went all mysterious about not seeing me, and now dramatically takes centre stage again. You can't be a doctor and assume everyone's dealing the cards straight off the top.

It wasn't Mrs. Waterhouse they were calling me about, for which I was profoundly grateful. I just couldn't stand to have two of my own patients going sour on me at once. The intern had done all the right things before I got there: he was pouring in saline and cortisone and had started antibiotics. It took me about twenty minutes to bless the proceedings and to run over and look into Mrs. Waterhouse's room, being careful not to be seen so I wouldn't have to spend another twenty minutes talking to her. It took me three more minutes to get down to the ER.

160

Maureen had been there ten minutes: they'd drawn the bloods, started an IV and given her a blast of IV sugar, and she was waking up.

"How do you feel?" I asked her.

"Like a fool," she said, trying to keep her eyes from rolling up into her head. She was very pale and her clothes were wet with sweat. "What a headache."

"What happened?"

"We were sitting there at brunch, having our Bloody Marys and I started feeling just awful."

"Awful? How? Shaky? Palpitations?"

"The whole gazoo," she said. "Very hot and very nauseated. And now this headache."

"Did you eat anything this morning, before your drinks?"

"Yes. And I hadn't had that much to drink before it hit me." She was irritated. "This is not alcoholic hypoglycemia."

"What did you eat?"

"English muffins and orange juice and a banana, before I even left for Houlihans. Then a croissant at Houlihans."

The resident stuck his head through the curtains into the examination cubicle and said hello, and he told me the sugar would be back within half an hour. He said someone wanted to talk with me. I pulled the curtains back so the nurses could watch Maureen from their central station and walked out to the waiting room.

"Dr. Abrams?" said a nice-looking man, offering me his hand. This had to be the mystery brunch date who'd called me from Houlihans. I wondered if he was the "friend" who needed some help with his limp penis. He was spare, very clean-looking skin, almost pink, with light hair and greying temples. I could see how she might go for him.

"She was fine, until about five minutes before I spoke with you," he said.

"She was okay when you picked her up this morning?"

"Yes, fine," he answered without missing a beat. Either they hadn't spent the night together or he was very good. "She had about finished her drink and suddenly flushed and then blanched. Then she got sick on the floor and sort of slumped over."

"Did she actually lose consciousness? Did she actually not answer questions? Did she move in jerks or twitch?"

"No. She just put her head on her arms, like this," he demonstrated, "and slumped on the table and told me to call you. She had your card in her wallet."

I grilled him for a while, and it sounded as if she had simply drunk her drink and greyed out, but nothing to suggest chest pain, seizure or prior distress. I walked back into the treatment area, leaving her "friend" – he said his name was Timothy Moore – stewing in the waiting room with a scant "She's doing better, now." I knew I shouldn't take it out on him. He seemed nice enough.

The blood sugar came back at thirty-two – less than half normal. The C-peptide would take a week to ten days, the insulin level longer. She had hypoglycemia, but how she got it was anyone's guess until the other tests were ready.

"Maybe I should've got insulin antibodies," said the resident.

"Why?"

"If she's a surreptitious injector, she might have them."

"Even people who've never injected insulin can have antibodies. What we should have drawn was proinsulin levels."

"Don't think I got enough blood for that."

"Call the lab and see. What did you send off?"

"Grey and red top," said the resident, referring to the tubes of blood. "You admitting her?"

"Wouldn't you?"

Maureen refused to be admitted. She felt much better after the IV sugar and wanted to go home.

"That sugar was for real," I told her. "You were pissed I hadn't taken you seriously. Now I'm serious. You've got to come in."

"What're you going to do for me in the hospital?"

"Work you up for insulinoma."

"Christ, a three-day fast?"

"Right."

"I'm all right now," she said, sitting up, looking woozy. "It was just something I ate. You know what really came up?

162

Orange juice. Helen made some fresh-squeezed this morning and that's what came up."

"Did anyone else drink the orange juice?"

"I don't know. I didn't see Helen have any. She was on one of her three-hour diets, not eating, making everyone breakfast."

"Who else had the orange juice?"

"My friend Tim. No, he didn't. He had coffee. Maybe it was all those Bloody Marys. I had some pretty stiff Bloody Marys at Houlihans."

"Maybe you'd better stay," said a voice from behind me. It was friend Moore.

"Look, I'll come in next Monday. You can schedule it now. If I have any more episodes, I'll be here. Even if I don't, I may come, after this morning."

"What do you gain by putting this off?" I asked.

"It's just bad timing. I can't be out from work right now."

I watched them walk out of the ER. She didn't lean against him and he didn't put his arm around her, although she grabbed his forearm once, to steady herself. This had to be the Tim Helen had mentioned.

Something real had happened this morning. This wasn't neurotic hypoglycemia. This morning Maureen's blood sugar had been measured in a reputable hospital laboratory at thirty-two, just eight points higher than the sugar General Dhieu had at autopsy. The number of explanations for that sugar was limited: she had either gotten some insulin, or something that made her release her own insulin, or she had a tumour which made insulin on its own.

She was probably profoundly crazy. She probably shot herself up with insulin before breakfast, then orchestrated high drama in the ER. She'd managed to bring her sugar daddy face to face with her new younger suitor and then she marched bravely out, like a good little trooper, having got both of us cooing and fretting over her.

If she were a nut, she was a calculating and full-blown one. If she wasn't a nut, she might really have a potentially lethal tumour.

# 36

Monday morning I didn't think about Maureen more than every five minutes. It was a busy morning with phone calls and patients and I was trying to get out to go over to the National Institutes of Health.

The first call was from Dr. von Dernhoffer, smooth voice, just wanting to know how I was and how my morning was going and what I thought of the nice cool weather we were having and had I solved the General Dhieu case because the newspapers kept calling. I told him what I knew and what was cooking and that I was going to the NIH this morning if I could ever get off the phone.

"I won't keep you then," he said. "I know you have to do things your own way."

"And I have to pay my own way, too," I said. "Which means seeing a few of my own patients right now. I've got rent to meet, and I don't make much as a medical investigator."

I had to weigh Mrs. Simpson, who slipped into my office and planted herself there and went through her catalogue of I-have-an-itch what-should-I-take. And there was a nice lady with a thyroid nodule, which I stuck a needle into and biopsied, and mounted the biopsy on a slide.

Then I pulled on my jacket and waved good-bye to Mrs. Bromley who knew where I was going because she had set up my schedule and told me where I was supposed to be.

"You will stop by and check on that man in toxicology?" she called after me.

This morning even I knew where I had to go. I like that drive to NIH: it takes you past all those pristine suburban neigh-bourhoods Maureen had maligned so exquisitely. Bethesda is very high-density in churches, country clubs, Country Squire station wagons with fake wood on the doors, women who shop in tennis outfits, formerly restricted neighbourhoods (no Negroes, no Jews) now restricted only by the money it takes to buy there, swimming pools and perfect green lawns fronting colonial houses.

The National Institutes of Health campus fits into Bethesda as gracefully as weeping willows on a plantation. I parked in the visitor's lot and hiked over to the Clinical Center.

The Clinical Center is the hospital for the NIH, with all the wards and patients and clinical laboratories that do all the tests on what they take out of the patients. I walked into the first lift and pushed the button for ten and was lucky enough to recognize the corridor I needed. The tenth floor was done in government modern: green and grey. It looked exactly like the corridor in my government workers' clinic building. I wondered how anyone could work there for more than a week without jumping out a window.

Stewart Stapler was in his lab. He looked pleased to see me until he saw the slide and specimen bottle. He did the staining and histologic evaluation for me because I sent him patients for his studies. Stewart was the author of at least a hundred papers on thyroid disease and his mission was to produce New Knowledge. My little biopsies were just time lost from his pursuit of same, unless one of them turned out to be something he was studying.

He asked about the patient the biopsy had come from, hoping she might be worth studying. He listened while I presented her case, sitting there at his microscope, tieless, ink stains on his shirt pocket, glasses with very thick lenses.

"Either she's got thyroiditis or she's taking some thyroid pills and not telling you."

I asked if he had ever seen a patient who faked illness by surreptitiously taking medication.

"About one a year," he said. "Usually a nurse or somebody medical."

"Any idea why they do it, Stewart?"

Stewart shrugged. "We had a nurse who worked on the eighth floor last year, dating one of the clinical associates.

Weight loss, erratic menstrual periods, tachycardia. We put her through the million-dollar workup when the scan showed no uptake over the thyroid. Nobody thought about the possibility she might be taking pills. She was such a nice girl. Girlfriend of a doc. Finally, it was the only thing that would fit all the data."

"But why do they do it?"

"All I know is you're talking big-time psychosis. It's not just a neurotic who needs to be sick because life's too much to face. I didn't believe that until this nurse. Shrinks said, big-time disease. I thought, what do shrinks know? Sent her home. They found her hanging from a beam in her basement."

"By the neck?" I said. "By a rope?"

"Dead. Left a note and everything." Stewart was studying my face. "You okay?" he said. "You look a little green around the gills."

"I've got this patient might be taking insulin – surreptitiously. I'd rather she took thyroid if she wants to play games," I said as if I were talking about just another patient. "When her blood sugar drops she gets a little comatose."

"How low does she get?"

"Thirty-two, last time."

"You'd better get her to a shrink, if you can be sure she's doing the dirty deed. Or next time she misses an appointment, send them to check her basement."

Stewart clasped his hands behind his head and leaned back in his chair. "You're sure she doesn't have an insulinoma? Shrink wouldn't help much there."

I left Stewart's lab intensely sorry they did not have a bar in the Clinical Center. I took the lift to the cafeteria in a fog.

I don't remember pouring the coffee or paying for it, but I was stirring in the sugar when my beeper went off. There was a phone in the back of the cafeteria and my fingers couldn't seem to dial the numbers fast enough. It was Mrs. Bromley. I waited for her to say they had Maureen with a rope around her neck.

"Saint George's just called," she said. "That insulin level is back."

"Yes?" I said. Thinking it was on Maureen.

"We *are* still interested in General Dhieu, are we not?" said Mrs. Bromley.

"Don't keep me in suspense."

"It's twenty-four," said Mrs. Bromley. "They told me to tell you the concurrent blood sugar in the sample was twenty-four."

I thanked her.

"Well," she said. "What's it mean?"

"It means either General Dhieu's nurse gave him too much insulin, by her own error or by Biocon's error, or someone else did."

"The insulin's high then?"

"With a blood sugar that low, the insulin should be undetectable. Zero," I said. "They didn't think they had interference from antibodies?"

"It was Dr. Potter, the lab director. He said it was a 'clean' assay. He said they were most sure of the result."

I thanked her and tried to hang up.

"You are going to check with that man in toxicology?"

"Yes, mum." I did hang up, then.

The toxicology lab was in the Clinical Center building six floors above the cafeteria. I stepped off the lift on five and found it with only a little wandering around. There was a sign by the door: TOXICOLOGY: NIDMD.

I stepped in and saw someone in a white lab coat behind a lab bench. She was very nice to look at. She was undoubtedly the lab tech Sumner had told me about. She was also very familiar. She looked up and met my eyes and I realized she was my disappearing Neil Young fan from Mr. Smith's. Her name tag said MAI NGUYEN.

"I thought you liked daiquiris," I said. "And here I catch you drinking coffee."

She put down her cup and looked at me, trying to understand. She was every bit as pretty as I had thought she was the first time. Everything about her, physically, was clear and unblemished.

"Oh," she said. "Mr. Smith's." She smiled.

"You're a lady of many talents," I said.

"Not so many," she said.

"You have a talent for language," I said. "You speak English like a native."

"I had lots of practice in my native land," she said with enough irony to make me stare at her.

"And you work here? I thought you worked at Saint George's Hospital."

"Why?"

"We shared a lift there one day. I remember you were carrying an Igloo ice chest."

"You have a good memory. I was collecting samples. We collaborate with Saint George's on a number of studies."

"But you work here? In this lab? In toxicology?"

"I was raised in Mekong. Toxic substances was a subject which seemed, as you say, a natural."

I think I smiled when she said that, but she didn't. As perfect as her English was, I couldn't be sure when she was joking, or if she knew when I was.

"And now you have read my name tag," she said. "And your name, I have not been told."

"You're interested?"

"Of course. Why should I not be?"

"You weren't interested last time."

"You came back from your phone call with another woman. I do not ménage à trois. Not on the first date."

"You were gone."

"You didn't see me."

I told her my name and she gave me her phone number, writing it on the back of a lab slip. *Ask for Mai – 521–2947.*

"You're a doctor," she said.

I was wearing a beeper and had a stethoscope in my jacket pocket.

"You picked right up on that," I said.

"Oh," she said, "I am very quick."

"Actually," I said, "I'm here on business. Your chief is running some insulin and some other pills for me."

"Dr. Smirnopoulous is running samples?"

"Yes. That's his name."

"Insulin?" she said, and she walked over to a green cloth-covered lab log, and turned some pages. "When did you send them?" she started to ask, and then she looked up. "Oh, wait. I know which ones. The insulin isn't ready yet. That's a toughie. The pills, however, are done."

She told me the pills were quinine, digoxin – just what they appeared to be.

I asked her when the insulin would be ready.

"I'm setting up the stuff this afternoon. I can tell you it is insulin, though."

"But I want to know how concentrated, how potent."

"I'm still working on that," she said. "What's all this about? Can't the drug company tell you the units per cc?"

"I know what the drug company thinks," I said. "But the patient got his usual number of cc's and got very hypoglycemic."

"I understand," she said. "And you're going to cost the drug company *beaucoup* bucks, if this insulin's too hot."

"I'm only trying to find the truth."

"That," said Mai Nguyen, "can be the most dangerous game."

I smiled.

"I'll call you when we have the results," she said. "We have your number. You call me, when you'd like to listen to some Neil Young."

I left on that good note. She was a very fetching young thing. When it rains it pours. A month ago, a big evening for me was watching the cars go by on MacArthur Boulevard from my front porch. Now I've got three lovely females in various stages of solicitation all springing from the same fountain – Mr. Smith's. I thought about that and tried to imagine how that could be more than a coincidence. I couldn't get very far with it, so I tried not to think about what really bothered me. I thought about Mai Nguyen and about Mrs. Que's legs and about all the possibilities there. But pretty soon I started seeing Stewart Stapler's eyes behind those thick lenses and hearing him tell me about women who take drugs to fake illness and where patients like that are headed.

# 37

Tuesday I was still thinking about Maureen. More than thinking. I was worried. I was worried when she walked out of the ER, but I was sceptical enough to shrug it off and let her play her hand. Now I kept going back and forth – suppose she's taking insulin to fake it, or suppose she's really got an insulinoma? Either way, it was not good news. I think the insulinoma idea bothered me more. *That* was my responsibility.

The whole morning I had forced myself to think rationally and to consider how very insane she probably was – despite all her protestations of not wanting to be ill. Walking out of the ER was a nice touch, especially after she'd made sure I'd be there to see it.

But she couldn't have been sure I'd be there to see it.

If she was injecting insulin on the sly, then she was one very sick pyscho. And if she were nuts, all her good looks and quick wits wouldn't stay interesting long. She'd become tedious very quickly.

But if she wasn't faking, she had something that wasn't going to just go away. Maybe it was the alcohol. Who was I trying to kid? Alcoholic hypoglycemia happens in starving winos who never eat, not in healthy young women who tipple a few at Houlihans.

I went through it all like that, back and forth, and decided not to call her. The rational thing to do was to let *her* call. But who's ever rational, in the end?

Mrs. Bromley glided in with the mail, and asked, "How's Miss Banting?" and I reached for the phone and called Maureen at work.

"Don't keep me, Doc," she said. "It is five past noon and

I am feeding myself on schedule, mercilessly, warding off hypoglycemia."

"It's a bad feeling."

"Tell me about it. That was the pits Sunday. Never felt so rotten."

"Then that was your worst episode?"

"It won the prize," she said. "I was most glad to see your face."

"I'm glad I could make it, even late."

"Were you late? All I remember is looking up and seeing your wonderful gorgeous face."

"I was late."

"You were wonderful. I was so impressed," she said. "So was my friend."

"Moore?"

"Yes. He's been looking for a doc. I gave you a terrific recommendation."

It must have been pretty terrific – soon as I hung up, Timothy Moore was on the phone asking for an appointment. He had some "medical problems" he wanted to consult me about.

He arrived later that same afternoon.

"Maureen appreciated your attention very much," said Moore. "She thinks you're a very fine doctor."

I nodded, agreeing that I was a very fine doc.

"And she was a nurse. She ought to know."

"I know," I said, and he looked at me trying to understand exactly what I meant by that. I asked him if he had known Maureen long.

"Oh, we go back a long way," he said, leaning back in his chair, smiling, putting his hands behind his head.

"New York?"

"Vietnam."

Now that was interesting. He looked too old to have been in Vietnam, unless he was a doctor or some kind of career officer or something like that. I never got it out of him. I asked him why he had come. He said something about a growth on his foot, but when he took his sock off, it looked like nothing more than a mole and he looked embarrassed at having brought it up.

I sat there wondering why he really had come when he said, "Another thing, my libido isn't what it used to be." He sounded as if he was talking about his putting game.

"Is it the drive or the performance that doesn't seem up to par?"

"Both," he said, laughing a little. He wasn't comfortable. "I guess I'm just getting older." He was forty-seven, but looked more. "My own GP tells me I'm just slowing down."

"Has he evaluated you for this?"

"No, he just told me to stop trying to be a young stud."

"Is that what you've been trying?"

"I don't know."

"I'd like to see his records, so I don't repeat things he may already have done. You can sign a release with Mrs. Bromley, out front."

"I don't think he's done any tests for this particular problem."

The particular problem was that he could get an erection, but it didn't last and ejaculation was problematic. I began to feel better about Maureen and him, and I began wondering what her message was in sending him. But I wasn't sure what I was really being told or, for that matter, by whom.

"There are several reasons why men have the problems you've mentioned," I said. "We can do a testosterone and a prolactin to rule out some basic problems, but there's always the psychological area, when it comes to sex." He didn't say anything. "Could there be psychological reasons you're having problems?"

"I can think of about a hundred, offhand," he said, laughing.

I began to like him a little, and I wondered whether or not that was what was supposed to be happening according to Maureen's scheme. He had an imperturbable quality that went down well.

Then I went through a few medical history questions like a real doctor and discovered Timothy Moore was a diabetic. He'd been taking Diabinese for ten years.

Now of all the reasons for bona fide, one-hundred-percent mechanical impotence, diabetes leads the list. Timothy Moore hadn't awakened with a morning erection in six months, and

172

the more I talked to him the more I became convinced the only way he was going to be put back in business was with a penile implant.

I told him I might need to refer him to a urologist for nocturnal tumescence studies. If he wasn't getting spontaneous erections during sleep, he'd need a plastic rib put into his penis to keep it in constant extension.

"Wouldn't that get," he thought how to phrase it, "in the *way* quite a bit?"

"I can't speak from personal experience," I said, and watched his eyes, "but the patients I talk to are always enthusiastic."

"But are they orgiastic?"

"All it does is take care of the erection problem. It won't give you ejaculatory prowess."

He said he'd have to think about it.

I sent him off to get his blood drawn and he shook my hand and looked me in the eye and told me it was a pleasure to see me again. I told him to make a return appointment with Mrs. Bromley and tried to read his eyes but saw nothing. I had the feeling he approved of me, but I couldn't say why, and didn't really know why he should have to approve of me. Was the old love being asked to endorse the new one? Or was I just being too convoluted?

I walked back to my chair, once he'd gone, and looked at the Viet Cong photo on my wall and thought about Maureen and about Timothy Moore and about her hypoglycemia and tried to imagine the connection between her and him and it.

# 38

Von Dernhoffer's unwelcome unctuous voice came over the phone Wednesday morning.

Mrs. Bromley had warned me when she buzzed back the call. "It's that oily man from Saint George's," she had said.

"And how are you doing this morning?" he asked.

"Splendid," I said. "Just ever so."

"Well, I'm glad to hear that," he said.

Isn't that nice you're so glad. I'm so glad you're glad. "What can I do for you?" I said out loud.

"Has Dr. Potter spoken with you?"

"You mean about the insulin level? Yes. I know it's high."

"Now what do you make of that?"

"It means the General had too much insulin for that level of blood sugar."

"Too much insulin? And what could account for that?"

I love being asked questions when the questioner already knows the answers. "Well, Dr. von Dernhoffer, I believe we've discussed the possibilities."

"Yes, but I thought it was pretty clear that high insulin, low sugar meant either insulinoma or insulin overdose," he said. "And the autopsy ruled out insulinoma."

"I agree."

"So you've concluded the patient got an improper dose of insulin?"

"Well, he got too much. How that happened is what I'm still working on."

"I'm not sure I see what you mean. He got too much: the nurse made a mistake."

"That's the most likely, but not the only possibility."

"And what other possibilities are you working on?"

"Dr. von Dernhoffer, has anyone from Biocon been to see you?"

He paused just long enough to give it away. Biocon had got to him all right.

"I've got some people at NIH looking at the insulin," I said. "Just covering all the bases."

"I appreciate your thoroughness," said the Chairman. "Of course, it's important, while we try to be complete, that we not go around making potentially serious allegations," he said. "That's only fair."

"Dr. von Dernhoffer," I said. "I'm a busy man. I'm not going to try to guess what those Biocon men might have told you, because that would waste my time and yours. So why don't you

174

just come to the point and tell me what's bothering you?"

"I'm not applying pressure," he said, voice a lot less friendly.

"I've really got to get to my next patient," I said, looking at my empty schedule. "So if you don't mind."

Von Dernhoffer managed to say that two men from Biocon had been in his office that morning, and they were most upset that Dr. Abrams had not seen fit to hand over the insulin bottle from which the fatal dose was drawn. They had not been able to get the bottle from the NIH, either. They were sure Biocon was about to be unjustly slandered and they were hinting, none too subtly, at a big-bucks lawsuit.

"I'd really like your report as soon as possible," said the Chairman. "The paper called this morning. That Shaw woman. I don't want to interfere, but I have to be sure you're not being diverted into unpromising avenues."

"As soon as I have the results from NIH, you'll have my report," I said. "They may vindicate Biocon entirely. It'll be a better report, all the way around."

That seemed to shut him down and he said a few more ingratiating things about my credentials and hung up.

Biocon was upset, burning with resentment. I could see their point of view. I leaned back in my chair and thought about those Oriental followers who kept popping up everywhere. Was I supposed to know they were following me? Were they gathering the dope on Dr. Abrams, womanizer, bar rat and Vietnam war veteran – read Vietnam druggie? Or was I supposed to wonder why they let themselves be seen? A subtle message from the big boys at Biocon? We know where you live.

# 39

It had been a long two hours at the government workers' clinic. More and more civil servants were succumbing to stress-on-the-job, acute and chronic inertia and endemic ennui. Which is to say, morale was low. After two hours of torpor, it was all I could do to close up my briefcase and slump towards the door. Before I could reach it, the phone buzzed and I was caught.

"Aren't you lucky?" It was Maureen. That energetic voice and her rush of words cheered me up.

"Am I?"

"I'm taking you to a play tonight."

"Suppose I'm busy?"

"Then you're not so lucky."

I told myself to be rational, restrained, and to tell her no. I still hadn't worked out what that Timothy Moore referral was all about and anyway, she was a probable crazy. Big-time crazy, as Stewart Stapler had said. Crazy enough to make you love her and then jump out a window or go down to the basement and put a rope around her neck. I considered all that for a full microsecond, and asked her when and where she wanted me to pick her up.

The play was a grim little morality drama set in the sixties. It was playing at the Kennedy Center. I do my best to avoid Vietnam memorabilia-cum-art, but being with Maureen improved it considerably. It was called *Deaf Abraham's Children*, and concerned parents and their quandary about letting their kids go fight in Vietnam. The title, of course, was an allusion to the biblical story about acting in blind obedience, placing loyalty above reason and all that. The none-too-subtle point was that one ought to listen to inner voices, and ask, "Would God ask me to murder?" The parents in this little production hear the voice from above and send their kids off to slaughter.

"So the hand came down again and again, for five years, fifty thousand times."

That's when Maureen leaned over and whispered, "And that's just counting our guys."

That's when I decided it wasn't all that essential if she was a nut who injected herself with insulin just to get my attention and to give her semi-impotent semi-boyfriend fits.

She had a sense of perspective.

After the play we joined the dash to the exits for the

176

underground parking lot. It was a weekday night and most of these people worked for or around the government and had to be at work the next morning.

Before we could reach the lift to the car park, we were caught in a standstill. The anchorman for one of the national evening news shows was standing talking to a famous former cabinet officer. Rubber-necking was causing a massive traffic jam.

"What are they all gawking about?" asked Maureen.

I identified the major players for her.

"So what?" she said. "A guy who looks good reading the TV monitors talking to a has-been. So everyone's stopping dead in their tracks."

"Celebrity counts."

"Fame is all," said Maureen.

"That's what Mrs. Bromley says."

"Oh, yes. She was very proud of you for getting in the papers with the murdered general."

"You know something I don't know?"

"About what?"

"The General: I didn't know he was murdered," I said. "And I'm the one who's supposed to find out."

"Oh, he was done in, all right, with malice aforethought."

"What makes you so sure?"

"He was a general, wasn't he? And a Vietnamese? Someone had it in for him. None of 'em die natural deaths."

We walked to the garage and took the car to Georgetown.

We had a pitcher of sangria at Café des Artistes and I asked her why she still went to plays about Vietnam, visited monuments to the war, ate at Vietnamese restaurants.

"As opposed to forgetting the whole thing?" she said. "Tried that, and failed. Drank to forget. Didn't work. Couldn't forget the babies." She looked at me for my reaction, then smiled.

"Burn cream was my speciality at Binh Thuy," she said "Napalm. Great paediatric affliction."

She smiled when she said that.

"Don't see much of that in Washington," I said.

177

"Tell me about your downtown clinic. The one for the inner-city people. You never talk about it."

"Not much to say."

"Why not?"

"It's just a clinic. Usual inner-city stuff. Crisis medicine. Folks down there don't have the prevention concept. They get a pain, they come in."

"Don't most people?"

"Most people have heard of strep throats, bacteria, heart murmurs, hernias, meningitis. Those are foreign words on Sixteenth Street. If it's not on TV commercials, they haven't heard of it. They get whatever's selling. Diagnosis? What's that? Hey, doc, what's good fo' a knot in the stomach?"

I don't know why I got so worked up. Maureen got all silent and looked at the sangria in her glass. So I was a neoconservative. At least I'd taken the blinkers off.

We finished the pitcher and she looked at my hair and suddenly said, "Why do you straighten your hair?"

"The only thing I straighten is my tie, and that not often."

"No, but you blow-dry it. Takes all the curl out."

"I like it that way."

"Because you're a Hebrew Son of the Confederacy?"

"I pass for white."

"So you're defensive. You cultivate the whole WASP patina. Your office looks like some London men's club."

"I'll have to talk to my interior decorator."

"I'm talking to him now. There's nothing *wrong* with all that. It's just that there's more to you and you won't admit it."

"I deny it?"

"You obscure it."

"Where did all this come from?"

"You don't like yourself, so you take it out on other people. I mean it's no tragedy, a little self-hate, but it interferes with your sympathy for other people."

"I just like people who work hard, don't expect much, and sacrifice for their kids," I said, and watched for her reaction. She didn't react at all. She just studied my face.

"One of the things I liked about you was that you did that ghetto clinic. I guess I was just kidding myself."

178

"Why would that make you like me?" I asked, astonished.

"Maybe I misjudged you," she said. "I mean the modest little house, the beat-up car. You didn't seem to care about all the things doctors get caught up in. So I thought you must care about more important things. But you'd probably love to have the big house in Potomac with the pool and the Maserati."

"Not particularly."

"You're just too beat to work for it," she said.

"Those aren't what I want," I said. "But I wouldn't apologize if they were."

"Of course not," she said. "The neoconservative."

I looked at her flaring eyebrows and tight mouth. She looked down at her fork, playing with it. I asked, "So why don't you work in the Martin Luther King Clinic? They can always use nurses."

"Maybe I will."

"Or maybe you're afraid."

"Afraid?"

"It wouldn't be a fantasy any more. It wouldn't be grateful patients or even people who really needed care."

"They need care."

"So come on down. I'll get you a job."

"If I ever went back to nursing, it'd be where they need it the most."

She didn't say where that might be. I waited. Then I asked, "Why did you send me Timothy Moore?"

"Speaking of questions from left field."

"That's an evasion. He's your boyfriend. And you sent him to me to fix his limp penis. Why?"

"In the first place, I didn't send him to you. I told him what you said about that workup. He went on his own."

"Now who's not being honest with herself?"

"And he's not my boyfriend."

I waited for her to say more, but she just shook her head the way she often did, to make her shiny hair swirl and fall back into place. It was her way of regaining composure.

"Want to go away with me this weekend?" I asked.

"I'm not sure I like you enough."

"I wasn't asking you to elope. Just to go somewhere."

179

"I've got plans for this weekend."

"With Timothy Moore?"

"With whom is my business."

"Why'd you call me today?"

"I thought you might like the play."

"That was the excuse. And now you're pissed at me and I can't even figure out why."

"I wanted to get to know you better. I'm not sure I like what I found."

"Why?"

"I'm just disappointed," she said. "I saw that photo on your wall and I liked you. I hear you dumping on a bunch of ghetto people just because they're black and didn't go to Swarthmore, I don't know what to think."

"Black, poor, none of that matters. I just don't like people who think family means have the baby at thirteen, shove it off on grandma who's on welfare. People whose idea of self-improvement means graduating from smack to cocaine."

"They just don't measure up to your lofty standards."

"I'm discriminating. I don't apologize for that."

"So you go around hating half the world."

"More than half."

"You hate people with no money, no education, no hope."

"Just because I don't help them abort their foetuses doesn't mean I hate them."

That was a low blow, and I regretted it immediately. Her face went red and tight.

"Let's get the bill," she said, waving for the waiter.

"I'm sorry," I said. "I know you wouldn't waste your time in that clinic if you didn't believe in it."

The waiter came and Maureen took the bill and dug in her pocketbook. I let her pay. She was in control now.

She got up and walked out and I caught up with her on the street.

"I said I'm sorry. What do I have to do?"

She whirled around. "You're a real misanthrope, aren't you?"

"Oh, I'm a great fan of mankind," I said. "And I didn't even have to smear on the burn cream."

# 40

Thursday afternoon, I walked into Mrs. Que's room at Saint George's to discover her bed occupied by a woman on a respirator who looked about eighty years old and must have weighed fifty pounds. The surgeons had sent Mrs. Que home that morning. I had sent Mrs. Waterhouse home Wednesday. That left me with only one patient in the hospital.

I walked over to Seven West to see Mrs. Sambawe. Mrs Sambawe was a nice Ethiopian lady, sixty-three, with metastatic adenocarcinoma. It wasn't clear where the malignancy had originated, and since adeno CA from the breast would be treated differently from adeno CA which had started in ovary or colon or lung, the hunt for the tissue of origin was under way.

She was very cooperative about the whole thing. Her husband was with the Ethiopian embassy, and they were very elegant people, erect and with fine, thin faces that looked like they'd been carved from ebony. He had a degree in architecture and she liked her suits from Lord & Taylor, and she spoke Arabic, Italian, French, English, not to mention Ethiopian.

We had run her quite a chase. She'd had a sigmoidoscopy, looking for colonic CA, and when that turned out clean, she got the castor oil and Fleet enemas followed by the barium enema, which was also negative. Then she got her post-barium enema clean-out – more enemas – then some magnesium citrate to clean her out for the upper GI series, which was also negative. Along the way, she had a bone scan, liver scan, gallium scan, and she had just come back from her abdominal CAT scan and mammograms, which had taken all morning.

I looked through her chart. Her chest X-rays, sputum cytology, IVP and stool guaiacs were all negative. If the CAT scan was negative, Monday she'd have an ERCP, which meant having her swallow a fibre-optic telescopic about the size of a clothesline and then squirting some radiographic dye into her pancreatic duct, to look for pancreatic CA. It can be quite a procedure. I wouldn't look forward to having one.

Her husband was with her when I walked in.

"I think she needs a respite," said her husband, with his lovely Ethiopian lilt. "Your technological advances have quite worn her out." He smiled when he said that, and I could see he didn't mean it as a complaint, just as a simple statement of fact. She'd been through the wringer.

"You must be very frustrated," I said to her.

"Terrified, first," she said. "But then, after you told me what I had, and I woke up, still alive, the next day, it was better. I could face it. But the tests have worn me out."

"I was hoping I could take her out to dinner, and perhaps a movie, Saturday, if you would agree," said the husband.

"I don't see why not," I said. "When is your ERCP? Monday?"

"Yes."

I went out to the nurses' station and wrote an order for a pass for Saturday. When I looked up, I saw the Head Nurse in her white nurse uniform, standing about ten feet away, taking orders off a chart. The Head Nurse and I had met before. She looked about as happy seeing me as she would have seeing a cloud of locusts.

"I'm writing a pass for Mrs. Sambawe for Saturday night."

"I'm afraid that's not possible."

"Of course it is. I just wrote the order."

"There are no passes for inpatients any more."

"Why on earth not?"

"Because we've had a memorandum from the Director of Nursing."

"The Director of Nursing doesn't write orders on my patients."

"I'm sorry."

"Did she give any reasons, or doesn't the Director have to do things like that?"

"The memo was very clear about this."

182

"But it doesn't make any sense. This lady's having nothing done to her over the weekend. She's just going to sit here. She needs a break."

"You'll have to speak with the Director of Nursing."

She said that with an unnecessarily satisfied little smile. She really liked her little measure of control.

"Maybe I can help," I heard a voice say. I turned around and it was Helen.

"I didn't hear the whole thing," she said.

So I explained about how Mrs. Sambawe very badly needed a little vacation from all the diagnostic efforts on her behalf and that her presence wouldn't be missed over the weekend since she had no tests scheduled until Monday morning.

Helen explained that the big blue insurance company in the sky had, in its infinite sensitivity to the workings of hospitals, decided that if patients were well enough to go out on pass, they weren't sick enough to be in the hospital, hospital days being very costly to the company.

"You're telling Mrs. Sambawe with the adenocarcinoma in her bone so she walks with a limp, who's just been invaded by every test known to man, and who has just one more to go on Monday, she has to be kept prisoner here over the weekend?"

"Hey, don't take my head off, Doc," laughed Helen. "You've got a shorter fuse than Maureen even." She smiled a multichinned smile. "I think I may have the solution to your problem." She looked at the Head Nurse who had been listening to all this with an expression of great suffering impatience. "If she has adeno CA, why don't we just put her on the adeno CA protocol, as a control?"

"That's fine with me," said the Head Nurse, looking at me as if I hadn't changed my underwear in three weeks and she could smell it.

I didn't understand what had happened. Helen explained: they had switched responsibility for Mrs. Sambawe's nursing care over to Helen by the simple expedient of declaring her a protocol patient. Helen was the Head Nurse for clinical protocols and Mrs. Sambawe could now go out on pass because protocol patients were not covered by the Director of Nursing and her infamous "no passes" memo.

"It's easy, when you know how," said Helen. Her eyes looked glad, with none of that anger they usually had.

"It's nice to know someone in power," I said.

"Nurses run the world," said Helen. "Don't you forget it."

"I appreciate your help."

"You're someone I gotta take care of. Don't want anything bad for you. Maureen wouldn't let me hear the end of it."

"I see."

"Where you guys off to this weekend?"

"I don't know where Maureen's off to," I said.

"Oh," said Helen, looking distraught. Then she recovered and said, "We're having some people over for a TGIF. You're invited, you know."

"You mean you're inviting me."

"Maureen told me to tell you."

"If you happened to see me . . ."

"Yes."

"No, she didn't. She'd call me herself. She's not real happy with good Dr. Abrams right now."

"She came home all upset. She wants to see you, but she's got pride up to here. It's just a TGIF. Lots of people, beer, very low key. She really told me to get you to come."

"I'll try to make it."

"Promise."

"I'll try."

"I'll page you every ten minutes Friday afternoon. I'll cancel Mrs. Sambawe's pass."

"You really know how to hurt a guy."

"Don't give up on Maureen," said Helen. "She fights with everyone, especially the ones who mean the most to her. But then she forgives you right away and doesn't know how to say it. She holds a grudge for about ten minutes. And she's a good friend, in the long run."

Helen flashed a big grin, turned on her heels and lumbered off down the hall. Coming after that dinner at Mr. Smith's, her affirmation of the depth of Maureen's friendship was very interesting. I still couldn't figure out why they lived together. Even if they were bosom buddies, they didn't do well on a day-to-day living-together basis. And on what was this abiding friendship based? Helen the superhawk, who still smouldered about the lost cause against the forces of darkness in Nam and Maureen who thought the whole thing an atrocity? People don't just agree to disagree on something like that.

Of course, they had weathered some storms together, from Holy Redeemer to Vietnam. But in Helen's case, I had the feeling there was something more. The way she looked at Maureen, the way her eyes lingered and the places they went – it had me watching her. Helen wasn't easy to judge. Sometimes I wanted nothing more than to simply escape her, and at other times, like just now with Mrs. Sambawe, she was engaging and even kind.

My big problem with Helen was my associative mind. Burbling in the back of my skull was General Dhieu's case, a man who had enemies. And there was Helen, who worked in the same hospital, a woman who wanted to throw bricks through the windows of Vietnamese restaurants.

# 41

Friday morning I saw four patients, tying my own record for total number of patients seen on a single morning in the office. Mrs. Bromley was very happy.

"You'll be most impressed with the next one," she said over the inter-office phone.

"Rich?"

"Very fetching."

It was Mrs. Que, looking very fetching indeed in burgundy and green. Her belly was fine. She was in for her migraines.

"I was playing bridge last night and one of my friends gave me a little green pill for the headache, and presto, I was cured."

She sounded funny, saying *presto*. She must have picked that up from American TV. She wanted more of the little green pills. She had no idea of the name, but since it worked so quickly, I guessed it was some sort of ergot compound. We went through the product identification section of the *PDR*. She picked out propanolol without any doubts.

"Fine way to get your medications, from a friend at a bridge game."

"What can be the harm? All my friends were there, if anything happened."

"Did your friend ask if you were asthmatic, before she gave you the pill?"

"Asthmatic? I had a headache."

"Propanolol can do nasty things to asthmatics. Had an asthmatic patient once, took his wife's propanolol. Died before he could get to the hospital."

That wasn't a true story, but, then again, it didn't impress Mrs. Que very much anyway. She wanted her magic pill and I told her how to take it and she got up to go.

"I'd like to examine you," I said.

"I would enjoy that, too," she said. "But I am in a hurry."

She stood up. "I will be calling to you sometime soon. We can go fishing on a boat, and I will bring a basket picnic and wine and I will have you examine my lovely scar."

"Then you don't think I'm a CIA agent after all?"

"Oh, my husband was most frustrated. You are a most harmless citizen."

"He checked me out?"

"You and your Miss Maureen Banting."

"Really? What did he find?"

"You were in the war. So was she. You were given a Purple Heart medal and an honourable discharge. Miss Banting was also given an honourable discharge, and a Bronze Star medal. But she was a bad girl and was thrown into the stock-cage."

"The stockade? What for?"

"Oh? You did not know this, then?"

"No, tell me more."

"You are most interested in Miss Banting? Perhaps I am wasting my time fishing with you."

"I'm sure you know all there is to know about me and Miss Banting."

She smiled. "She is a very pretty young girl. Perhaps you are not interested in an old lady like me."

"You are ageless. Why'd they throw her in the stockade?"

"She was striking an officer. A fight."

"That sounds like her."

"She has a hot temper?"

"Scalding. Who'd she strike?"

"Ask her," said Mrs. Que, annoyed now. "What is a Purple Heart?"

"It's what they give you when you say you want to go home but they still want you to fight."

"You were fighting? I thought you were a doctor."

"I was collecting medals."

She laughed and walked out of my office. I leaned back in my chair thinking what a nice firm body Mrs. Que had, and thinking about Maureen, who also had a very nice firm body, and then I phoned the laboratory at Saint George's. Maureen's insulin level was not ready and wouldn't be for another week, but they had the insulin antibodies done, and they were absent, which at least was reassuring if you wanted to believe she didn't self-inject insulin.

I hung up thinking about her tests and about how Maureen was probably going to turn out to be very psychotic and how I'd just have to wait for all the lab tests to be sure.

Mrs. Bromley looked up as I hurried past her desk on my way to the government workers' clinic. She would be gone by the time I got back to the office and she said, "Have a nice weekend."

"You too."

"Any plans?"

"That seems to be a popular question lately."

"Who else asked? Mrs. Que? She's a hot number, that. Better watch her."

"I should be so lucky. No, Maureen's room-mate, Helen, asked."

"How *is* Miss Banting?"

"Hard to figure."

"Good for her."

I drove down to the clinic, which dragged even more slowly

than usual. There was an outside phone call from a lady. But it wasn't Maureen. It was only Mrs. Simpson who thought she felt a new heart murmur.

After clinic, I drove home through Georgetown, along M Street, and considered stopping off at Mr. Smith's. But then I thought, that's where all this trouble began, and I continued on down Canal Road and on home.

But I couldn't settle down. I went from room to room, picking things up, folding and closeting clothes until the place was so neat there wasn't anything left to do but turn on the stereo. They were playing Jackson Browne, a song I knew well and sometimes liked:

> People go just where they will,
> I never noticed them until I got this feeling
> That it's later than it seems.

I listened to it all the way through, then turned on the TV. *The Big Sleep* was on the four-o'clock movie. I sat there watching, wondering what Maureen would think of Bacall, when my beeper went off.

## 42

It was Helen. "You're coming, aren't you?"

"I just got home."

"No excuses. Come on."

Half the street was in shadows when I got there, but Maureen's house was on the sunny side. I could see people sitting in the rockers on the porch, but I couldn't be sure who they were, looking at them through the screens.

I stayed in my car trying to decide whether or not to get out.

"Dr. Abrams, paging Dr. Abrams," Helen's happy voice rang out.

I got out and walked up to the louvered door Helen was

holding open. She held a brimming mug of beer in one hand. "Don't be shy," she said.

Helen stepped back so I could move past her onto the porch. I looked around for the party. There was Creedence Clearwater Revival coming from inside the house, but the only people on the porch were Maureen and Timothy Moore. They were sitting in adjacent rockers, with an empty rocker on either side. The empty rocker at Maureen's elbow was still moving – Helen must have been there. It had to be a tight fit for Helen.

Maureen looked up and smiled. She looked dreamy, as if she had just awakened and she said, "Glad you could come." She held a joint pinched between the fingers of one hand and held a bottle of beer in the other.

Timothy Moore didn't appear any friskier than Maureen: they both had that slothful look of sunbathers lolling. Creedence was doing "Bad Moon Rising." Moore rolled his eyes towards me and looked me over but he didn't say anything. He looked back out across the lawn to the street where nothing in particular was happening. He was probably thinking about impotence and about how much I knew. Maureen's arm was covered with his hand.

I heard Helen's too cheerful, over-buoyant voice, "What can I get you, Doc?"

"Whatever you're drinking."

"One Molson, coming up." She sounded like a TV commercial.

She disappeared into the house.

"Sit down," Maureen said, with a languid gesture towards the chair. It was strange seeing her so lethargic. Must have had something to do with what she had pinched in her fingers. She was like a different person entirely. She smiled and put down her bottle and held up her hand to me. I sat next to her but didn't take her hand, not with Tim Moore hanging onto the other side.

Helen brought me a mug of beer. She squeezed herself into the chair on Tim Moore's other side.

"How was your day, Timothy?" asked Helen. "You never told us."

"Oh, spectacular," said Moore, still looking at the street, in

189

the general direction of my car. I looked at my car. It was a pretty banged-up-heap.

"Did anyone invite you to speak on 'Wall Street Week' or 'Washington Week in Review'?"

"Helen, that happened twice," said Moore, with a little more life in his voice. "You make it sound like I'm a regular item."

"You are, Timothy. You under-rate yourself all the time." Then to me, "Timothy is a very respected financial analyst. He's been on 'McNeil/Lehrer,' 'Wall Street Week,' 'Washington . . . '"

"Oh, Helen. They invite me when things are slow and they need fillers."

"Timothy Moore, that's not true," said Helen. She inflated herself, which in someone of Helen's proportions was a little frightening. "I don't know why you keep putting yourself down. You're very well respected. Your newsletter's taking off. You're really something."

"Helen, I don't know what I'd do without you. I finish a week of disasters, come over here, and you prop me back up again and send me back into the fray."

Helen beamed, "I'm only saying what everyone but you knows."

"Tim isn't doing badly," Maureen said to me. "Give Benjamin a stock tip, Tim."

"Right now I could use a bank account," I said. I can be very clever.

"A widespread condition," said Tim Moore, not to me, to the street.

"How's the dragon lady who's got no spleen?" Maureen asked. She took a swig of beer and looked my way.

There was a long silence. I get uncomfortable during long silences, especially when I'm sitting next to a woman I admire and her arm is being held by the guy sitting on the other side of her. Usually, in situations like that, I either restrain myself or leave. But Maureen asked me how Mrs. Que was, so I had to stay to answer.

I supposed bringing up Mrs. Que was supposed to divert me from Tim Moore hanging all over her arm.

helplessly on the ground, trying to catch his breath. Helen leaned over and swiped at the bird, catching it with a sweeping gesture. Leaning over and plucking anything from the ground was a difficult anatomic proposition for anyone of Helen's girth, but she captured the pigeon deftly.

Then she dropped the rubbish bag and took the bird in both hands and wrung its neck.

She opened the bag and dropped in the limp bird body, resealed the bag, and carried it over to the rubbish bins, dumping it in.

I left my window in a hurry, running down the hall to be back with Maureen before Helen returned. I was sitting in the rocker when Helen bounced back in.

"Can I offer anyone coffee?" she said with a bright little smile.

I said no, and got up to go. Helen lurched over and sank into the rocker I'd vacated on the other side of Maureen.

"Have a nightcap," said Maureen. Timothy Moore was asleep now, his head against her shoulder. Helen leaned her head on Maureen's other shoulder.

"I'm fine," I said.

"Thanks for coming, Doc," said Helen, with a dreamy smile.

I think she really meant it.


# 43


I had just pulled up in my driveway when my beeper went off, and when I reached my door the telephone was ringing.

The whole way home the image of Maureen sitting there in her cannabis haze with Timothy Moore's head on one shoulder and Helen's head on the other rode with me. So I was still in a daze when I got to the phone.

"What the hell you doing home on a Friday night, boy?" It was Sumner.

"You'd be proud of me. I was at a party."

"Good man. Got anyone with you?"

"No."

"Well, let's not degenerate into celibacy, boy. There's a whole city full of women out there. Best female-to-male ratio on the East Coast."

"Tonight, I think you just might have a point," I said. "Where are you?"

"Hallelujah. The worm turns. Down at my office. I'll meet you at the Shanghai Palace. Know it? Bethesda, off Wisconsin, on Del Ray."

"I can find it," I said. "But I just got a page. I could be delayed."

"You on call this weekend?"

"I'm always on call."

"Private practice. What a ballbuster. Why don't you join the army, boy? You'd work every fourth weekend."

"Let me answer this page. I'll call you if it's trouble. Otherwise, I'll meet you there."

Sumner was reluctant to let me off the phone but he had no choice. The answering service said it was a Miss Gwen calling and gave me her number.

"Full moon," said Mai Nguyen. "Feel strange?"

"I always feel strange, talking to you."

"That's just the way you should feel. Take me out for a drink."

"Now why would I want to do that?"

"Maybe I'd tell you about that Biocon insulin you brought me from Saint George's."

"You did the assay?"

"All finished."

"And so?"

"You buying the daiquiris?"

"We're going to have company," I said.

"I only do ménage à trois if I like her."

"She's a he."

"Same rule applies."

194

Mai arrived at the Shanghai Palace at the same time I did.

"You got here fast," I said.

"I was still in the lab," she said. "Finishing off an assay."

"The Biocon insulin?"

"You have a one-track mind. That we finished this morning. No, we're setting up a new assay. Takes two hours just to pass it through the column," said Mai.

"There's a new poison you don't have an assay for?"

"There's always new poisons. They call 'em drugs. This one's called Hyporide, and it's a bitch to assay."

We walked into the restaurant and waited for someone to seat us.

"What's the news?" I asked.

"You're so eager," she said. "Don't you want to have a drink first?"

"No."

"The stockholders and board of trustees of Biocon can breathe easy," said Mai. "The insulin is U-100, just as it says on the bottle."

That meant either Karen Sweeney gave the General too much insulin by mistake, or someone else supplemented the dose later on. At least these were the only possibilities I knew of then.

"You don't look happy," said Mai. "You look as disappointed as Chester did."

"Chester?"

"Dr. Chester Smirnopoulous, the guy you talked to on the phone. The Chief of Toxicology, my boss."

"He wanted it to be Biocon's problem?"

"It would've made him famous."

"Everyone in this town wants to be famous."

"Not you."

"You're right. I just want to be a humble country doc."

We had been standing in a little screened-off atrium. A woman holding menus approached us. I told her we were meeting someone and tried to describe Sumner.

It was dark and pretty empty and Sumner was waving enthusiastically from a booth table. He had seen Mai and was very enthusiastic. We sat down with Mai between Sumner and me. Sumner couldn't take his eyes off her. I made the introductions, which wasn't made any easier by Sumner's detailed inspection of all Mai's parts.

"Nguyen?" said Sumner. "I believe I had the pleasure of spending a year in your native land." He was in uniform and only a little high from his Singapore slings. He had two empty glasses in front of him and he was working on a third.

"But I never met a native as lovely as you."

"Who is this guy?" Mai asked.

"He's a steely-eyed killer from Walter Reed."

"He's an idiot if he thought Nam was a pleasure," she told me, looking straight at Sumner.

"Ah, to be in Saigon in September," Sumner said to his drink. "All those exquisite nubile young things in their light cotton dresses."

"Exquisite young things? You mean us pineapples?" said Mai. "Don't you know all we're good for is a case of the clap and a quick blow?"

Sumner sat there with his mouth open, his tongue moving but no words coming out. Things appeared to be getting out of hand so I tried to start over by telling Mai about Sumner's thyroid research and by telling Sumner about Mai's toxicology lab, about which I knew nothing except that they were setting up a new assay. Sumner, at least, had heard of Hyporide.

"It's gonna replace Diabinese someday," he said, sobering up a little. "It's in clinical trials now. They're trying to establish a dose. You come to that Endocrine Society meeting, you'll hear all about it."

"I don't know about all that," said Mai. "But it's tough to assay. If you can't get blood levels worked out you're going to have a hell of a time figuring out a dose."

Sumner looked impressed.

"That's true," he said. He waved to the waiter for another Singapore sling.

We ordered chicken and shrimp and snow peas and mushrooms and pork.

"You eat pork, don't you?" Sumner asked me, with a quick little twinkle to Mai. She didn't smile back.

In my more paranoid moments I would have thought that

was Sumner's attempt at elbowing in on Mai, pointing out that I might be strange and kosher. But maybe he was just being considerate. Mai didn't like him, whichever.

The food wasn't bad, but "Shanghai Palace" was something of a hyperbole. It was a dreary suburban place with local talent on the electric organ. Local talent had run through "The Impossible Dream", "My Way", and "Mack the Knife", when Mai leaned over and whispered to me, "Meet me in the head." She slipped out of our booth with Sumner following every move of her body along the way.

I left Sumner with his third Singapore sling a few minutes later.

I stood around outside the bathrooms and tried the men's room, but it was locked. Mai stuck her head out of the men's room door and said, "Come in."

She locked the door and I saw her paraphernalia spread out on the sink counter: wax paper, white powder. She held a silver spoon to her nose and snorted.

"Great stuff," she said, offering me the spoon.

I shook my head. I had the feeling I was supposed to be impressed.

"You don't know what you're missing," she said.

Well, what did she expect from a guy who hangs out in small-town bars with redneck soldiers and electric organ players? She was wearing a violet knit dress and she pulled it off over her head. That left a green bra and panties. There were burn scars over both her thighs. She caught me looking.

"Napalm," she said. "Turn you off?"

"No."

She was standing there in her high heels and she sent her panties sliding to the floor.

The bathroom door heaved and Sumner's voice came through it. "Open this sucker up."

"Use the women's room," I called out. "You can lock it."

"I'm going to be sick," he said.

"Use the ladies' room."

I heard the door close next door.

Mai was wrapping herself around me, entwining legs, pulling at my belt buckle and zipper.

"Not here," I said.

"I want you here," she said. "Right now."

It wasn't easy, under the circumstances, but she wanted to time things with the coke, and she seemed to like it. Better sex by chemistry. We dressed and walked back out to the table and said good-bye to Sumner, who looked very grey and sweaty.

"Let me give you a lift home," I said.

"No," he waved me off. "I'm okay."

"Leave him alone," said Mai. "He'll wake up and find himself a pineapple to take home."

Mai followed me home in her car. I parked in my driveway and stood by the car looking at the stars. She pulled in behind and got out of her Corvette. I considered how a lab tech might afford a Corvette. She stepped out and walked to me. She had such a nice body, and I kept wondering why I couldn't keep my mind on her.

Maybe it was the burn scars. Not that they bothered me. They seemed to fit. But they started me thinking about Maureen, which was the one thing Mai was supposed to prevent me from doing.

We looked up at all the stars and listened to the night sounds.

"Far out," she said.

Now that was a well-tooled phrase. Maureen would never have tolerated a *far out* from anybody on a night like this.

"I should have dropped Sumner off. He was four sheets to the wind."

"He's a steely-eyed killer. He can manage."

We went inside and I watched Mai snort some more white powder. She made a big production out of it, as if it was supposed to excite and inflame me and convince me that she was one fast and flaming item.

Then she took a shower and wrapped herself in my bathrobe and sat on my lap. It was the same bathrobe Maureen had wrapped herself in. Mai suffered from the comparison. I kept thinking, too, about Maureen wiping burn cream on the kids and became unshakably convinced that she had taken care of Mai.

I asked Mai where it had happened and where she was treated and by whom. But she didn't want to talk about it.

198

# 44

The telephone woke us at ten A.M. Mai rolled away from it and pulled a pillow over her head. It was the ER at Saint George's.

"Dr. Abrams?" said a voice. "We have a comatose lady brought in here a few minutes ago. We understand she's your patient." I tried to clear my mind sufficiently to follow. "Maureen Banting."

"How is she?"

"Better now," said the voice. "Gave her some glucose, Narcan and thiamine, IV bolus. Woke up pretty quick. She may be postictal though."

"She was seizing?"

"Don't know. I mean, she wasn't seizing when they brought her in, but she could have been postictal. Hadn't bitten her tongue or wet her pants or anything, but she was really out."

"You sent off a sugar before you gave her any?"

"It's not back yet."

"Why don't you grab an insulin level, proinsulin level and C-peptide?"

"Too late now. Already gave her the glucose."

I told him to hold her there, that I'd be in to admit her. He said she wasn't going anywhere.

"She pretty out of it?"

"She's waking up. But I don't know how many squash cells went down with her sugar, if hypoglycemia's what did it."

The last remark ricocheted around inside my head as I stumbled trying to find clothes and get dressed. Maureen could knock off a lot of brain with these episodes. The brain lives on oxygen and sugar. Deny it either for more than a matter of minutes and cerebral cells can be most unforgiving.

"Hospital?" asked Mai from under the sheets.

"'Fraid so," I said, watching her crawl towards me like a cat, back arched.

"I want something to remember you by."

At first I thought she meant money, but then I understood what she meant. I didn't have time. Maureen was lying in the ER.

"Duty calls, darling," I said, and started getting dressed.

Mai's face fell, and she crawled back under the sheets.

Maureen looked bright and alert when I arrived, which was a great relief. The sugar was back: nineteen. A hundred's normal. She was lucky to be back among the mentating.

"We were driving on the Beltway and boom, it hit," she said, "like a hammer."

"You do any drinking this morning?"

"I did not. Even ate breakfast, like a good girl."

Timothy Moore slipped through the curtains and stood at the foot of Maureen's stretcher. His hair was neatly parted and his skin looked scrubbed fresh, but he looked a little dissipated about the eyes.

"You've got to come in this time," I told her.

She never took her eyes from mine. "Okay," was all she said.

I went over to the nurses' station, leaving Timothy and Maureen behind the curtains together, and I called admitting and asked for a bed on the metabolic ward.

They put Maureen in a wheelchair and Timothy Moore and I took her up in a lift. Once they had her in bed, Moore started looking uncomfortable and took her hand in both of his and patted it. Then he said good-bye and kissed her on the forehead while I stood there. He shook my hand and asked to be kept informed. I watched him from the doorway of Maureen's room as he walked down the hall and stopped at the nurses' station, asking about visiting hours.

"Well, I've done it this time," said Maureen.

"Meaning?"

"Nineteen. That a good enough number for you?"

"It's your ticket to a three-day fast."

"Benjamin, I want to ask you something that's going to sound crazy. Promise not to pull out the straitjacket."

I was considering that already, but I promised.

"You haven't noticed anybody . . ." she stopped, thinking how to phrase it. "You haven't seen any one person repeatedly, over the past few days?"

"You mean, as if I was being followed?"

"Like that, yes."

"You know me, in my own little cloud. Why?"

"Oh, nothing," she said. "This hypoglycemia's making me paranoid is all."

"You think you're being followed?"

"Did I say that?"

"What are you trying to say?"

"You think I'm neurotic enough already. I'm not giving you any more ammunition."

"It's just Mrs. Que's husband's boys. I told you. They got all out of joint and paranoid after that accident. So they're checking us out." That was my best guess at the moment. I could have gone through other possibilities for her: they could be some Biocon hirelings, out to shadow Dr. Abrams; or they could be parties interested in General Dhieu; or . . . who knew who they were? You live in Washington, D.C., you don't worry about a little observation.

"I don't like it," she said. "But I hope you're right and that's all there is to it."

"Who else could they be?"

"I don't know," said Maureen. "I've just got this spooky feeling."

"What spooky feeling?"

"That someone's after me. That all this hypoglycemia's not an accident or an act of God. It's just that I'm so normal most of the time, how could I have an insulinoma?"

"You think Mrs. Que's boys are giving you your hypoglycemia? What're they doing, sneaking in your window at night and sticking you with insulin?"

"I told you you'd call me crazy."

"Let's just worry about the insulinoma. When we exhaust the natural causes we'll start thinking about other things."

"Okay."

She smiled up at me and squeezed my hand. I looked at her

and somehow she looked different. For one moment, she looked unattractively like so many other crazy people I'd seen on various psych wards – impenetrable, stubborn and unruly. Then I thought about how I'd felt noticing that one-eared follower every time I turned around. That kind of thing can unnerve you. And I started focusing on her face with her eyes shining.

I turned to go out to the work station where the nurses sit and where the phones were and I heard Maureen say, "Would you be a prince and call Helen? I've got to have my robe and my scuffies."

"Why," I asked, "do you live with Helen?"

"What kind of question is that?" Her face was suddenly angry.

"You don't like her. She likes you, that's evident. But I can't see your side."

"What's that supposed to mean? She likes me."

I knew she knew what I meant, but I decided to stay on the track. "You have ugly scenes. You don't seem to enjoy each other, or to have much in common. It doesn't add up."

"We have known each other since grade school," she said, squeezing off each word like a shot. She was much more over-wrought than I had expected. Her eyebrows clenched together and her mouth grew hard and white and she looked past me.

"We have our differences, but we've known each other a very long time."

"You're not buddies now," I said. "Anyone can see that."

"You see a lot more than most people," said Maureen hotly. "You've known us for what? Two weeks?"

She was bright red, swinging her legs over the stretcher, ready to spring off it.

"Calm down," I said. "I'll call her."

I walked out to the station and dialled. Maybe I saw a lot more than most people and maybe I didn't see anything. I could see that TGIF party right before my eyes and I could see Helen sitting shoulder to shoulder with Maureen, with Tim Moore on the other side. Maureen and all that adoration.

Helen answered on the first ring.

"Maureen's had another episode," I told her. "I've

admitted her to Saint George's. She'd like you to bring her robe and her scuffies."

"Is she all right?"

"She's fine. We've just got to get to the bottom of this."

"What happened?"

"She lost consciousness," I said. "Her blood sugar was nineteen."

"Dear Mother in Heaven."

I gave her Maureen's bedside phone number.

"I'll come right in. I'll special her today."

"Fine."

"Where was she, when it happened?"

"Don't you know?"

"No. I went out early this morning, before she left the house. I went to church."

"She was driving on the Beltway," I said. Then for some reason I felt like saying it so I added, "With Timothy Moore."

"Oh," said Helen. I couldn't tell anything from the way she said it. But something bothered me about what she had told me. There was too much explanation about why she didn't know where Maureen had gone. She didn't have to say she had gone to church. We hung up and I went back to Maureen.

"Spoke with Helen."

"Good."

"She'll come."

"Great."

I turned to go, then turned back.

"Did you eat breakfast alone this morning?"

"No," she said. "With Helen. Why?"

"She didn't seem to know where you had gone, or with whom."

"Pumping Helen for information now?" said Maureen.

She was too angry to talk to, so I went back out to the nurses' station and wrote her admitting orders and my admitting note.

The admitting intern came by as I was finishing. He was glad to be getting Maureen because she was young and female.

"Got fifteen octogenarians on my service right now," he said. "All men. Be nice to make rounds on her in the morning, even if she does turn out to be a psycho."

"You'll like her."

"If you're getting C-peptides, why not get a check on her urine for oral hypoglycemics? If she's getting worked up for self-abuse, might as well cover the ground."

I don't know how red I turned, but I could feel how hot my face got. I'd forgotten that angle. She wouldn't have to inject insulin necessarily – she could be popping Diabinese, Orinase or whatever oral hypoglycemic she could get her hands on. There was some argument in the medical literature about whether or not the pills could make a normal person's blood sugar drop severely, but most textbooks list it as a cause to be looked for in suspected self-abuse.

I told the intern to go ahead and send the blood and urine for hypoglycemic drugs.

The laboratory part of Maureen's workup was nothing too fancy. It was designed to take advantage of the differences between the way the normal pancreas works and the way the sugar-lowering agents work. When the insulin is coming from a normal pancreas, there's an appropriate amount of it, and there's the wrapper it comes with, C-peptide. And when the bottom drops out of the sugar because someone's taken drugs, you can detect the drugs in the urine. If you remember to look for drugs in the urine.

I thought about my work on General Dhieu and realized I hadn't checked his blood for oral hypoglycemics. He had had a drug screen, but I wasn't sure sulfonylureas would show up in a standard screen. In fact, I doubted they would. But all that seemed, as Dr. von Dernhoffer would say, an unpromising avenue of investigation.

I started to go back to tell Maureen good-bye, but somehow it didn't feel right. Maybe I was just embarrassed at not having thought of the angle the intern had come up with. When that sort of thing happens you begin to worry about losing your good stuff. Not yet forty and already the interns are making me feel like a turkey.

I walked down to the lobby and out to the parking lot, ready to implode, thinking about the intern, and thinking about how I hadn't been such a great doctor where Maureen was concerned. I'd been other things to her, but not your average

204

anal-compulsive physician. I looked at the leaves across Reservoir Road, more and more turning fall colours, but felt no rush of pleasure that morning.

I thought about Maureen and about Helen and about Timothy Moore and I arrived at my car and got under way.

I stopped to put my magnetized plastic card in the gate machine and watched the wooden plank rise up and drove out of the lot, watching the plank come down in my rearview mirror. It was then that I saw a certain one-eared ex-fisherman starting up his car in a row of cars behind me.

I kept checking the mirror along Canal Road and continued glancing up along the Parkway to Cabin John. He was with me all the way.


# 45


I pulled into my driveway and sat there thinking. My one-eared friend had turned off about a block before my street. Funny how your mind connects things – little un-pleasantnesses. Things kept popping up and coalescing: it was bad to think I'd missed ordering the urine for oral hypoglycemics, and it was disconcerting to see Maureen turn snappish and hostile over a little probing about Helen. And now this other unpleasantness – someone following me. What really connected those things was their unpleasantness and the fact I didn't like thinking too long about any one of them.

And I didn't like seeing Maureen come unhinged. She felt threatened by somebody. It wasn't just the Asian shadows, either. When you started thinking in terms of foul play and ill intent, the possibilities multiplied exponentially. Who was this Timothy Moore character who always seemed to be with her when she dropped to the floor with a blood sugar falling faster than a barometer in a typhoon?

I had to stop thinking like that. For one thing, I hadn't been taught how to think like that. For another, you had to investigate the most likely thing first, which in this case had to be insulinoma. But insulinomas are not common tumours. Statistically speaking, there were undoubtedly more homicidal psychotics than insulinomas in Washington.

And there was that most unpleasant thing of all – the blood sugar of nineteen – which no self-respecting and unmolested metabolism would ever allow. When you got right down to it, I knew a lot less about Maureen and what ailed her than I thought I knew.

But I knew how I felt about that round head with the shiny hair and I knew how she looked in the ER all pale with her hair wet and pasted on her cheek. And I knew how I'd feel if anything happened to her.

And then there were her friends. The rejected, increasingly impotent suitor, Timothy Moore, who had his own supply of Diabinese and no doubt had the opportunity to crush up a few and mix it in Maureen's beer or coffee or whatever she was drinking when he was with her. She was teasing him with me, when she felt like it, and he couldn't be feeling too happy about himself lately, and taunts wouldn't help that. And, as I said, when you started considering ill intent, anything's possible. The urine for hypoglycemic drugs was becoming more and more pertinent. Mix Helen into the equation and things really got interesting. Helen, my main booster. Helen might smile oh so sweetly, but she wrings the necks of pigeons.

I guess I'd feel a little uneasy too, if I were Maureen, with friends like those.

# 46

Helen was there Sunday morning at nine, when I arrived to see Maureen. She was arranging a big pitcher of daisies.

"Aren't they beautiful?" said Maureen.

"Lovely," I said, watching Helen who was smiling, cooing and drawing up the blinds so they wouldn't touch the flowers on the windowsill.

"How are you?"

"No more problems," said Maureen. "I'm all cured."

I looked at her for some sign of irony.

"Oh, don't look like that. I'm not leaving the hospital. I'll go through with your sadistic little workup."

"There's a lab sheet with your name on it that shows a blood sugar of nineteen," I said. "I'm going to paste a copy to your wall. Any time you feel like bolting, you look at that."

"She won't bolt," said Helen. "We're getting to the bottom of this."

"I'll go through with it," said Maureen.

"And you'd better swear off the booze for a while," I said. "It just makes everything more difficult to interpret."

"After yesterday, no problem. I felt like one of those reformed alcoholics taking that stuff that makes you puke when you drink. Makes you turn colours and puke. That's what happened to me."

"I thought you hadn't touched a drop, yesterday."

"Did I say that? I might've had a small one."

"Maureen, you've got to keep me part of the team here."

"I'm sorry," she said. "I really am."

I marched out, for good effect. I wanted her to know I was angry. Holding out on me. Who knows what else she wasn't saying?

Helen waddled out into the hall to find me.

"She's sorry," said Helen. "But she always drinks when Timothy comes over. They just bring it out in each other."

"He seems to like her."

"Timothy's in love with her."

"Where's Maureen stand?"

"She waffles. She knew Timothy in Nam. That's where it all started. It went downhill from there."

I could imagine nothing on the face of the earth which could go downhill from Vietnam, but I didn't say that. I said, "Has Maureen had problems with drinking before?"

"She never drinks much, unless she's with Timothy. They sit up until all hours drinking and lately Timothy's been drinking a little more. I guess Maureen's been trying to keep up."

She didn't look as if she were finished, and I waited for her to say more. Finally she added, "I don't think Timothy's been very happy lately. I think he senses Maureen may have someone new in her life."

She looked at me to see if I caught that last comment. I had caught it.

I watched her to see if she was going to say anything more, but she just looked uncomfortable and shuffled her feet and walked back into Maureen's room.

I walked down to the car park. I wasn't sure what Helen was trying to say, but ill intent was getting all kinds of notice lately. Helen had pushed my nose in the direction of taunted, haunted, long-suffering Timothy Moore, although I wasn't sure she meant to. But if a list of suspects had to be made, Helen, as they say in the movies, had had all the opportunity. Maureen had mentioned Helen's making the orange juice she thought made her sick the first time. Of course, there was the question of motive. That took all of five seconds. The big question was what kept Helen from sitting on Maureen and squashing her long ago. Helen the fat. Helen the angry. Helen the patriot. Helen the pigeon killer.

It was all very exciting, considering the possibilities: jilted lovers, jealous roommates, shadowy followers, a patient who was possibly a big-time crazy. But as they tell you in medical school – common things occur commonly. Start looking for the bizarre and unnatural and you miss the mundane real disease.

On the other hand, as with General Dhieu, you had to keep an open mind. And Maureen could really hurt the ones she loved.

47

It felt good to be home and to be alone, except for missing Maureen.

I had the rest of Sunday to myself, barring emergency calls.

I walked into the bathroom and washed the mirror. Mai had been gone when I returned from seeing Maureen at the hospital Saturday, but she had left her mark: *You're one Great Lay,* in pink lipstick on the bathroom mirror. She'd probably seen that lipstick trick in some movie.

I was getting too old for all that. At my age there is no such thing as a great lay: there are only those occasional exceptional women. Having someone like Maureen in the picture made all the other exercises seem like calisthenics.

None of it happened on a very rational level – I just knew I did not want Maureen to leave and I was delighted to come home and find Mai gone. I'm not saying a little frolic can't be enjoyable, and when Mrs. Que called that morning, the juices flowed – but it wasn't the same kind of anticipation that began whenever I knew I was going to see Maureen.

Mrs. Que could quicken my pulse. But then it was over and gone. Like being in heat. She just radiated a scent, but it was gone when she left. And for Mai Nguyen, I was just one of the accoutrements, like her spoons and coke. But Maureen was more and more with me. Time not with her was just interlude. I could clean up the house, go to the office, answer phone calls, see patients, do paperwork. It just killed time now. I wanted to be with Maureen. But I resisted that feeling. I knew I had to, for everyone's sake.

Sumner called to find out what had happened Friday night.

"You were there, as I recall," I said.

"No, I mean with the pineapple, afterwards."

"She went home. I went home."

"What was going on in that bathroom?"

"She was showing me she knew how to snort."

"No shit!"

"You liked her?" I asked.

"Yeah, but she dumped all over me."

"She does that when she's turned on."

"By me, you mean?"

"Sure."

"You're pulling my chain."

"You're right. I am pulling your chain. She did not like you – you were dressed all wrong."

"She's got bad memories of the boys in olive green, huh?"

"I think she sees you as the rough equivalent of a storm trooper."

"You said she works at NIH?"

"The toxicology lab."

"Of course! I should've known. I'd heard Smirnopoulous had a real piece of work working for him in that lab. Maybe I'll go over there sometime."

"Bring a little coke to warm her up."

"Yeah, I might do that."

"And wear some real clothes."

"Yeah, blue jeans and love beads."

"You've got it."

Sumner thanked me for the advice and hung up. Then Mrs. Que called.

"Hello, my Kind Samaritan," she said.

I said hello.

"I have my picnic basket all packed," she said. "Are you free for a picnic?"

"Are we having company for this?"

"I certainly hope not."

"Your husband has arranged a chaperon for me and for Miss Banting. You never can tell when they'll pop up."

"I will make sure we are not chaperoned."

"Maybe you can call the dogs off permanently. It's starting to unnerve Miss Banting. And all she did was make me stop the car to come to your rescue."

"And now she is in the hospital, herself."

"Oh, your boys told you that?"

"I have a sixth sense."

"And it's got one ear and drives a blue Toyota and doesn't mind much if he's seen by the folks he's shadowing."

"Is Miss Banting going to be all right?"

"She's going to be just fine," I said. "But I'm surprised your sixth sense hasn't read the hospital chart and told you that already."

"You are angry with me."

"Good Samaritans don't expect to be paid, or haunted."

"I will see to it you are not haunted."

"And Miss Banting."

"Yes, of course," she said. "Now, what about our picnic?"

I said I'd meet her and she told me to drive out to Swain's Boathouse on the Potomac, near Great Falls.

It was a bright clear-sky day, cool and dry, and every leaf in every tree was moving. A steady wind made the water ripple and it was a nice time to be in Washington.

"Gorgeous weather," said Mrs. Que.

She wasn't bad herself, with her long hair blowing and her Lacoste shirt and white shorts.

We rented a rowboat and I rowed.

"A canoe would have been more romantic," said Mrs. Que.

"Not with this wind," I said. "Nothing too romantic about winding up the river."

"You are like all doctors, too practical."

We rowed straight out from shore and I watched for one-eared fishermen, boaters and other prying eyes, but saw nobody suspicious. Mrs. Que watched the wind on the water and I watched the sun play off her lovely high cheekbones and I watched her move her legs around. The muscles of her inner thighs were well developed.

"You are looking at my legs and making me feel like a young girl," she said.

"You have very pretty legs," I said. "The horse riding keeps them in shape."

"It develops you in here," she said, rubbing her inner thighs. "Which, of course, has other advantages beyond horse riding."

She smiled when she said that.

We rowed past an island and Mrs. Que pointed out another one about fifty yards off and we reached that easily, with the wind behind us and the current with us. She took off her Topsiders and hopped into the shallow water near the shore and pulled the bow of the boat onto the sandy riverbank.

"Watch yourself, pulling boats," I said. "You just got out of the hospital."

"I am quite recovered," she said, "and ready for my recreation."

We had lunch first, cheese and Finnish dry bread and wine,

211

and she took my hand and led me through the trees to get away from shore and found a secluded spot without too many sticks and bugs and took off her shorts and we recreated. I thought about getting poison ivy the whole time, romantic that I am. But it grows all over Washington and even in September you can get it. She had lovely skin and her scar was well healed and she certainly showed no ill effects of her surgery.

She was lying with her head on my arm afterwards, and I said, "I hope your husband's snoopers don't carry binoculars."

"You will not be followed again."

"How did your husband find out about us? About Maureen and me being in Vietnam, and what happened?"

"My husband is a businessman. He has many friends."

"I've got lots of friends. But I can't get information like that."

"You have to have them in the right places."

"And what did you find out about us, for all the trouble?"

"Nothing more than what I've told you."

"But you didn't tell me much."

"What didn't I tell you?"

"Why did Maureen Banting get thrown in the slammer?"

"I told you, hitting another officer."

"But what happened?"

"Why don't you ask her?"

"I doubt she'd tell me. Or she'd tell me what she wanted me to know."

"She had a brawl with a nurse captain. She beat the nurse and they had to hospitalize her. That's all I know."

"But why?"

"I suppose the injuries required hospitalization."

"But why did they fight?"

"Did you bring me out here to ask me about your Miss Banting?"

"I didn't bring you out here. We came together."

"Well, you can take me back."

She was definitely not pleased. We didn't say much until we were dressed and in the boat. Then she said, "Miss Banting accused the other nurse of mistreating patients. There was an investigation later and some nurses were questioned. That is all I know."

"She punched a nurse over that?" I asked, more to myself than to Mrs. Que.

"Is that so surprising?" said Mrs. Que. "Do nurses not get upset about what happens to their patients?"

I thought of Karen Sweeney as soon as she said that, and I almost convinced myself Mrs. Que had Karen in mind. "Did you mean the nurse in charge of General Dhieu?" I asked.

"I was not thinking of that case specifically," she smiled. "But, as an example, was his nurse not alarmed by his death?"

"Everyone was concerned," I said. "It was so unexpected."

"And unexplained," smiled Mrs. Que.

"Oh, there's no lack of explanations. Everyone has one: the Chairman of Medicine, the Director of Nursing. Even the General's widow."

"You must discount her," laughed Mrs. Que. "She can't be objective."

"I don't discount anything, or anyone," I said. "Not even the widow. Perhaps she doth protest too much."

"That's Shakespeare, isn't it?"

"Yes," I said. "Did you know Mrs. Dhieu?"

"The General's wife?"

"Yes. Your husband knew Dhieu. I thought you might have met her."

"I have made her acquaintance."

"What's she like?"

"Like most generals' wives: ambitious, and not to be trusted."

"Then you don't think she's right about what happened to the General."

"She may be. The General had many enemies," she said, looking at a cardinal flitting around a few yards off. "What do you really think happened?"

"Haven't decided. Maybe the widow's right. Or maybe the General just died suddenly of old age."

"That may be hard to sell," she laughed.

"Tell me one more thing," I said. "What was the name of the nurse Miss Banting slugged?"

That was not a well-timed question. Mrs. Que's face hardened and she said without amusement, "You are a most exasperating man." She stood up. "Perhaps we should have invited Miss Banting for this picnic."

We rowed back to the boathouse and I don't think Mrs. Que said more than six words the whole way.

"It was a lovely afternoon," I said, when we were walking back to the car park.

She looked at me and smiled and kissed me on the cheek.

"You are a lovely man," she said. "But your mind is elsewhere."


# 48


You had to give Mrs. Que credit – she was perceptive, and she was correct. My mind was elsewhere.

I had begun to believe my own press about being the great hypoglycemic maven. By local standards that might have been true, but there were things I didn't know or hadn't thought of – Maureen's intern had reminded me of that with the oral hypoglycemic suggestion. One thing they teach you in medical school: there are humble docs and there are stupid docs, just those two kinds. There were authorities in the world, and it was time to consult them.

I was back at Saint George's, in the medical school library, at six o'clock. I was sitting in front of a computer terminal. It was a pretty wonderful computer, and its terminal had a happy green glowing face. I punched in *Hypoglycemia* and got fifty-five references. That was too many, so I punched in *insulin* as a cross reference, which narrowed the list to seventeen. I had the printer rattle those off. Then I decided to get really cute and punched in two other words: *quinine, malaria*. I punched the buttons for all the articles that discussed those index words together.

That's when it happened. I sat there stuck to the glowing screen, squeezing the arms of my chair so hard it left grooves in the vinyl. There was a title on the screen. It had my mouth dry and my heart going full gallop: SEVERE HYPOGLYCEMIA AND HYPERINSULINEMIA IN *Falciparum* MALARIA. It was in the *New England Journal of Medicine*.

I ran upstairs to the shelves where they kept the bound volumes of the *New England Journal* and ripped the volume I wanted off the shelf.

It was a nice little study. Seventeen patients with acute malaria had been found to have blood sugar levels as low as nine, averaging around twenty-three, lower even than General Dhieu's level of thirty-two. Their insulin levels were as high as the General's and most were on quinine. The researchers had then given quinine to normal volunteers, and the insulin levels in the normals jumped up, but none of the normals got hypoglycemic. The combination of malaria, quinine and acute illness seemed to be what did it.

I read and reread that article and then went downstairs and photocopied it, and read it again. It had been published a year earlier. I was two years behind in my *New England Journal of Medicine* reading. Always up to the minute with my *Sports Illustrated,* but two years behind on the *New England Journal.* That issue was buried under a pile of unread journals in a dark corner of my office. I excoriated myself for a few long minutes about not keeping up, and about having all the wrong priorities and about my dissolute attitude about life in general. Then I consoled myself with the thought that even if I had been up-to-date, I probably would have skipped an article about anything as arcane as malaria. Or if I'd read it, I would have forgotten the whole thing immediately.

But here, through the marvels of computer technology, was a paper by some group in a university hospital in Thailand, describing a group of patients who fitted the General's profile to an eyelash. It was a slick little paper. Timely, too.

Maureen was right, generals never die a natural death. The General undid himself with his own quinine, unwittingly.

Then again, maybe it was all too timely, too slick. Life is never that tidy. Why should the General decide to come to

Saint George's and die a year after this article appeared? General Dhieu had enemies. His wife said that. And the paper came from Thailand. I couldn't call the authors on the phone and ask them a few choice questions. Who knows who these Thai authors are, or who they were working for? When you start thinking like that, it never ends.

The General had malaria and no spleen and he took quinine by the boxload and he died from the combination. Fortunately for me, he waited to do it until someone had described his problem in the medical literature so I could figure out what had happened.

I couldn't prove the General didn't get the wrong dose of insulin. I couldn't even prove his wife hadn't tiptoed into his room with a loaded syringe. But there's an old clinical saw: When a diagnosis is staring you right in the face, don't spit in its eye – it may spit back.

I felt good for Karen Sweeney. They couldn't point the finger at her. The finger pointing in my report was going to be in the direction of quinine and malaria.

The computer was no help with Maureen. I sat there staring at its glowing green face trying to think of what to punch in. I just didn't have enough answers on her yet, to punch in anything.

It felt nice to have one case wrapped up, however. It felt nice, but vaguely unsettling. Somehow I had connected the General's case to Maureen in an irrational, associative way. She had appeared just after the General's case had heated up, and she had basically the same problem, hypoglycemia. They were connected in my mind, if only temporally. Working on both problems alternately, I had, without thinking about it, expected not to solve one without the other. But now I could put the General to bed, so to speak. I could write my report, forget about him and concentrate on Maureen.

# 49

Monday morning, I pulled into the car park at Saint George's thinking about how I had not been covering bases. Anyone looking at the way I'd been operating would wonder whether I could throw from home plate to second base on two bounces.

First, there was the little matter of checking the medical literature on General Dhieu's case. That was something you're supposed to keep up with in the first place, and it was something you're supposed to check early on no matter how up-to-date you are on your reading. I could have saved a lot of people a lot of trouble if I'd gone to the computer initially.

Then there was the problem of checking Maureen's urine for hypoglycemia drugs. If the test were positive and Maureen's urine had, say, Diabinese, I'd know how her blood sugar had happened to fall to nineteen. Give a girl a little too much Diabinese and her pancreas might be persuaded to pump out enough insulin to drop her blood sugar to nineteen.

A positive urine would narrow the question from how to who: Tim Moore, who had his own supply of Diabinese; Helen, who as a nurse could easily get some; or Maureen herself, who was resourceful enough to come up with an easy drug like Diabinese or another sulfonylurea. Knowing what to make of a positive urine was the easy part.

But if there were no drug in Maureen's urine, I'd be back to square one, and I had a prickly feeling I was going to have to explain Maureen's blood sugar of nineteen without the help of a urine specimen full of drug. A clean urine would mean that either Maureen's hypoglycemia was not drug-induced, or the urine tested was not Maureen's.

That's what I meant about not covering all the bases. Just

suppose Helen had spiked Maureen's orange juice: she wouldn't be eager for Maureen's urine to reach the lab, and she could easily prevent it. Anyone who worked in the hospital could read Maureen's chart, see that we were looking for drug in her urine, intercept Maureen's specimen and replace it with one of her own, and Maureen's urine report would come back cleaner than your average whistle.

And I had been the bright boy to call Helen in to babysit Maureen after she was admitted. I'd delivered the sheep right into the wolf's hands. Good work, Abrams.

I raced down to the laboratory and stood before the clerk at the receiving desk, trying to catch my breath. She looked me over briefly, decided I wasn't worth watching, and went back to the sports page.

"Did you get a urine for drug screening on a Maureen Banting, Saturday?"

"I wasn't on duty Saturday," said the clerk, without raising her head. The Orioles had taken a doubleheader from the Yankees, and I was distracting her.

"I'm going to ask you nicely," I said. "One more time."

She looked up and shook her head. "What was the name?"

I only had to tell her three times and spell it before she managed to punch the name into the computer correctly. They had received two urines on Maureen: one at eleven-ten A.M. and one at one-forty-five P.M. The computer didn't know whether or not they were running both specimens. That took a lab supervisor, who was more eager to please than the clerk, and who assured me they'd run both urines and report them out separately.

I left the lab wondering why they'd received two specimens two hours apart, and didn't have to wait too long for the answer.

Maureen's intern was standing by the lift outside the lab entrance with two medical students.

"How is she?" I asked.

"Hungry, I would think," he said. "She started her fast last night."

I asked him about the two urines and how the samples were transported to the lab.

"I brought one of them down," said one of the medical students. She was a little redhead who looked about twelve years old. "LeRoy was worried the nurses would screw up the collection or escort would lose it. So I took it down there myself."

LeRoy was the intern.

"About what time?"

"Eleven, eleven-thirty maybe."

"In the morning?"

"Yes. I handed it to the receiving clerk myself."

"Good job," I told her. "You're a good man, LeRoy."

I stepped off the lift feeling very much better than I had in the car park. I blessed the intern silently and said thanks for medical students and stopped grating my teeth for a while. If both urines were negative for drugs, I could commit that angle to the rubbish heap of outlandish ideas. If both urine specimens were positive, then I'd have to ask Timothy Moore some questions about how he used Diabinese. If Moore satisfied my curiosity, I'd have some questions for Maureen. But if the urine the medical student carried down was positive and the urine the nurses sent was negative, Helen would have to be hung up by her thumbs until she talked.

I stopped at the nursing station to pluck Maureen's chart from the rack. Things were beginning to roll. In my jacket pocket was my report on General Dhieu, all typed and signed and pretty coherent. And plausible, too, if not exactly compelling. At least most of the sentences had subjects and verbs. It even had a reference to a certain article in the *New England Journal of Medicine*, which is to say, it was authoritative. Now I had the chart for Maureen Banting in my hand and she was getting the workup for insulinoma, a screen for drugs and foul play. The world was under control.

# 50

Maureen was reading the *New York Times* when I walked in.

"Hungry?" I asked.

"Not yet," she said. "Just feeling a little confined."

"Well, you can roam around the ward," I said.

"But not off the ward. The intern wrote that order."

"He doesn't want you passing out with a blood sugar of nineteen in some stairwell."

"I know," said Maureen. "But it's not the intern that's worried. You want to keep a close eye on me."

"What's that supposed to mean?" I asked, knowing full well what it meant.

Maureen said, "I saw the lab slip for the C-peptide when the tech drew the bloods this morning. I've read enough about hypoglycemia to know what you're looking for with that."

"Maureen," I said, "I could tell you the intern ordered that test. But that would be a lie." She looked a little less hostile now. "I've got to cover all the possibilities."

"You think I'm injecting myself with insulin?"

"No."

"Then why the C-peptide?"

"I've got to do all the tests, or I wouldn't be your doctor. I'd be your friend, but you need a doctor now."

"I know," she said, but it wasn't going to be the same between us.

"You tell everyone about your crazy patient who self-injects insulin?"

"I don't tell anyone. But the orders – anyone taking care of you can read those."

"I don't think Helen knows. If she did, she'd be even less a fan of yours than she is now."

220

"I thought she was a big fan of mine."

"Not lately. What'd you say to her Sunday?"

"Nothing much."

"Right now I'm more concerned about what you think of me. What kind of crazy you think I am. Injecting myself with insulin."

"I don't think you're crazy."

"Why would anyone inject herself with insulin and make herself sick unless she was truly crazy?"

I stood there trying to think of something clever and light to say. I'd given considerable thought to what to say if Maureen brought this up, and decided to be clever and light, but I hadn't yet worked out the details.

"Craziness is not my line," I said finally. "I work with numbers and lab tests."

"You're too humble," said Maureen, looking out the window. Then she turned to me and caught me in a grey-eyed vice. "The tests you ordered were a trap. You think I'm faking it."

"No."

"What else can you say? You'll deny everything." Then her voice changed from accusation to inquiry. "What I really don't understand – I mean, would you tell me just this, honestly, for once? Why'd you bother with the whole seduction routine – the dinners, the walks in the park – if you thought I was such a flaming psycho? Were you *that* curious? Or is there some kind of prize for medical detective of the year?"

"I don't have a seduction routine," I said. That was a stall and I knew she knew it. When you can't answer the question, sometimes you can get away with changing the subject.

"What do you really think's happening with me?" she said. "From most to least likely?"

"If I had to bet, which I don't, I'd bet insulinoma first, alcohol to place and foul play to show."

"Foul play?"

"You didn't get a sugar of nineteen from nothing and nowhere. If the insulinoma workup is negative, I'll need an explanation."

"Like what?"

"Like maybe somebody slipped you something."

I wasn't sure at the time, but I know now, a smile crossed her face, just momentarily.

"How would they do that?"

"First we have to figure out how the sugar got that low. I sent off a urine for hypoglycemic drugs. If the urine comes back positive, we'll ask some more questions. If that's negative, we'll push hard on the insulinoma."

"When's the urine coming back?"

"Few days, at least."

"By then I'll be through with the fast."

"That's right. We'll rule out the insulinoma with the fast. Some things will be cooking in the lab in the meantime."

Maureen was happy now. She was doing a good job of covering, but I could see the light in her eyes even her tight mouth couldn't distract.

"Maybe they knew what they were doing after all," she said. "Giving you that dead General's case. You're a wily rascal – you might just figure out what happened."

"You got yourself a maven when you got me," I told her. "That's what you wanted, wasn't it?"

"What's that crack supposed to mean?" she said suddenly, all the amusement gone, even from her eyes.

"Just what I said. I'm the local authority on hypoglycemia and you've got hypoglycemia."

"Oh," she said, smiling faintly. "Well, at least you cover the bases. You don't miss much."

That should have made me feel better, but somehow it didn't. I had the feeling she liked the idea I trusted no one, not even her, and held everyone under suspicion. That pleased her for some reason. Not knowing why bothered me.

## 51

His secretary was sure Dr. von Dernhoffer would want to see me when I dropped my report on her polished oak desk.

"If you will just have a seat," she said, reaching for her

"She's wonderful," I said. When I'm nervous, I talk too much and say the wrong thing. I'd been doing that less often since I hit my mellow stride, but I slipped back into it now. "She's had her husband do some research on you and me. Apparently they get suspicious when their people get picked up by strangers on the street."

"Oh?" said Maureen. She didn't sound too interested. "Is there more beer?" she asked Helen. Helen extracted herself from her chair with some difficulty and hustled off into the house. She reappeared with a bottle for Maureen, and one for herself.

"Mrs. Que's husband's research indicates you're a war hero," I told Maureen.

"No foolin'?" said Maureen.

Timothy Moore's eyes drifted over, then he looked back out at the street, smiling.

"She tells me you got a Bronze Star."

"Oh, that," said Maureen, not seeming at all surprised that Mrs. Que's husband could discover that. "They were handing them out that day. You know how they were with medals. I wanted a Purple Heart to go with my green uniform. All they had was Bronze Stars that day."

"Maureen," gasped Helen. "That's not true." Then to me, "She carried about half a dozen patients out of a burning ward after a rocket attack."

"They were just gooks, Helen," said Maureen, looking over to me with meaning. Then she looked back to Helen.

Helen's forehead popped out with beads of sweat.

"Well, I suppose it was better fighting them in Nam than fighting them on the beaches of California, wasn't it, Helen?" said Maureen, looking at me.

Helen's face was now bright pink.

"Viet Cong oughta be showing up in the landing craft at Malibu any day now," continued Maureen. "If they don't have their hands full with the Chinese and Cambodians."

Then Maureen turned to me. "It's all world communism, don't you know? Forces of darkness. Viet Cong are who's down in Central America now. You can't tell 'em from the locals. All those dark-haired commies and they don't none of 'em speak English." Then to Helen, "They're organizing an American expeditionary force to Latin America right now. Let's join up, all of us. Get 'em before they get to the shores of Texas."

"They wouldn't take you, Maureen," said Helen with all the cheer and bounce gone now. She had real venom in that voice. She struggled to lift herself out of her rocker and started collecting beer bottles from the chairs and tables around the porch. "This place's a pig sty," she said.

She rattled around, scooping up things into a trash basket, all indignant and disgruntled by the un-Americanism rampant on the porch.

Maureen said, "You can have my Bronze Star, Helen, if it means so much to you. Wear it on your nurse's uniform. People'll think you were Phi Beta Kappa or something."

Helen stopped scooping and stood there with her mouth agape.

"Leave her alone," Timothy Moore told Maureen. "She's proud of you."

"You two ought to get married," said Maureen. "You're so in love with each other."

Helen moved quickly through the door and into the house.

"Why'd you do that?" said Moore.

"She's such a cheerleader sometimes," said Maureen. "I get sick of it."

"She's proud of you. That such a crime?"

"Helen thinks Lieutenant Calley was a war hero. That's her idea of heroism."

I stood up and asked directions to the bathroom and got pointed down the long hallway to the rear of the house.

Helen was lumbering ahead of me, carrying a black plastic rubbish bag. She went out the door at the end of the hall and I went into the bathroom.

I could see her from the bathroom window. She was moving towards the rubbish bins at the end of the alley. Several pigeons waddled between her and the rubbish bins and I was surprised to see how fast she moved, kicking one savagely in the ribs.

If I was surprised, the pigeon was astonished. He flapped

192

telephone console and moving to press the intercom button. I caught her hand.

"Let him read it first," I said.

I was sinking into the inch-and-a-half-deep maroon carpet into which her desk was planted, and I began to move towards the door. Dr. von Dernhoffer's office had a lovely waiting room, but I had to get to my office.

"He'll see you now . . ." I heard the secretary say as I slipped through the door to the hall.

A stocky Oriental man with a flattened nose and wearing an Irish tweed hat was waiting at the lift. I'd begun to notice Oriental men lately. I took the stairwell exit to the car park. Using my plastic parking card, I negotiated both wooden barriers and escaped the car park and took Thirty-eighth Street and a series of turns through Glover Park to Tunlaw Road. It was a tortuous way to get to my office, but it would be hard to follow me without my knowing it, unless you knew where I was headed.

They knew. A dark green Saab picked me up by the Russian compound, staying two cars behind me all the way down New Mexico Avenue to my office.

Mrs. Bromley looked up and followed me back to my sanctuary in the back of our suite carrying a fistful of telephone messages.

"The Chairman, Dr. von Dernhoffer, called. Can't get used to his secretary's accent. What *is* that language she speaks?"

"Alabaman," I said. "Can you get Mrs. Que on the phone?"

"Is she still lurking about?"

I looked up and caught her eye, "What do you mean, lurking?"

"Figure of speech," said Mrs. Bromley, startled by my tone. She retreated to her desk in the waiting room and buzzed back with Mrs. Que on the line.

"My sweet Samaritan," she said. "How nice of you to call. Is this business or sensual?"

"I thought you were calling off your husband's blood-hounds."

"Bloody hounds?"

223

"Don't go simple on me, your English is better than mine. I'm still being followed."

"I have talked to my husband," she said. "I think I can believe him on this subject. He says he has no one-eared men in blue Toyotas."

I did not want to believe that. She sounded genuine enough, and she had picked up my reference to one-ear and asked her husband. So I believed she believed it. But there was no reason for me to believe her husband. And there was good reason for me to want not to believe what she said – if one-ear wasn't sent by Mrs. Que, I'd have to figure out who did send him.

"It's unpleasant, being followed everywhere."

"I am sure. But my husband denies he has sent anyone."

"What do I have to do, tackle one and haul him in to the local police?"

"If you think it would help, perhaps you should."

I didn't like her being so agreeable.

"Your husband's been snooping around about me. He's got my military records, somehow. He got Maureen's. He's been worried, though for the life of me I can't see why, unless it's because of General Dhieu."

I paused to see if she'd bite at that, but she said, "My husband worries about everything."

"But he was a friend of General Dhieu's and he found out pretty quick I was investigating what happened to the General."

"And why should that worry him?"

It was the very question that had stumped me. I took a wild swing. "Maybe he knows something about what happened to the General, and when I was so rudely introduced into his life, he thought he'd been set up. He thought he was being drawn into the investigation."

"This sounds reasonable. Is that what happened?"

"I had no idea who you were when I stopped at that accident."

"Then it is all a coincidence."

"Or maybe you followed *me* into Mr. Smith's because your husband knew I was on the case, and that van was something you hadn't planned on."

"Maybe."

"I'll give you a chance to make it up to me."

"I am making up to you?"

"Your husband's so good at digging up old army records: see what he can do on a Helen Sligo, Medical Corps, sometime about nineteen seventy-four."

"I'm sure he would claim to not know how to begin. And I would have to reveal I told you what he found on you."

"Oh, I bet it won't be too big a surprise."

"How do you mean that?"

"Somehow I don't think your husband's been totally in the dark about your seeing me. He might have even encouraged it."

"Why would he do that? You think he would like me to have been with you, rowing boats?"

"He might not like all the details of your approach, but if he wanted to find out more about me, sending his wife around could get him close in."

"Closer in than I would want him to know," she laughed. "Closer than *you* would want him to know. He has all kinds of friends."

I could imagine Mr. Que's many friends.

I hung up and dialled Sumner at Walter Reed. He wasn't in, but the secretary who answered his phone said he was Sergeant someone and I asked him how I could get service records on a former nurse who'd been thrown in the brig for striking another officer.

"The nurse was an officer?"

"Yes. It happened in Vietnam."

"The Adjutant General might have a record," he said. "Otherwise you'd probably have to go to the central record storage in Saint Louis."

That sounded like more than Sumner would be able to swing. I thanked the sergeant and hung up. I sat back and looked at my Viet peasant on the wall and thought about touching bases and about diverting energies and decided to stick to the here and now, until I stopped getting answers.

## 52

I was busy in the office that morning. Mrs. Bromley was thrilled. Mrs. Simpson was there. She was sure she had diabetes because she had lost her taste for sweets, which Mrs. Simpson was certain meant that her blood sugar must be very high and she must be about to lapse into coma.

She wanted to be admitted to Memorial Hospital immediately. I told her I didn't have any admitting privileges at Memorial and despite my intense desire to cut things short, asked why she wanted to go there. The *Washingtonian* magazine had ranked Memorial as the number one hospital in Washington, and Mrs. Simpson wanted in, forthwith. Eventually she calmed down and left.

Between Mrs. Simpson and the next patient I called the lab at Saint George's and asked for a rundown on Maureen's blood sugars. The Sunday blood sugars were all normal, but the Monday morning sugars weren't on the computer yet. Those computers could tell you anything. I probably could have found out what colour of tie I'd be wearing tomorrow from the computer. But the computer couldn't tell me if Maureen's urine had Diabinese in it or if her blood insulin levels were high. The techs hadn't finished those tests yet.

There was a new patient: a thirty-eight-year-old woman with a "busy consulting business" and a tender thyroid. She had thyroiditis. I told her the best medicine was aspirin in regular doses and she was not at all impressed. She didn't come to a fancy endocrinologist for aspirin. I placated her by ordering some fancy tests to confirm the diagnosis but sent her away on aspirin.

Mrs. Bromley brought in the mail as I was shoving things

into my briefcase. I was trying to get away to the government workers' clinic downtown. I took the mail and fled.

"You did very nicely this morning," Mrs. Bromley called after me.

"We're packing them in," I called back.

"Watch that Mrs. Que," she said. "She's a slinky . . ." The door closed behind me and I couldn't hear the rest.

The whole drive down to the clinic I thought about Maureen and what I would do if her sugar fell during the fast, or if the urine came back positive, or if I was confronted with any one of the possible outcomes of the tests.

It's a nice drive to the clinic, through Rock Creek Park, with the road winding down the hills and along the creek under the bridges and all along the river past the Kennedy Center. But I hardly noticed it.

I saw the usual lineup of patients at the clinic: two black women telephone operators who had pelvic exams and Pap tests as part of a free cancer screening programme, and a man who had a cholesterol of 168. I know patients who'd kill for cholesterols of 168, men with cholesterols in the 400s who've had three heart attacks and still lay down cholesterol plaques in their coronary arteries, despite their low-fat American Heart Association diets. This particular guy with the cholesterol of 168 said he ate four eggs a day. Some people are just metabolically blessed.

Then there are those people who have blood sugars of nineteen for no readily apparent reason. Those people are not metabolically blessed.

A Pap exam patient called to cancel out, which left me with ten gift minutes. I reached into my briefcase and retrieved the mail I hadn't had time to open. There was a brown envelope from Timothy Moore's GP with a photocopy of his medical records.

I flipped through the chart, not being very impressed by the completeness or legibility of the record. Then I noticed a little item in the social history section. The handwriting was scrawled and wasn't easy to decipher, but one notation was unmistakable. After "Occupation": *Management consultant, former priest, S.J.*

I read that over about twelve times, trying to get something

227

more from it, but that's all it said. I reached for the phone, and picked up the covering letter with the doctor's phone number on the letterhead.

The GP was an old guy, judging from his voice, and he didn't seem at all outraged or surprised to hear that I would call about the priest question.

"That's what I thought the problem was all along," he said. "Got maybe two dozen priests or ex-priests in my practice. Never charge 'em a dime, of course. Never charge a man of the cloth, unless he gives it up of course. But I never ask 'em if they're impotent. I mean, it'd be kind of insulting. But the ex-priests, now, like this Moore, they come in with the damnedest complaints: sexual, psychosomatic, you name it."

"Well," I said, "I was just asking in case his hormone levels come back normal and I have to tell him it might be there's a psychological component."

"Hell, of course there's a psychological component. Don't need hormone levels to know that. This guy was brought up to think masturbation's a cardinal sin. You think he's just gonna take off the collar one day and start screwing?"

"Do you know when he took off the collar?"

"Moore? Let me see. He's been my patient since about the early seventies. He was already out of the clergy when he came to see me."

"So he'd already been to Vietnam?"

"Oh, sure. That's right. I remember now. He was back from the war. He was a priest when he was over there, though. I remember thinking it was the war that made up his mind about that – leaving the fold."

"Ever ask him?"

"No. Have you?"

"No. But thanks."

I'd taken a very competent social history from Timothy Moore, erstwhile S.J. I didn't know the first thing about him. Usually I get my patients to account for every year. But something about the whole thing kept me from asking. It was almost as if I'd been set up and I didn't want to appear too interested. Well, now I was interested, and I hadn't covered all the bases.

# 53

I arrived at the nurses' station at the metabolic unit at four-thirty. I checked Maureen's chart but all her sugars so far were fine – nothing below ninety. The urine and blood tests for exogenous agents weren't back on the chart and they weren't in the computer.

"Well, here's Dr. Marquis de Sade," said Maureen as soon as I walked through the door. She was standing looking out her window, looked at me, and then back out again.

"Enjoying your diet?"

"Delicious," she said, holding up her water jug. "Try some. Perrier and water with a twist of hunger."

"How's it going?"

"Not bad, considering." She was smiling and her eyes looked bright, a single shade of grey against very clear white. Her skin was milk white.

"Your blood sugar's behaving itself."

"Ninety-three at noon. What was the three o'clock?"

"Ninety-four."

"Jesus, it's going up! I'm starving and it's going up."

"That's really the same number. The lab isn't that accurate."

"But I'm not eating. What's keeping it up?"

"Your liver. And your hormones and your fat stores."

"I've got plenty of those."

"Sure, all hundred pounds of you."

"I told you, I've gained weight since all this began."

"Your body looks wonderful."

"Thanks, Doc."

I sat down in the chair next to her bed and she sat on the bed cross-legged. She was wearing blue jeans and a T-shirt with NOTRE DAME printed across the chest.

"I like your shirt."

"Thanks."

"Timothy Moore give that to you?"

"No," she said, suddenly serious. "Tim went to Holy Cross."

"Just as good."

"For what?" she said slowly.

"For the priesthood. Good place to prep, don't you think?"

"Well, you do poke your nose around."

"I'm curious about my patients."

"And what have you found?"

"Nothing you don't already know."

"How do you know what I know?"

"I know you knew Timothy Moore in Nam. And I know he was an Army chaplain there. So I know you knew he was a priest."

"You deduced that pretty well."

"Oh, I'm just warming up."

"Why are you so interested in Timothy? You want to know if I'm sleeping with him?"

"I'm interested in why you slept with me."

"What's that supposed to mean?"

"Just what I said."

"Because I liked you. And I found you attractive. I was charmed."

"Past tense?"

"Excuse me," she said. "One moment you're all doctor, the next jealous lover. One moment you're checking me out for surreptitious drugs, telling me you don't really know me all that well – the next moment you're checking out my love life."

"That's as easy to understand as the girl who climbs out of my bed and tells me she's referring me a boyfriend who can't get it up."

"That's not what I said."

"What did you say?"

"I said I had a friend, who had some problems in that department."

"And how would you know about those particular problems?"

"Maybe he told me."

"Maybe he did."

"Look, I don't ask you about your life," she said, standing up off the bed suddenly.

"I know, you like the fact I never pry."

"That's right."

"Sorry I asked," I said, getting up. "Somehow I thought it might be relevant."

"Relevant?"

"You're right. I should never have brought this up."

"Well, don't go away mad," she said. I could have tried a dramatic exit then, but she looked like she might open up a little without it.

"How'd you find out about that Bronze Star?"

"I told you, Mrs. Que had us checked out. They got hold of our service records. Don't ask me how."

"Now how would they get those?" said Maureen. "You sure you don't have other sources?"

"Other sources? Like what?" I said, all innocence. I considered trying Sumner Barrington's name on her, but I thought of that as my ace in the hole.

"Like other people."

"That's all I know," I said.

"I don't think so," she said, and I just looked her in the eye and left.

She was right, of course. I knew that Timothy Moore was the father of her baby. Sumner had told me that. At least I knew it when I knew who the priest was. But there were other things I didn't know about what happened back then. Helen had intimated that this whole problem started back in Nam. I thought Helen meant the whole problem with Timothy Moore, but now I wasn't so sure. She might have meant she thought the root of the blood sugar problem went back that far.

# 54

The house had lights on and it looked like someone might be home, so I stopped and rang the bell. Helen came to the door.

"What a surprise," she said, beaming and bright, my biggest fan. "How's Maureen?"

"Holding up."

"I'm working evenings," she said. "I'll see her in about an hour."

She offered me a beer and we sat down on the porch and she waited for me to say why I'd come. I just sat there and rocked and looked at my car on the street and let her get nervous.

"Well, is this a social visit or business?" asked Helen finally.

"Both. Curiosity mostly."

"About what?"

"Was Tim Moore angry when Maureen aborted his baby?"

It was aimed for that spot between her eyes and I believe it found its mark. Helen shuddered and blanched and looked sideways and up and down and everywhere but at me and finally worked up a little fury and looked me in the eye and said, "I don't know what you're talking about."

"That's why you almost fainted just now," I said.

"That's one of those how-often-do-you-beat-your-wife questions."

"True. But it's fair. We're not in a court of law."

"Did Maureen tell you about the abortion?"

"No."

"Then I don't think I should."

"You were the one who told me how bad Tim Moore and Maureen were for each other. You said they were 'poison' for each other. That's not an easy word to forget. Now every time

Maureen gets sick Tim Moore is right by her side. He's taking Diabinese, which lowers blood sugar pretty well, especially in big doses. Now I have opportunity, and I'm looking for motive. She aborted his child. He may never have another one."

"I don't think I like you any more," said Helen. I could see the pigeon killer in her eyes. "Not one bit."

"I'm sorry."

"Did the tests for Diabinese come back positive?"

"Nothing's back yet. I'm just trying to stay a step ahead."

"Why don't you find out whether or not Maureen's got Diabinese before you start throwing accusations around." She was really hot. "Sure Timothy was hurt. He's crazy about Maureen, and always has been. He left the clergy for her and he's still knocking his head against the wall while she can't make up her mind. But she doesn't love him. And it's very sad to see. But he wouldn't hurt her in a million years."

"Okay," I said. I left my beer on the porch and walked to my car, a little weak at the knees.

She certainly did not act like a woman trying to cast suspicion in the direction of Timothy Moore. Playing detective was no fun at all. I decided to wait until I had some evidence before I played again.

## 55

Maureen was awake the next morning when I made rounds at seven-thirty. Her sugars had been rock steady the whole night and she hadn't had any sweats or headaches or any other symptoms except fatigue, and the nurses' notes mentioned she had been a little irritable.

"Never realized how much I liked Helen's bacon and eggs," said Maureen. "I'll never rush past one of her breakfasts again. My mouth waters just thinking about it this time of the morning."

"You can eat all you want, Thursday morning."

There were no patients scheduled for the office that morning, which made Mrs. Bromley edgy and which didn't do wonders for my state of mind either, since it left me with nothing better to do but call the lab doing Maureen's urine for hypoglycemic drugs and pester the lab supervisor about the results.

"This must be a pretty special case," said the supervisor. "We don't get all that many requests for urine sulfonylureas and we don't get doctors calling twice in two days."

"This is a special case," I said. And I didn't know, even then, how special.

Then Dr. von Dernhoffer called. His voice wasn't quite as honeyed this day, and he seemed in more of a hurry to get to the point.

"About your report: you list three possibilities for the patient's death," he said. "What I need to know is your final diagnosis."

"You didn't ask me to take a multiple choice test," I said. "This isn't the Boards of Internal Medicine. I don't have to guess the answer you're looking for."

"But you haven't given a diagnosis."

"Did you really expect me to?"

"You list them in order. You think the most likely is number one?"

"Yes. I think the most likely thing is that the General took too much quinine and that that, given his malaria, pneumonia, asplenism and coronary heart disease, did him in. It's all in there. He probably dropped his sugar with the quinine, just like the patients in that report from the *New England Journal*, and his heart couldn't take the strain."

"But those patients had acute falciparium malaria. The General didn't have falciparium."

"Nobody's perfect. He had malaria. What difference the species? He had rigors and chills and he thought he had malaria. He was sure enough to take his quinine."

"Pneumonia can cause rigors."

"I think he had both," I said. "Look, I can't be sure. That's why I list the other two unprovable possibilities."

"But as long as those are in there, that's all anyone's going to see."

"Who's going to see just those two?"

"Stephanie Shaw. You know what she's going to latch on to."

"I can't stop the press from misrepresenting the facts. Bigger men than you and I haven't stopped that from happening, ever."

"But you say he might have received 'an excessive dose of insulin, either inadvertently through a nursing error or from another source.' Now what do you mean by 'another source'?"

"You know very well what I mean. You want me to say his widow or some nonfriendlies might have penetrated your nonexistent defences and slipped him forty units of insulin?"

"Then in another part of the report," von Dernhoffer went on as if I had never spoken, "you say it's unlikely the nurse made an error because the insulin level was so high she would have had to draw up twice as much volume in her syringe as the prescribed dose, and she probably would have noticed an error that big."

"Makes sense to me."

"But that leaves the other 'source' as the most likely explanation."

"No," I said. "It leaves the explanation I said was most likely as the most likely explanation: quinine, malaria, no spleen."

"But that's not the way Stephanie Shaw's going to read this."

"I can't help how Miss Shaw reads things."

"This is going to be trouble."

"Real sorry to hear that."

"This is really not going to do."

"What do you want me to do?" I asked. "Delete part of my report?"

"I'd like you to give your honest opinion, and to come down on a diagnosis, whatever you think, so there will be no ambiguity in the conclusions."

"You can't have me see a patient's chart a week after his death and expect an unequivocal answer. Too many unknowns," I said. "You've got my report. I'm sure you can find someone else to do another."

"Well, now, I'm sure that won't be necessary."

"I'm sure it will be, if you want me to change anything."

He mumbled something I didn't quite catch about trying to explain this report to someone and hung up. I didn't hear the word *thanks*.


# 56


Maureen fasted all Tuesday and her blood sugar level dipped to seventy, but she felt only hungry and a little dizzy – none of the real severe sweating, palpitations or panic. We drew an insulin level with the blood sugar of seventy, just to be sure.

She was drinking water and walking around the ward, looking out the windows, probably for a way out.

"There's just the rest of tonight and tomorrow," said Maureen. "This is going to be a breeze. Nothing's happened yet. I feel fine. The nurses keep asking me how I feel and I say 'Great' and they write it down. They probably think 'This one hasn't got an insulinoma. She's just crazy.' They think I'm as crazy as you think I am."

"I don't think you're crazy."

"You're not sure though. You're reserving judgment."

I couldn't say she was wrong. So I changed the subject. We talked about how long it would take for the results to be ready and what would have to be done if she had an insulinoma.

But she didn't have an insulinoma.

I knew that. I knew that even before the insulin levels were ready because her urine was loaded with ketones and even minute levels of insulin will clear ketones away. If she had an insulinoma, she'd have lots of insulin and no ketones in her blood or urine.

There were still about forty hours to go with the fast, though. Anything could happen in forty hours.

Pulling out of the hospital garage I checked my rearview mirror. Checking the mirror had become a habit lately. There had been lots of positive reinforcement. The mirror check yielded results again: my one-eared companion was with me. I'd begun to get quite a lot out of the rearview mirror. Just a flick of my eyes and I could pick up all kinds of details. One-ear was wearing a knit hat which covered his ears, but I knew the rest of his face now. He often chewed a toothpick, and he had one now.

His being there made no sense now. I couldn't see what purpose he served if he was Mr. Que's boy. Maybe Mr. Que didn't know I'd handed in my report and signed off the Dhieu case. Or maybe one-ear worked for someone else who didn't know I was through with General Dhieu. Or maybe I wasn't as finished with the good General as I thought.

He stayed one or two cars behind me the whole drive home along the Parkway. He kept going on MacArthur Boulevard when I turned off to my street. I told myself not to think any more about it.

The phone was ringing when I got home at six-thirty. What a surprise. I don't really need a bell on my phone: I can just pick it up whenever I'm home – someone's going to be on it.

This time it was Mai Nguyen.

"You don't call. You don't write. Have you forgotten all about me?"

"I've been busy."

"Saving lives?"

"Pursuing diagnoses."

"Take me out to dinner and forget all that serious business."

I really did not want to go, but there was no graceful way of avoiding it without hurting her feelings. I know, that's egotistical. She could survive without my attentions. But she sounded as if she did not want to be turned down. I told her I'd pick her up in an hour.

"Oh, I'll meet you there," she said. "Don't bother."

"No reason to take two cars," I said.

237

"Suit yourself," she said. "But I'd be glad to drive in and meet you there."

I understood why Mai was not eager for me to see her digs when I got to her neighbourhood.

It was in Little Saigon.

Mai's address landed me at a red brick apartment building. Her Corvette roosted among a collection of souped-up Trans-Ams and Firebirds, scattered vans with over-sized wheels and hand-painted panels depicting eagles and settings suitable for the Marlboro man. Bumper stickers proliferated: KEEP ON TRUCKIN', and LET'S DO IT IN THE ROAD. Vehicles owned by people who had nothing much else to spend their money on. The door to her entrance had a cracked glass window and I pushed the button next to "Nguyen" and was buzzed in. Opening the door, I realized I needn't have bothered with the security system – the door lock was broken.

A boy of about ten answered her apartment door. It had been a three-floor walk-up and I was catching my breath and he stood there looking up at me curiously. He was interesting to look at: sandy hair with a little curl, oriental eyes and the fine high cheekbones of the Vietnamese. He mixed the two worlds prettily, that kid did. An Asian woman appeared behind him and bowed the jerky little bow villagers did, and said, "In please. Mai come soon."

There were at least ten people, of three different generations, in a room which served as living and dining room. They were watching television, "Family Feud," and most of them turned around to look at me. The woman who had answered the door pulled up a folding chair for me, so I could watch "Family Feud" too.

Two little girls, about four or five years old, came to inspect me. They were wonderful little girls, with straight black hair in fringes and big dark eyes, and they smiled and stared at me, one at each shoulder. I was much more interesting than "Family Feud." They smiled and looked at their own shoe tops and then checked back to meet my eyes and then looked down again and bit their thumbs and swivelled their little hips and kept me entertained until Mai appeared in her slit-sided dress, looking stunning.

"Are you keeping the doctor company?" she asked them.

Everyone in the room turned all attention now to Mai, who was certainly better to look at than anything on TV. Two little girls I hadn't noticed before came running up to and around her, all giggles and energy, excited by seeing their aunt dressed up for the night.

I was introduced to various aunts and uncles and sisters and a grandmother who spoke good English.

"You are the one who investigates the death of General Dhieu," she said.

"Yes. Did you know him?"

"Everyone knew of him," she said with a smile I had no chance of reading. "The important thing is that he is dead."

I wasn't sure if she was pleased about that or not.

"She's pleased," Mai told me in the car. "She's just sorry she couldn't have been in on it."

"On killing him?"

"Yes."

"They think he was killed?"

"They hope he was. My grandmother did not hold much affection for the good General."

"Was she very political when she lived in Nam?"

"Everyone was political in Nam," said Mai.

"Who's your favourite suspect where General Dhieu's concerned?" I asked.

"What makes you think I have suspects?"

"Everyone else seems to have one."

"*Cherchez la femme*," she said.

"Now there's a great help."

"It means . . . "

"I know what it means. Which *femme*?"

"How many *femmes* are there?"

"You mean how many women connected to General Dhieu? How should I know?"

"Well, what women *do* you know connected to him?"

"I don't know," I said. "I don't know much about him. He had a wife. She's been screaming he was murdered."

"Perhaps she doth protest too much," said Mai.

I had to smile. "Why would she do that?" I asked. It was a point that bothered me. "She could have let the whole thing go away. There would never have been any investigation. The hospital was only too eager to sweep it under the carpet."

"The hospital might have been. But Mrs. Dhieu does not live in the hospital. She lives in Washington, and there are lots of Vietnamese who have their own ideas about how her husband died."

"Now, that's interesting," I said. "What're they saying in Little Saigon?"

"They're guessing. Lots of rumour. You are the investigator, and not to be swayed by idle talk."

"But I'm interested."

She just smiled and it was clear I was going to get nothing more from her.

She took a cassette out of her handbag and popped it in my car stereo. It was Neil Young, "The Needle and the Damage Done." It was probably the same cassette I'd seen her steal.

There was nowhere to park near Dupont Circle. We wound up five blocks away.

We walked to the restaurant in the purple evening. They still had the sidewalk tables out at Kramers and Afterwords and people were sitting outside in the cool air, eating and drinking wine and reading books they'd bought in the bookstore part of Kramers. We reached Le Petit Garçon and Mai led me inside. She stood there in her olive green silk dress with the slits up the sides which opened so that you could see only the sides of her thighs, not the scarred parts. She was speaking French to the maître d'.

He seated us and Mai ordered us both wine and she ordered the dinner, all in French. Then she turned to me.

"Why so pale and wan, love?"

"That's a quote, isn't it?"

"Yes. But you avoid the question. You're not a happy man tonight," she said, scrutinizing me.

"I get depressed watching you."

"Watching me? Am I not a great joy?"

"No, you're not."

She looked at me, with what I thought must be something

240

like fear, if she could feel fear any more. I decided to knock off the heavy stuff.

"Why am I depressing?" she asked.

I just shook my head.

"Your little Vietnamese pineapple brings back sad memories?"

"That's not it," I said. "It's you. You're such a . . ." I couldn't think of how to put it.

"A what?"

"Seeing you tonight, with your family . . ."

"Kind of a turnoff, huh? Ten in a four-room apartment. Little Saigon."

"No, that's not it," I said. "Just the opposite. I liked you better tonight than I ever did."

She looked at me with enough surprise in her face to make me want to say things very carefully, but I didn't know how.

"I mean, the cocaine, the Corvette you couldn't possibly afford on a tech's salary. The quick fingers on the street."

"What?"

"It's just that you're so bright and young and you speak French and Vietnamese and absolutely dazzling English and yet you're so marked."

I saw her recoil and realized that was exactly the wrong word.

"I don't mean the legs. That's not nearly as disfiguring as you think. It's just that to look at you sitting here, anyone would think you're on top of the world, but you're one of the walking wounded."

"What do you mean about not being able to afford the Corvette? What do you think I do for my money? Do you think I turn tricks in the bathroom at the Clinical Center?"

I tried to think of a denial, but I couldn't deny it. That's what I thought.

"Who would pay to have me?" she said, holding my eyes with her own. "Who would pay to touch these legs?"

"I'm sorry."

"What else can I spend money on? Can't get my own apartment. Can't go on vacations."

"Why not?"

"You saw the reasons tonight."

"You bring it all home?"

"I'm one of the lucky ones, one who could find work. In Saigon, I was an instructor at the university. Here I'm a lab tech. At least it pays. My sister – you saw her boy, with the curly hair – her English is not so dazzling as mine, and with the children, she cannot work."

"I see."

"And as for the dissipated life, I'm not doing anything half the people my age don't do. In fact, with my living arrangements, I don't get a chance to do anything very often, except very unusually when a nice man invites me to his place. Usually the invitations come from men who are not so nice, and I don't go. I've never had herpes or the clap, even though I ball guys in bathrooms on the first date, very rarely."

"Oh," I said. I can be very quick and clever.

We looked at each other across the wide divide of the table. It was a very wide divide now.

"I guess I met the wrong kind of people in Nam," I said. "Ever since I got back I seem to think the worst of people."

"I don't buy that," said Mai. "That whole lost generation sob story."

Her café-au-lait-coloured eyes held mine.

"Vietnam turned into a sewer," she said. "But it wasn't any worse than a lot of other sewers before or since."

"That didn't make it any easier to take."

"All those bleeding hearts," said Mai. "Came back feeling sorry for themselves, crying in their beer what a tough time they'd had. Forget that. They were soft when they went. Blaming Vietnam for their alcohol or heroin. Forget it. If it hadn't been Nam, it would've been something else. They had something wrong before they went."

"Am I a bleeding heart?"

"I never heard you sound like one, until tonight. You never did any crying about your own wounds."

I think she realized she had let more slip than she intended, and I said, "I never told you I'd been to Nam."

"Your friend from the bar was there," she said. "The obnoxious one, with all the medals," she said. "I thought you must have been too."

It was plausible but not convincing. Suddenly I began seeing connections and possibilities I never saw before: the one-eared hessian might not belong to Mr. Que and maybe I didn't follow Mai to Mr. Smith's that day. Maybe she laid down a scent.

Those thoughts slipped by as a vaguely discomforting ripple, and I fastened on Mai's point. Until recently, until Maureen, I hadn't thought of myself as harbouring any smouldering wounds. Since Maureen, I'd been aware of a bleakness, an absence. She'd made me remember how it felt to be really alive.

"This whole thing isn't really about us, is it?" asked Mai.

"Not about you," I said.

"Well, don't make your hang-ups mine," she said. "The great American tragedy doesn't become you."

"Is that what I'm playing?"

"I don't know what you're playing. But I get very tired of ennui and I don't need anyone passing judgment or talking about victims. Americans are the wrong people to talk about victims."

Dinner came, and it was very nice and very French and I had no idea what I was eating. It was a lovely dinner and I liked Mai more and should have enjoyed the evening thoroughly, but I was thinking about Maureen starving on the ward while I ate, and I was thinking about those urines being set up for tomorrow's assay. And I was thinking Mai was right, maybe it wasn't Nam after all. Maybe Maureen was one of those borderline personalities just looking for a ledge to trip over.

## 57

Wednesday was more of the same. Maureen getting hungrier and weaker and more light-headed but denying any symptoms like the ones which got her to the emergency room.

"It's just not like Saturday. I'd know that feeling. It wasn't one bit subtle."

It made me feel better hearing her say that – she sounded so unpsychotically straightforward.

"You said we could end it tonight," she said.

"That's right. Seventy-two hours is up at seven P.M."

"But I haven't had any hypoglycemia."

"Your sugars are drifting down a little."

"But that's not the real thing. Not like Saturday."

"The test runs seventy-two hours."

"But how do you know the insulinoma will fire off within seventy-two hours? I mean, do they always blast off in seventy-two hours?"

"That's the way the test is done."

"Now you're sounding like the bureaucrats you can't stand."

"You've got to draw the line somewhere. We could wait until you starve to death."

"But I feel okay. Let's keep going until tomorrow morning. Just until then. If I haven't had anything by then, we'll call it quits. I don't want to go through all this and miss it just because we stopped too soon."

Times like that scared me. She started looking like so many other people, people on psych wards.

But I let her have it her way. She wasn't going to have an insulinoma, though. She still had plenty of ketones.

That night, the drive home along the canal seemed to go on and on. The Asian reconnaissance effort had expanded to two people. My one-eared friend and a second man, just as small and wiry and expressionless. They drove the same Toyota and followed me from Saint George's to MacArthur Boulevard.

It had turned cool during the day, cool for Washington in September anyway, and I drove with the windows up, listening to the traffic helicopter guy talk about the snarls on the Beltway.

The phone was ringing when I reached the door and it kept right on ringing the whole time I fought the lock. It was seven-fifteen and dark. I got to the phone on the eighth ring.

"Dr. Abrams?"

"Yes."

"Karen Fox, Chemistry lab. Your answering service gave me your home number."

244

"Yes?"

"It's about that urine on Maureen Banting."

I waited for her to go on.

"I rushed it through, as I told you I would."

I waited. I didn't have the heart to ask.

"It's clean."

"Both samples?"

"Yes. Both the eleven-ten A.M. and the one-forty-five P.M. Nothing."

"What did you test for?"

She listed the drugs. Sounded like a complete list.

I thanked her and let it all rattle around inside my thick skull. It gave me a headache. First pangs were related to the realization that I didn't have any explanation for that sugar of nineteen. The second wave of head pain came from the sad but clear memory that I had hurled groundless accusations at Timothy Moore, and harboured similar but unspoken suspicions of Helen, with no evidence that anyone had slipped Maureen anything.

I called the lab back and asked for the results of the insulin levels and C-peptides, which I knew could not be ready yet. Amazingly, they had the levels from Saturday and from Sunday and Monday samples, but none after that. Saturday's samples showed high insulin and C-peptide levels and Sunday's showed normal for everything. Monday's levels were all suppressed, which is normal for a fasting patient.

The results eliminated surreptitious insulin injection. But they really didn't make sense. It was all wrong for Maureen's insulin to be high on Saturday when they brought her to the ER with such a disappearingly low blood sugar. Her insulin should have been turned off – she should have had no insulin at all in her blood. That finding was compatible with insulinoma, or with blood-sugar-lowering pills. But her urine drug screen was negative for pills, which left insulinoma. But in three days of fasting her blood sugar hadn't done anything unusual, which is not supposed to happen with insulinoma. Her blood sugar had been a model of decorum for three days. How could you figure that?

Unless the tumour hadn't read the textbook.

I'd been some fine physician. Suspected everyone. Pointed the finger quite a lot. But now I knew where to point it. The first thing the good doctor does when he suspects insulinoma is to get the patient to the hospital.

Now I had her where I should have had her all along and I didn't know what to do with her.

# 58

Thursday morning, I arrived at Maureen's room at seven-forty-five. Timothy Moore was already there.

"They're going to feed me," said Maureen. She was sitting cross-legged on her bed in shorts and a Holy Cross T-shirt. She did not sound happy.

"She doesn't want to eat," Timothy Moore told me. "She has to eat something."

"But nothing's happened," said Maureen. "All this for nothing."

"Eat," I said. "There're other ways of looking for insulinoma."

"Like what?"

"CAT scan. We might even think about trying to provoke it. I'm not saying we'll do it, but I'll think about it. For now, you eat."

"How would you provoke it?" said Timothy Moore.

"With tolbutamide. It's a drug like your Diabinese which releases insulin from the normal pancreas. If Maureen has an insulinoma, tolbutamide could really open the flood gates."

"Isn't that dangerous?" asked Moore.

"That's why I'll have to think about it. First I want that CAT scan. If I can see something, there'd be no point in trying anything risky."

"Have any of the tests come back?" Maureen asked.

246

"Some. When I've got the complete picture, I'll sit down and go over them with you."

"But right now, there's nothing definite?" asked Tim Moore.

"Not yet."

"Well, that's a relief. No news is good news," said Moore, standing up from his bedside chair and tousling Maureen's hair. "Hang in there, champ. You're in good hands." He folded his *Wall Street Journal* under one arm and picked up his pretty attaché case of maroon leather and stood there smiling at me in his blue pin-striped suit. "Slow but sure, doctor. She's always impatient."

"I know."

He smiled at Maureen and walked out of the room.

I looked after him, feeling pretty silly. It was inconceivable, seeing him with her, that he would ever do anything to harm her.

"When's the CAT scan?"

"I'll try to get you on for today. If not, tomorrow. Just relax and enjoy breakfast."

"I don't even feel like eating."

"You don't have to make up for all three days at once."

"Three and a half days," she said.

I went out to the nurses' station and checked the computer for the sugars from Tuesday and Wednesday, but the ward clerk told me the computer had been down all morning.

Back at the office, Mrs. Bromley asked how the hunt for Maureen's tumour was going and I told her.

"Don't despair," she said. "I have great faith in you."

"Faith is about all we have left."

"Something will turn up," she said.

I got only two calls that day. One was Mrs. Que.

"My husband is out of town," she said. "If you buy me a drink tonight I might tell you what I've found out about Mrs. Dhieu."

"I'm not interested in Mrs. Dhieu anymore," I said.

"Why not?"

"I've handed in my report. I'm finished with the case. Or didn't your husband tell you?"

"He can be as difficult as you. Besides, I told you. He's out of town."

I didn't say anything. I wanted to get off the phone.

"What did you conclude, in the end?"

"I concluded that nobody can draw any conclusions at this late date. We'll never know."

"How unsatisfying."

"Medicine's like that."

"Will we have our drink?"

I said yes. I don't know why I said yes, but it seemed easier than dealing with her and it got her off the phone.

The other call was from Sumner reminding me about the Endocrine Society meeting that night, at Walter Reed. Just before I left my downtown clinic Mrs. Que called and I told her I'd meet her after the meeting.

I drove from the clinic directly to the meeting. I didn't have time to stop off at Saint George's to see Maureen beforehand. You have to allow an extra hour for the rush-hour evening traffic. Even allowing for that, it was nearly seven before I reached the sentry station at Walter Reed. There was no soldier to salute me, for which I was grateful, and I found a parking space immediately.

"What took you?" asked Sumner, by way of hello. "You missed dinner."

"You didn't send the helicopter," I said. "I had to drive."

The speaker was a guy I knew. At least I felt I knew him – I'd read a hundred articles with his name on them. He was a diabetologist, now at NIH, and he was talking about the latest generation of hypoglycemic drugs.

They were testing three new ones in human trial. One of them was Hyporide, the drug Mai had mentioned. The director of her lab was there and he mentioned they were having a tough time perfecting an assay for Hyporide. Assaying the concentration of the drug in the blood is a nice thing to be able to do: it allows you to predict the blood level of the drug for a given dose.

"We've got a good urine assay now," said the chief of the lab. "So we can tell you whether or not the patient's actually remembered to take his pills, but the serum assay is tough."

The diabetologist liked Hyporide in particular because it was effective even in very fat diabetics. It was being tried in a multicentre study and seemed to be well tolerated, except for an unpleasant reaction with alcohol.

"It appears to be the same Antabuse-like reaction seen with some of the sulfonylureas: flushing, nausea, sweating. It's very unpleasant. The patients have to be warned about all that, if they're going to drink alcohol."

I'd been drifting off for some of the discussion, but that woke me up. It sounded so familiar. It was just what Maureen had described in her own episodes.

"Hyporide is not a sulfonylurea, then?" I asked.

"No, it's not even that close structurally, which is why it doesn't show up in the sulfonylurea assays."

"So if a patient were taking Hyporide and you checked her urine for sulfonylureas, it would be negative?"

"Of course."

"How often do you get hypoglycemia with it?"

"I can't answer that," said the diabetologist. "It's only been under clinical trial for seven months. We haven't had any unusual number of reports of hypoglycemia. But it is apparently quite potent. Even in patients more than twenty percent over ideal weight. Some of that has to do with the enhanced peripheral sensitivity to insulin." He went on about its mechanism of action.

"How soon will it be available?" I asked.

"To the public? Not for at least two years."

Nice try, Abrams. But you can't get the stuff unless you're a patient involved in one of the trial studies. Not real likely Maureen could have run afoul of Hyporide.

The discussion ended at nine and Sumner wanted to search the local bars for talent.

"You're in for a special treat, tonight," I told him. "We're having a guest appearance."

"The pineapple?"

"Someone new."

He followed me down to Kramers and Afterwords and we went in the bookstore entrance.

"What is this?" said Sumner. "A bookstore? I haven't met a

249

broad in a bookstore since college. I was talking about having a drink."

We worked our way to the rear of the book department to the bar and tables in the rear. Mrs. Que was waving from a corner table. Sumner looked much happier.

"I have a table for two," said Mrs. Que.

"No problem," said Sumner. "Abrams can leave."

She smiled one of her dimpled smiles at him, with her eyelids at half mast. Sumner looked happier than I'd seen him look since Mai Nguyen.

"We can get a bigger table outside," she said. "It may be a little cool."

"Fantabulous," said Sumner in my ear.

She did look smashing, in a red dress, a different dress than the one she wore for her accident, but a very nice, contour-hugging dress.

"You are afraid of me now?" asked Mrs. Que. "You bring a chaperon to protect you."

"It's only fair," I said. "Until your boys give up their chaperoning."

"You have not noticed any lately." It was a statement, not a question.

"Beg to differ. One-ear's still with me, and he even has a friend now."

"I told you, I know nothing of this one-eared chaperon."

Sumner was looking back and forth between us.

"Were you taking evasive action?" she said. "Is that why you were late?"

"We were at a meeting," I said.

"He's a handsome man," said Mrs. Que, looking Sumner over. Sumner looked like a puppy being petted. "More mature than you, perhaps."

"I'm very mature," said Sumner. "Urbane, too."

We had white wine.

"Do you like this place?" asked Mrs. Que.

"Oh, it's a favourite," said Sumner. "You can leaf through Updike or Cheever or Erica Jong or whomever, and then have a chablis."

"Do you like Updike?" she asked, smiling. I'm sure it was

250

an ironic little smile she was trying to suppress, but I suppose I'll never know.

"Well, I haven't made up my mind about him. All that urban angst."

"I think he does better with suburbia," said Mrs. Que. "But Erica Jong is a favourite of mine."

"Really?" said Sumner, eyes ablaze. "She's one of my favourites, too."

"How surprising," said Mrs. Que. "I would have thought she would appeal mainly to women."

"Oh, no. She's very appealing."

"But, you know, my English is not so very good. I cannot understand some of her idioms."

Sumner stood ready to explicate idioms for Le Van Que.

"What is this 'zipless fuck' she mentions so often?"

For a moment every feature of Sumner's face was frozen. I think all his neurons and synapses were firing at once, like a power station hit by lightning. Then his face slowly dissolved to joy.

"That's not something you can really explain," said Sumner. "You have to experience it."

Mrs. Que was sitting there, cool as the underside of a pillow.

"You have a car?" she said.

Sumner gulped hard. I watched his Adam's apple bounce up and down and he looked over to me and I shrugged and he managed to say, "Yes, I do."

They left together.

I sat there drinking my wine, having absolutely no flushing, nausea, or other unpleasant reactions.


# 59


It bothered me the whole way home, about the Hyporide. As soon as I walked in the door I called Sumner. The phone rang a long time but he answered it, sounding very unhappy to be disturbed.

"Sumner, about that Hyporide."

"I cannot believe you are calling me at this moment."

"Where are those multicentre trials going on?"

"Abrams, is this some kind of a joke?"

"Sumner, you owe me one."

"There are twenty hospitals involved. You want me to list all twenty?"

"Is Saint George's among them?"

"I'd have to look it up."

"Can you do it now?"

"Abrams!" Sumner sounded desperate.

"She'll understand, Sumner. You're a doctor."

He was back in a few minutes.

"Yes," he said. "Saint George's is one of them," and he hung up.


# 60


Early Friday morning they were thawing out Maureen's frozen urine – both the eleven-ten A.M. specimen and the one-forty-five P.M. – in the Saint George's lab. I had them pour off fifteen cc's of each into a separate container.

Then I called Mai Nguyen.

"Hi, sweet doctor."

"Mai, I need a favour."

"For you? Name it. I hope it's kinky."

"Need you to run some urine for Hyporide."

"Hyporide?"

"I think I have a patient who may have got some inadvertently."

"Not likely," said Mai. "It's only available on protocol. You can't just buy it at your local Dart Drug."

"I know that," I said. "I'll bring it by. It's thawing out in my pocket."

"Thawing?"

"It was frozen."

"Sorry, Doc. You're out of luck."

"Why?"

"Freezing denatures the stuff. So does heating. This assay's what you call finicky. We need it warm and wet, like me."

"How long's Hyporide hang around?"

"When do you think he got it?"

"Last Sunday."

"Five days? No can do, Doc. Stuff's cleared in one, outside two days."

Mai wanted to know how a patient could have gotten a dose without being in a study, and I evaded two or three minutes' worth of questions and hung up.

Then I went down the hall to the Clinical Research Center end of the ward and walked into the nurses' station. The ward clerk had seen me around, talking to Helen, and said hi.

"Helen around?"

"She's off today."

"I think I left something in her office. A paper."

The ward clerk opened her drawer and grabbed a ring of keys and led me to Helen's office and unlocked it. Then she went back to her desk.

I looked around. There was a very neat desk, with little on it except a plastic sign that said HELEN SLIGO, RN, CLINICAL RESEARCH CENTER. Her file cabinet was locked but the key was in her desk drawer. One of the file drawers was labelled PROTOCOLS. It had manila folders with project titles neatly typed on labels. I went through each one. The thirteenth one said: NIH HYPOGLYCEMICS TRIAL. That one had eight names on it listed as investigators. Helen Sligo was one of them. I read through the protocol and saw that Hyporide was one of the drugs, and that it was distributed in clinic. And clinic, I presumed, was supervised by none other than Helen Sligo.

Helen Sligo, slayer of Glover Park pigeons, fat, lovelorn room-mate of Maureen Banting who suffered unexplained hypoglycemic episodes with clean urine and flushing attacks when those episodes were preceded by alcohol. It made a nice little story.

But all I had were the same things I had had when I went around pointing the finger at Timothy Moore – negative urine tests and a bunch of inconclusive blood tests. The tests would be compatible with an oral hypoglycemic drug causing the sugar of nineteen, except I had to find the drug in Maureen, or in her urine.

I locked the door to Helen's office behind me and used the computer terminal at the clerk's desk to check the results on Maureen.

Then I walked down to her ward. Her chart was on the metal holder next to her door, and the door was closed. I carried the chart down the hall to the nurses' station and started thumbing through it, as if there were an answer somewhere in it, as if the chart could tell me whether the flushing and nausea Maureen had Sunday past was caused by Hyporide.

"Dr. Abrams?"

The voice had come from behind me and I just about jumped out of my socks.

"Didn't mean to startle you," she said. It was the Head Nurse. "Can I talk with you for a moment, in my office?"

I followed her in.

"It's about Miss Banting."

"Yes."

"I had to call security about it this morning. I'm not sure what to think. But I thought you ought to know."

"Yes?"

"Barbara Wendel's my charge nurse on nights. She's a very reliable gal. Worked for us for three years."

"What happened?"

"I'm not sure. Neither is Barbara. But we had to report it." She drew in a breath and spoke very clearly, taking breaths to keep herself from going too fast and sounding out of control.

"Barbara was working the night shift with an LPN and a nurse's aide last night. Barbara was in one of the rooms at the far end of the hall and the LPN had left the floor on a break.

254

The aide came to Barbara and told her there was a man in the visitors' bathroom with a chart, Miss Banting's chart."

"Miss Banting's chart?"

"The aide was sure she saw the man take the chart from the chart rack outside Miss Banting's room, and he went into the bathroom with it. She thought he was a cleaning man, until she saw him with the chart."

"A cleaning man?"

"Well, he had blue trousers and a grey shirt with a photo ID like the cleaning man, but he plucked that chart right out of her rack very fast. The aide had stepped out of the room right behind him and saw him."

"He probably knocked it out of the rack and was putting it back."

"That's what Barbara told the aide, but they went out to see and the chart was gone. The aide said he was in the visitors' bathroom. She followed him down there, if you can believe that."

"Why didn't she call security?"

"She did, later. But the aide's new and I don't know her very well, but apparently she's got more nerve than brains. She pushed the door to the bathroom open and tried to see if he was in there with the chart."

"And?"

"She didn't see him," said the Head Nurse, pausing for effect. "But she heard him."

"*Heard* him?"

"He was taking pictures. You know, it sounded like this – " She imitated the whirring noise a camera with an automatic advance motor makes. She did a very nice job. I knew what she meant immediately. It sounded like a presidential press conference.

"They called security of course, but the man was gone."

"I see."

"I thought you ought to know, as her physician."

"Thanks," I said. "What did he look like?"

"Medium build. Medium height."

"White? Black? Asian?"

"Don't know. You could ask the aide. She was the only one

who actually saw him. But, as I said, she's not superbright."

"Wonderful."

"Do you have any idea," said the Head Nurse, looking at me carefully, "what this is all about?"

"Have you told Miss Banting about this?"

"No. We thought you might want to do that. Or we could let security."

"I'll tell her," I said.

Then I went to see Maureen.

She was lying on her bed, watching Jane Pauley interviewing somebody.

"Jesus Christ," said Maureen. "You think Jane thinks those questions up herself, or do they hire a half-wit to do it for her?"

"Have you eaten?"

"It's on the way. They woke me up to draw a sugar at some black hour. Anything back on the insulin levels?"

"Not yet," I said. "We have some news, though." I tried not to pause dramatically, but I couldn't decide what to tell her first, or how.

"Okay, the suspense is killing me."

"Actually, there's two bits of news," I said. "The first is that your urine came back negative."

She was watching me closely now.

"Did you expect to find something there?"

"If drugs had anything to do with it, we might have."

"Well, that's a relief at least. You'd have called for the straitjacket if I'd had anything in my urine didn't belong there. Big time psycho pops hypoglycemics. What do they call it? Münchhausen syndrome?"

"I wouldn't call you a psycho, even if your urine had been positive."

"But you'd think it."

"I wouldn't even think it."

"Why not? What else do you call someone who tells you she's not taking anything, but has urine full of drugs?"

"A victim, maybe."

She laughed. It was a sudden, explosive laugh, like a balloon blown out. "A what?" she said. "You mean like your General

256

what's-his-name? The guy the widow says got helped along to the morgue?"

"It's just one possibility. Not likely. A rule-out, with a very doubtful rating."

"But there's nothing in my urine," said Maureen, shrugging. "So the Agatha Christie angle's not working."

"We can't test for all the drugs. We only find what we look for."

"You're really something," said Maureen, grinning. She looked very amused. "You're really into this cloak-and-dagger routine."

"I put it way down the list. I just don't want to forget it. No, I like natural causes," I said. "But you haven't asked me about the second headline."

"I'm not sure I can take another headline."

"Last night, someone was seen photographing your medical chart."

She looked at me for meaning. She was either very, very good, or she really did not comprehend. She went on trying to assimilate and finally said, "Say that again."

"Your medical record. Someone was here. He took your chart from the rack outside your door and took it to the bathroom and photographed it. An aide saw it all and reported it."

"Ho-oh, no," Maureen croaked. "Your General, maybe, but not me. They might have wanted him, but why would anyone want to get me?"

"I'm not sure anyone wants to get you. I'm just telling you what I've been told."

"You're just telling me . . ." said Maureen, sputtering. She was holding together that enamelled front very tenuously – the cracks were showing. But she looked more annoyed than frightened, more confused than alarmed. "You think this snooper had anything to do with my blood sugar?"

"I'm keeping an open mind," I said, watching her re-gel. "But no, I think whoever it was didn't know what's going on with you any more than we do. What he was trying to do was find out what we know."

"I don't like this at all."

"You're taking it pretty well."

"Give me a chance and I'll decompensate for you."

The door opened and we both jumped. It was an aide with her breakfast tray.

"Until recently, I would have bet it was just Mrs. Que's husband's boys doing a little research."

"The dragon lady in the red dress? Why?"

"Look at it from his point of view. A car smashes into his nice Mercedes. Soon as he looks up, there's Dr. On-the-spot Abrams. Pretty soon, his wife's a patient of Dr. Abrams. Mr. Que does a little checking, and what do you know? Dr. Abrams has some interesting connections. Dr. Abrams is investigating the death of one of Mr. Que's former business buddies, General Dhieu."

"The dragon lady's husband was a buddy of Dhieu's?"

"I'm not sure what the relationship was. But they knew each other and Mr. Que didn't like the idea that I was snooping around about the General and then turned up in his own backyard."

"All very interesting. But what's all this got to do with me?"

"You were with me. They check you out, and what do you know? Maureen's got some Vietnamese connections of her own."

"So do two million other Americans. That doesn't explain why he'd be interested enough to send somebody after my hospital chart."

"It might and it might not. Then again, this guy last night might have nothing to do with Mr. Que."

"I like that even less," said Maureen. "Who else you been antagonizing lately?"

"That's the problem, I don't even know. Maybe the widow."

"The widow's investigating the investigator? Or maybe the guys who got the General?"

"Anything's possible."

"So someone did knock him off?"

"I didn't say that."

"But you think it."

"I'm an agnostic, where the General's concerned," I said. She was tough to divert whenever the General came up. "But I think the time has come for a little quiet reflection in peaceful surroundings, unobserved."

"Then you'd better leave town," said Maureen. "Washington's a goldfish bowl."

"I was going to invite you."

"Why?"

"So you don't have to sit home alone."

"I don't know," she said, smiling. "Why should I trust you? I mean, how well do I know you?"

I smiled. I recognized that line.

"I mean, all this started about the time I started up with you."

"You had your episodes before me. That's why you came to see me."

"I don't know," said Maureen with enough of a smile, "Helen always told me not to trust you."

"Now there's a great source of advice."

She laughed.

"See how it feels when people don't believe you?"

# 61

I discharged Maureen and gave her a lift to her place and went on to my office. We had no patients scheduled, and Mrs. Bromley was restless. She was not pleased to learn I was leaving for the weekend, that I wanted her to call Skyline Drive for reservations – "Rather like getting Redskins tickets, reservations at this time of year, at Skyline Drive" – nor was she happy about calling the government clinic to tell them I wouldn't be in that afternoon.

"Shall I say you've been called out of town to consult on some world leader?" asked Mrs. Bromley.

"Sure. Say the Ayatollah's sick. Tell them he has hypoglycemia and Dr. Abrams's being flown to Teheran to work him up."

"You'll leave a number where the answering service can reach you?"

"No. Doolan's on call for me this weekend. I'm just taking off a little early. I'll call him."

Before I could sit down and phone Doolan, Sumner called.

"Big night for you," I said.

"Not half as exciting as my morning," said Sumner. He sounded tight and unhappy.

"What happened?"

"Got to my office this morning and it's crawling with CID."

"CID?"

"The army version of CIA."

I sat down quickly in my swivel chair and did not swivel – the room was moving round fast enough.

"Seems they'd been asked to talk to me by some friends of theirs. They wouldn't say who. Had to be CIA," said Sumner. "This Le Van Que turns out to be a real hot item, it turns out."

"How's that?"

"They've been keeping an eye on her and where does she spend the night? At the apartment of one lucky lieutenant-never-to-be-full-colonel, Medical Corps."

"Why were they watching her?"

"You think they're going to tell me? They ask the questions, friend. I answer what I can. But I think they may have let something slip. I'll tell you in a moment."

"What'd they ask?"

"This and that. But not a few questions were about you."

"No foolin'?"

"Would I kid you?" said Sumner. He sounded certifiably morose. "That's what I was getting to. This Mrs. Que. You know about her husband?"

"Some kind of 'businessman', with a lot of 'connections' is all I know."

"Try again, big boy. Her husband's got no connections, least not in this world. He's dead. He's one dead general. *Your* fuckin' dead general, Dhieu."

If you could crack a telephone in your hand, mine would have cracked. I let my heart rate settle down below a hundred and said, "What was that you just said?"

"I said, Mrs. Que is Mrs. Dhieu. Que's her maiden name. Very trendy, Mrs. Que, uses her maiden name."

"But I met her husband."

"I don't know who you met, but it wasn't her husband, unless he's come back to life. One of the CID boys let it slip who she was, and the other gave him a look. I had Bernie, my staff sergeant, run over to the microfilm room at the library and go through some back papers and get me some photos. They weren't real good photos, but they were good enough to be sure of Mrs. Que-Dhieu."

"Did they have a photo of her husband?"

"Dhieu? Yeah."

"What'd he look like?"

"Broken nose, scar on his cheek. White temples, black hair. Distinguished, tough-looking old bird."

That was not the man I'd met at the accident, the man who'd come to the hospital in the ambulance.

"How'd you meet this dragon lady, anyway?"

"I more or less ran into her."

"Benjamin," said Sumner. "That's no answer. This is my job. I got CID men crawling all over my office."

"I spotted her in a bar in Georgetown. On the way home, her car passes mine in a dogfight with some bimbo in a van. They crashed and we stopped to help."

"Sounds like a setup."

"I can think of easier ways for her to meet me. That crash cost her her spleen."

"And she told you her husband's still alive."

"The guy driving the car was supposed to be her husband."

"Well, he's not."

"So the spooks were watching Mrs. Que. Then they see us all at Kramers and decide to move in?"

"So now I'm a security risk," moaned Sumner. "Wonderful."

"Seems to me, if they'd really thought that, you'd never have heard a thing."

"Come again?"

"If they thought you were part of something, they'd just keep watching. No, they asked you, which means they trust you for some answers."

261

"Hadn't thought of that," Sumner said, sounding brighter.

"They didn't tell you not to call me?"

"'Course not. They told me to let them know if I heard anything."

"You do that. Tell me too."

"Just do me a favour," said Sumner. "Don't throw any more women at me."

We hung up and I looked at my wall for a few minutes and tried to remember what it was Mai had said about Dhieu's wife. Something about protesting too much. *Cherchez la femme.* There was plenty of speculation around Little Saigon about how General Dhieu happened to meet his end at Saint George's. Maybe it was informed speculation. I couldn't see that Mrs. Que being Mrs. Dhieu really proved anything. Even if she had tried to meet me, picked me up at Mr. Smith's, it wouldn't have proved anything. She was interested in my investigation.

But what about the demolition derby on Canal Road? Big crash, could have killed someone. That couldn't have been planned. That was no setup. She might have gotten into her big Mercedes and followed me from Mr. Smith's, but that Mercedes-squashing wasn't in the plan. Mai said she had plenty of enemies. Someone must have spotted her, recognized her and given chase. I just happened to be in the vicinity because she was keeping an eye on me. So we get introduced a little more abruptly and a lot more dramatically than she'd planned.

It sounded plausible. I might be able to sell it to the movies. But I didn't like it. No, the movies wouldn't have it. It didn't have the smooth flow of fiction. It had the tangled woof of fact. It's probably what really happened.

I thought about it all a little more and got nowhere. There was no reason for Mrs. Que-Dhieu to not want to meet the man investigating her husband's death, given her interest. And there was no reason for her not to have me followed, watched, investigated. Knowing who she was didn't change anything. It just made me wonder why she was trying so hard to know what I knew.

There were easy enough explanations for why she might be

262

so interested. Either she killed the old boy herself or by proxy, or enough people thought she did that she had to know who did, or she was just eager to know who her enemies were.

I'd done enough wall-staring and thinking for one day. I called Maureen and told her to wait for me at her place.

"You sound strange," she said. "You okay?"

"Fine."

"What's happened?"

"Nothing," I said. "I'll be right over."

"You don't want to talk about it over the phone?" she laughed, a little uncomfortably. "You think they've bugged my phone? I hope they have. Listen, schmucks, whatever you're looking for, you've got the wrong marks. We are non-combatants. White flag. Yellow streak. Go snoop somewhere else – the ACLU, League of Women Voters, wherever."

"Just stay there," I said. "I'll be there in a few minutes."

"I'll be here," she said. "Alive, hopefully."


# 62


Maureen was alive when I arrived. Alive and amused enough by my plans for hasty departure to annoy me. I didn't tell her about Sumner's call, but I assured her I wasn't kidding about the man who photographed her chart. The whole incident seemed to have rolled off her, leaving no mark at all.

"You recover quickly," I said. "A little while ago, you weren't so equanimous."

"Oh, it's just Washington," she said, waving her hand. "Roadblocks, breath tests, snoopers. Let it get to you, you're really in trouble."

"Pack your bags. Sweaters, jeans, woollies. And hiking boots."

"Hiking boots?"

"I'm taking you away from all this madness."

"I like it. Heard that line before somewhere."

"You'll love it. Fresh air and . . . "

"Don't say anything more about it. The walls have ears," she said, rolling her eyes. She laughed, not a crazy laugh, just happy. We were escaping.

It took her ten minutes to throw things into a suitcase. I stood by her in her room and pointed to things in her closet and chest of drawers. She had a satiny red bra and panties and I pointed to those. "Oh, this *will* be fun," she said. When it was all in a big suitcase, I carried it downstairs. She dragged a long woollen coat out of the closet but I pointed to the down vest and she put that over her sweater.

It was light outside and we paused at the front porch door. I peered around, up and down the street, but saw nobody.

"You don't think they're that dumb," said Maureen.

We walked down the stairs and I tied the suitcase onto the trunk rack of the Triumph.

At my house we didn't talk much. They had followed me, too, and we were thinking about bugs and all that cute espionage stuff. Maureen turned on my stereo very loud and whispered in my ear, "I feel like a total fool, playing spy movie." I laughed. But we kept the stereo turned up anyway.

I shoved my bag into the hole behind the seats, checked to make sure I still had the tickets for the cabin, and we drove off.

"Think they've bugged the car?" she asked.

"I checked it out while you were packing."

"Clean?"

"How the hell would I know?"

"Where're we going?"

I looked at her and brought a finger to my lips.

"Oh, they don't need to bug your car. They can follow us. Neither of us would spot them."

"We spotted them before."

"Yeah, I know. That's always bothered me."

"Why?"

"Because we're amateurs, and they're not."

"So?"

"So either they're amateurish, or they wanted us to know we were being followed."

"Why would they?"

"That's what I can't figure."

"Maybe your faith in professionalism is misplaced."

We followed the Beltway and Maureen looked out her window as we flew by the big eighteen-wheelers. From the level of a Triumph, all you could see was the wheels and undercarriages. It was early enough that we hadn't hit the Friday rush and we were to the Route 66 turnoff quickly.

Then Maureen remembered she had forgotten to leave Helen a note saying she was all right and wouldn't be home. She looked at her watch. "She'll be home by now. She's already stopped off at the ward to help bring me home and they've told her I was discharged. She'll call home, get no answer and go wild."

"Call her from Warrenton. That's not far."

The Route 29 turnoff came up fast and we were in Warrenton by six o'clock. Maureen called from the Howard Johnson's. I went into the dining room and looked over the menu in a booth.

Five minutes later, Maureen slid across from me.

"She was frantic. She would have called the police in another ten minutes."

"Maybe we should have let her. Maybe they could figure this thing out."

"She wasn't too happy to learn who my driver is."

"Better than Timothy Moore."

Maureen smiled, "I'm not sure. She might prefer Tim now."

A fifty-year-old waitress with bubble-bouffant, skirt above the knees, took our order. I watched her swish away in her black rayon waitress uniform.

"Right out of *Five Easy Pieces* isn't she?" said Maureen. "All she needed was the chewing gum."

The cheeseburgers weren't too greasy and the strawberry ice cream soda had real ice cream. Maureen ate everything on her plate, cole slaw included. She had an ice cream sundae with hot fudge for dessert.

"Getting your appetite back?"

"I can see why those Arabs are always fasting," she said. "It's so nice when you start eating again. And there's no guilt. I lost four pounds on that fast."

"Don't think the Arabs have any guilt about eating."

I looked at her. She smiled back.

"Arabs don't have guilt about anything," she said.

"You know how to play to a Jewish audience," I said.

"That's the first time I've heard you refer to yourself as Jewish."

"Did Helen tell you this was all a Zionist plot?"

"I didn't tell Helen about anything. Just said the tests were cooking and we went away for a holiday."

"Tell her where?"

"No."

We went back to the car and drove down Route 211 towards Skyline Drive. It was dark along the road, no lights, only the stars and moon, more stars than you can ever see in Washington. The country road was rolling and fast and the car heater was working well, for once, so it was a nice drive.

"Like a space ship," Maureen said. "Black, black all around, except for the sky."

I smiled in the dark.

"You're being nice again," she said. "Not asking, when you really want to know."

I didn't know what she meant, but I looked over as if I did.

"Timothy Moore and I were friends. In Vietnam. He had his breakdown over there."

"Breakdown?"

"Everything was collapsing. It wasn't a good place to be a priest."

"Why not?"

"Promising rewards in heaven. It didn't wash."

"Not with you?"

"Especially not with me."

"You'd rather laugh with the sinners than cry with the saints?"

"The big sin is throwing away life."

"I can think of bigger."

"What did Timothy say, when he saw you in your office?"

"Not much. He's had some trouble with sex."

"Don't most people?" she said and looked off into the dark. "Except us."

"Helen adores him, doesn't she?"

"Yes, but she'll never admit it, not even to herself."

"Why not?"

Maureen kept looking out her window. "Can't you guess, knowing Helen?"

"Ex-priest?"

"Of course."

"And she doesn't approve of a good Catholic girl like you dating one?"

"Once the vow is taken," said Maureen, looking back to me, "it's forever."

"Apparently Timothy Moore doesn't look at it that way."

"No. He's through with all that."

We came to the base of the mountain and began up the winding mountain road. "Do you mind if I roll down my window?" asked Maureen. "I just know there's pine out there. I want to smell it, even if I can't see it."

You could see the outlines of the trees against the starry sky as we came around bends and it got cooler as we ascended. There was a van behind us, which made me nervous for a while, but it passed when I slowed. For most of the climb we were alone. Alone except for the forest eyes along the roadside. We would catch them in the headlights. Deer. Sitting by the roadside grazing. Big bucks with antlers, so close you could see them through the dark.

A ranger at the toll gate entrance to the Drive took our coins and gave us directions to Skyland. It took us twenty minutes to find it in the dark. No illuminated signs up there – just reflectors and headlights. We pulled up into a big car park behind what looked like a long low motel, with a big main building at one end. Maureen got out and stood leaning on the car door, looking at a sign in front of a cabin ten feet away.

"Register here. Knock loud," she read.

A teenage girl with a park ranger's jacket over a sweater was huddled behind a wooden desk with an electric heater aimed at her feet, watching a little black-and-white TV.

"Crummy reception," she said, gesturing at the TV. "Except channel five. Can I help you?"

"My secretary called. I'm Dr. Abrams."

"You're one lucky man, Doc," she said. "These cabins are booked months in advance. We'd just got a cancellation, when your secretary called."

She logged my name into a book and handed me a key and told us how to get there. It wasn't a cabin, just a room along the motel line. "You're in time for dinner at the main lodge," she said. "If you don't waste a lot of time in the cabin." She smiled at me, but she didn't wink.

"Impudent little tart," said Maureen outside. "She think we'd rush in and go on screwing through dinner?"

"She didn't mean it like that."

"Of course she did. She took one look at you and thought the same thing I did first time I saw you. But I wouldn't miss dinner, not tonight."

# 63

Our place was one room with a picture window facing the Shenandoah Valley. Maureen stood there looking out at the lights below, wrapping her arms around herself. There were two beds and a warm bathroom. The walls were wood panelling.

"I think I'm going to like this place," she said.

"Wish it had a fireplace."

"We'll keep warm."

We walked down the path to the main lodge and stepped into the big hallway, struck by the immediate warmth and light of a tremendous fire hissing in an enormous fireplace. They seated us in the dining room, away from the fire and next to a window which must have been lovely to have breakfast next to when you could see the valley below. But at night it was drafty and cold.

"They want to distribute us for the waitresses," said Maureen. "Heaven forbid one should get one more customer than another."

"You'd better eat. You're getting irritable."

"I'm fine," she said. "As long as they don't seat one of that Que bitch's boys next to me."

"I'd almost forgotten about them."

"It does all seem very far away," said Maureen. "But it was nice in a way."

"Nice? You didn't seem to like anything about it at first."

"At least it distracted me from my real problems."

"And what are those?"

"A blood sugar of nineteen."

"That was pretty scary."

"That's a real problem," said Maureen, holding my eyes with her own. "These little twerps playing at spies, surveillance – making themselves feel important with all their sneaking around. Kids' stuff. A sugar of nineteen, that's a big problem."

"We'll get an answer."

"I know you're doing everything the way you should," she said, reaching for my hand. "You're a good doc, Benjamin Abrams, MD, really."

She looked like she meant that.

"But so far, we've got a big zero," she added. "It's kind of discouraging."

"You've got to know good news when you hear it," I said. "An insulinoma's no great bargain."

"Neither is an unexplained sugar of nineteen," she said flatly. That wasn't a criticism, just a statement of fact. "What do you have, after you've eliminated all the probable explanations?"

"The improbable," I said, without thinking.

She smiled. "Let's not talk about it. This must happen to you at cocktail parties all the time, patients cornering you about their heartburn."

"I don't go to many cocktail parties."

"What do you do when you're not doctoring or sweeping helpless young things off their feet?"

"Daydream about sweeping helpless young things off their feet."

"And you sleuth and make Mrs. Bromley proud of you, making the papers. What did you decide about the General, in the end?"

"I decided not to decide. I listed the possibilities and left it at that."

"Which were?"

"That he had malaria and quinine and that's been known to drop blood sugars and raise insulin."

"No kidding? Malaria can do that? Saw lots of malaria over there. Never heard of that."

"Malaria plus too much quinine can. Either that, or somebody gave him too much insulin."

"Like who?"

"His nurse. I don't limit it to her, though. With his wife making all those accusations, I just left it at 'excessive dose,' without saying who might have done it."

"Some day you may look smarter for that," said Maureen.

She met my eyes when she said that, and then caught herself looking a beat too long and looked aside, to her reflection in the window.

"You know something about the General?"

"I know he was a general, and I know he was Vietnamese. That's all I need to know."

"I'm beginning to come around to your point of view."

"Why's that?"

"They're still at it. I've handed in my report, signed off the case. If it was Mr. Que or even the widow, that should end their interest in me. But someone's still at it. They've even tried to see your chart."

"You really think that had to do with the General?"

"What else could it be? Somebody's too nervous. He had a following of people who hated him. I've met some."

"Vietnamese, you mean?"

"Who else?"

Maureen had been leaning forward, bright eyes following everything. Now she quickly lowered them.

"I don't know," she said. "General Dhieu had enemies of all colours."

"The most likely thing, the only thing I can really imagine is that whoever it was wants to know what I thought happened to the General. But they couldn't get their hands on the report, or weren't sure I'd finished with the case."

"Have you?"

"Sure."

"Why?" she asked.

"There's nowhere else to go. There's no way to dig out who slipped him a special bonus of insulin, if that's what happened."

"But why would they be interested in my chart?"

"Maybe they thought your case was connected."

"But that's ridiculous," said Maureen, with more vehemence than I could understand at the time.

The waitress came for our order and the food came quickly after. I was still sated from the cheeseburger at Warrenton, but Maureen finished off prime rib, a salad and baked potato, and a few glasses of red wine.

"My first alcohol," she said. "No problem. When I'm with my doctor, no problems. It's just when I'm left to my own devices, I get in trouble. With you, I'm safe."


# 64


We walked back to our room, breathing the pine smell in the air and looking out over the lights in the valley.

"Who lives down there?" asked Maureen.

"Farmers, Rednecks."

"They must live such uncomplicated lives."

"It's always other people's lives that seem uncomplicated."

We didn't turn on the lights in the room. Maureen wanted to undress with the drapes pulled away from the picture window. I looked around, satisfying myself I could see in all the dark corners and I checked the bathroom. The thermostat was in the bathroom and I turned it up to seventy and wondered why they didn't have fireplaces in the rooms.

Maureen was naked between the sheets when I got there. She pulled off my underpants. She was lying on her side and slipped her top leg up and down mine. She was very warm and silky and wet in places. But I started worrying about the uncovered window and extricated myself and pulled the drapes.

"Their eyes are everywhere," laughed Maureen.

"Your hands are everywhere."

"We're both ubiquitous."

And for the night we forgot followers, generals, widows, and horrible sweaty nauseating hypoglycemic attacks.


## 65


The sun poured through the fabric and seams and edges of the curtains and woke us in the morning. Maureen pulled on her Lanz nightgown and threw open the curtains.

"Let's go!"

We dressed and went over to the lodge and had pancakes and Canadian bacon and we looked at the valley while we ate. Then we went out to the shop and bought trail maps and a compass.

I read the descriptions of a few hikes and Maureen picked out one that would take us to the ruins of cabins built by incestuous clans of early mountain people.

"They sound like such fun people," she said.

We followed the asphalt road until the path marked with yellow blazes took off into the woods. The path wound around and took a sudden bend and we found ourselves in a clearing not ten feet from a pair of bucks locking horns. They went at it, pushing back and forth for about half a minute until one had had enough and bolted off into the thicket. The victorious buck stood there looking after him for a moment, then turned his attention to us.

"I think he just laid claim to this territory," said Maureen, taking a step back.

I picked up a good thick branch and held it like some pathetic club.

"Fat lot of good that's going to do, Tarzan. Look at the rack on that boy," said Maureen.

The buck did have an impressive set. He was something to watch – muscle slid in bulky waves under his hide with every movement.

"He's got no quarrel with us," I said. "He's on our yellow blaze trail. We're supposed to look at that graveyard."

The buck seemed to be listening to all this.

"Somehow I don't think he's gonna see it that way," Maureen said.

The buck turned away, and walked along the edge of the clearing away from us, past the gravestones, and trotted off into the forest.

"What a man," said Maureen. "Faced down Santa's reindeer."

"Sometimes a little intransigence pays off."

"Says the man who ran for ten days through the woods."

"You have to know when to pick your fight, and with whom."

We looked at the gravestones. Maureen liked the old names.

"Ezekiel Abernathy," she said. "Why don't people name their kids like that anymore?"

"Here's a Timothy Sloane Moore."

Maureen came over and looked at the stone. TIMOTHY SLOANE MOORE, 1787–1822: HE WILL FIND HIS REWARD IN HEAVEN, said the stone.

"I sure as hell hope he found it before that," said Maureen.

"His reward?"

"Yes. I hope he had some fun on earth."

"You're some swell Catholic," I said. "That's the Christian deal – you defer gratification."

"I'm through with all that. From now on, it's time to cash in the chips."

We continued following the yellow blazes. The woods were cool, dark and deep. Maureen carried the trail maps and I carried my reindeer club. The trail wound down the mountain along a fast stream which ran over dark stones. The water was cold and clear but the stream-bed was black and leafy and looked treacherous for wading.

We followed the path along its twists and corners and stopped to look down where it ran alongside a waterfall, some fifty yards ahead. There were two hikers by the falls: one on his haunches, the other lying on his side, talking to the first. The one lying down had a knit hat covering his hair and ears, but I knew him, even from that distance. I knew him by his lean rodlike body, by the way he moved. He was missing an ear.

I stopped short and Maureen ran into me from behind.

"What's wrong?" she said. "Snake?"

"In a manner of speaking."

I stepped off the path and drew her with me. "Our friends must have had reservations, too."

"Friends . . . ?" Maureen echoed blankly.

"The nice Oriental boys who've taken such an interest in me lately."

"Where?"

"Down the trail."

"You saw them?"

"They must be running a budget operation – keep sending out the same boys all the time."

"Were they coming this way?"

"No, waiting by the falls."

"Waiting?"

"Pausing."

"How can you be so sure it was them?"

"It was them."

"But from this distance?"

"You want to come down with me and make sure?"

"Let's get out of here," Maureen said. "This is creepy. In these woods. They could do anything. We'd never even be found."

"Maybe we could take them," I said, "by surprise."

"I liked the odds with the buck better. Let's fly."

We started back up the trail, Maureen ahead. I checked back over my shoulders for the forest troops. I didn't like the way they were lying around down there, calm, unhurried, sure of themselves. There was no one on the path behind us, but we had gone only a few hundred yards back up the path when I spotted them above us, higher up the mountain on a trail, moving fast.

"They're going to cut us off," I told Maureen.

I pulled her off the path and cut into the woods, running bent low at the waist, following the natural paths between the trees, working down the side of the mountain but still in the general direction of the Lodge. Maureen was falling behind.

I waited for her. She was breathless when she reached me.

"Those Cong taught you well. You just fly through woods," she said.

"Stay close."

You can understand about deer and other bounding animals evolving when you try to move quickly through a forest. At that altitude, it wasn't all evergreen, but the forest floor was dark. It wasn't too tangled to run through, but you had to keep springing over fallen trunks and vines.

Maureen could not keep up.

"Do you know where you're going?" she said, when we paused, sucking in air.

"Better than they do."

"Go on and get help. I just slow you down."

"No."

We picked up a stream in a little ravine and walked right into it, on the wet rocks, following it up the hill, the cold water soaking through our shoes.

"Where are they?" Maureen asked.

"Can't be sure."

"Maybe you should tell them you'll be happy to rewrite the report any way the widow wants it."

"Sure. We'll wait here for them. Maybe they even speak English."

"Keep going."

We followed the stream, slipping on the wet, algae-covered rocks of its bed, breathing so hard they must have heard us if they were close at all, and then I saw a sheer rock cliff rising up ahead.

The ravine veered off to the left and a path I hadn't been able to see before bent off by the right side of the cliff.

We took the ravine side up the rocky cliff and Maureen caught her breath on a ledge, while I scouted the trail side of the cliff. I rejoined her on her porch and we pulled back out of sight.

"When did you see them last?" Maureen asked.

"Ten minutes ago. But they came down below us. They'll be making their way up the ravine – have to decide which way we took. We better go."

"They'll catch us. It's at least two miles to the road."

"They'll have to check the trail first. If we're lucky, they'll split up to do it. One will go up on the dry path and look for tracks. The other'll stay in the ravine. If that happens, I'll take the one on the path and you make some noise so the other goes for you."

"What do I do when he gets here?"

"Look for me."

"The hell I will. I can throw rocks with the best."

I went down to the foot of the cliff and found a nice little overhang to crouch under on the path side of the rocky face. Maureen walked around to the other side of the cliff. A minute later, our pursuers came treading up the ravine, slipping less than we had, carrying no visible weapons, but wearing knapsacks.

I gripped my deer-crusher club and rolled it in my hands. It was good heavy wood. Then I began to think, which is never good to do in tight spots. It made my mouth taste brassy and I started to breathe fast. What if they both came up the ravine side?

276

And what was I really going to do? Crush a skull and ask questions later? This wasn't the Mekong Delta. Working my way up the ravine, I'd built up a nice, healthy, aggressive hate, the kind that can propel you. But who was telling me to kill? Don't follow leaders, watch your parking meters. Don't kill on command of voices.

They were close enough now that I could be sure it was my friend. He had removed his hat and his hair fell down and lay flat over the side where the ear should have been. Those two weren't just happening along because they liked rugged climbs.

No weapons visible, but the two-eared one had binoculars dangling from his neck and one-ear had his knapsack swinging heavily below his armpit. I could guess what he had in that.

They stood in the ravine and talked for a moment and one-ear split off for the path on my side of the cliff while the other waited in the ravine, looking up the other side where Maureen hid.

One-ear was looking for tracks. He was scanning the ground in front of him. As soon as he stepped out of sight of his friend down in the ravine, I fired off from my crouch like a linebacker going for a fullback and reached him in four good strides.

He never saw the blow coming. I hit him with my shoulder behind both knees and his legs flew up over his head, so he landed on his head and shoulders. It was a megahit, as they say in the NFL. He just lay there and for a moment I thought I'd broken his neck, but he started moving and trying to roll onto his knees. His knapsack was lying near him and I kicked that away and grabbed him by the hair, catching his neck in the crook of my arm. All I had to do to cut off his air was flex my biceps, and I did it once or twice to let him know. I had him kneeling in front of me and a nice solid crush on his neck and a very firm twist on his scalp.

"Call your friend. All I want to hear is a name, very natural, or you're a dead man."

"*Didi,*" he shouted. "*Didi mau len!*"

His friend came sloshing up and around the rocky ledge and his face showed astonishment. It made me feel better. A man bent on murder wouldn't look so disarmed.

"Drop your binoculars," I told him. I don't know what I wanted with the binoculars, but ordering him around seemed like the right thing to do, and I wanted him to get used to obeying orders.

He dropped them.

"If I wanted you dead, you would be," I said. I pulled back on one-ear's hair to demonstrate how easy it would be. "You will go back down the ravine for a few miles. I'll be watching."

I couldn't see my man's face, but I could smell him very well, and I could feel his heart pounding, which made me feel sorry for him.

"I'll let your friend go, unless I see you stop. In that case, you can come and pick up the pieces."

The binocular man looked at his buddy helplessly and turned his palms outward with a little shrug. Then he scrambled back down the rocky grade to the ravine. I dragged my hostage over to where I could see down the ravine and we watched his friend working his way down the stream.

I straightened my captive up and stood there feeling his heart pounding, trying to get control of myself. I could feel my own bicep tightening around his neck and that made him start to wriggle. I don't know why that set me off, his wriggling. I would have squirmed too, with someone's arm cutting off my air, but something took hold of me that had nothing to do with reason, nothing to do with him personally. It had to do with the woods, the chase, and his Vietnamese body. I could feel it pounding in my temples, feel my neck swell and feel his neck begin to give.

Then cold steel behind my ear and a calm voice.

"This is a gun, Ben," it said. "Let him go or, I swear, I'll pull the trigger."

It was Maureen. And it was a cold metal thing behind my ear. I let go and he fell at my feet. He reached for his throat, recovered a little and sprang away, scrambling down the path to the ravine and off down the hill.

I turned to Maureen. She was flipping a flashlight in her hand.

"Got it out of his knapsack," she said. "You would have killed him, you know."

I wanted to deny that, but I knew she was right.

"Thanks," I said.

She looked at me as if she were looking at a stranger.

"Where does that come from?" she said. "What is it? Hormones or what, makes you ready to break a trachea?"

"The Vietnam disease," I said. "Hell if I know."

I looked down the ravine. I could still make out the panicked figure of one-ear slipping and splashing down the hill.

One-ear had almost had to pay for my own ten-day terror in the woods. It made me think of Maureen's remark that Helen wanted to throw a brick through the window of the Vietnamese restaurants in Georgetown. If you can't kill the one you want, kill the one you've got.

# 66

Maureen and I didn't have time to talk until we were in the car with the suitcases on the back, taking the curves of the mountain road at good speed with ill-considered faith in the Triumph's brakes.

"If those guys really wanted to waste us, the easy thing would have been to fool with your brakes," Maureen said.

I slowed down and we stopped at the first petrol station which was at the foot of the mountain, just outside the parkland. The station attendant put the car up on the overhead rack and checked out the brakes and the hydraulic lines and everything looked fine. So we took off again.

Maureen asked what they had done and what they said.

"Not much. The one I had, just called out '*Didi*' or something like that. Does that sound like Vietnamese?"

"If it was Vietnamese, it means 'run'," she said. "How'd you know his partner wouldn't come up firing?"

"I was hoping they'd be convinced the one I had was in imminent danger of becoming a paraplegic. They weren't carrying much in the way of hardware."

Maureen looked at the binoculars.

"They were observers," she said. "Wonder if they observed us last night. Must have got an eyeful."

"What could they see? Lumps under a blanket."

"You don't remember last night so well."

"I remember everything about last night."

"Think we ought to return the binoculars and the knapsack?"

"To whom? The General's widow? She's not likely to admit to knowing those characters. We'll never know who they were, for sure."

"Then we get to keep the binoculars?"

"Spoils of war."

"Plus what was in the knapsack," she said. "Two peanut butter sandwiches and one pair of white socks."

"At least there were no grenades. Makes me feel better about what their mission must have been."

"But the binoculars are expensive."

"I've always wanted a pair."

"You still think this had to do with the General?"

"Can you think of anything else?"

"But why would they follow you?"

"The strange and mysterious workings of the Oriental mind."

"Oh, come on."

"We're never going to know. We're never going to know who sent those guys today, or the guy who worked over your chart, and we're never going to know who killed the General, or for that matter if anyone killed him."

"You have to have faith," said Maureen. "You may learn more yet."

# 67

We were back to Washington in time for dinner. Maureen wanted to stop by her place and drop off her things and change.

"Think this being followed will end now?" she asked as we unloaded the car.

"Time will tell."

"I'd prefer a note of apology and a promise they won't do it again."

Maureen unlocked the porch door and we were in the hall, me lugging her bag.

"Oh! I'm so glad!" It was Helen, throwing her arms around Maureen.

"I'm fine. Jesus, Helen. You act like I just got back from Khe Sanh."

"I was so worried. I didn't know where you were."

"I told you. I was with Benjamin."

"But you didn't tell me where you were going."

"Oh, Helen."

Maureen grabbed her suitcase and dashed upstairs, leaving me with Helen.

"Well, I hope you're pleased with yourself," Helen said, once Maureen had disappeared.

"What's all this about?"

"Just tell me this: are you her doctor or her boyfriend? Don't you think it's time you gave up one or the other?"

"For a while she won't need a doctor."

"How would you know?"

"I know."

"You have an odd way of showing concern for your patient. Taking her out to chase all over. Suppose she had an attack?"

"Not likely."

"You just had her admitted to the hospital for almost a week. Then suddenly you tire of that game and it's time for a ride in your sports car. You're not like any doctor I've ever known."

"I discharged her from the hospital. She could have taken off for the weekend with anybody."

"Now what's that supposed to mean?"

"At least if anything happened she was with me, not Timothy Moore."

Helen looked as if I'd just passed very malodiferous gas. "You don't care what you say, do you?"

"What have you got against Moore, anyway? Just that he gave up the cloth?"

"I'm not discussing him with you. He's a sweet, damaged man. You couldn't understand."

"I didn't realize you had it so bad."

"There's a lot you don't understand. You just chase after what you want. You are ruled by your appetites."

"Aren't we all?"

"No."

I looked at that pasty, grim face, those dark, cheerless eyes and that hair pulled back severely and I believed her. There were people in this world who were ruled by other things.

"What do you want, Helen? You want me to just fade away? You didn't mind me too much when it looked like I might pry Maureen away from Tim Moore. But you don't like her liking me any better."

Her eyes showed something close to fear, fear at what I might say next. I said: "What is it you don't like, Helen? Maureen and Tim Moore, or Maureen and any man?"

"They're bad for each other."

"How do you know that? You hear voices, or what?"

"I know."

"You believe, Helen. That's different from knowing."

She looked me right in the eye and I could see she had no idea what I meant.

Maureen saved me by reappearing with her suitcase repacked, ready to go.

"When will you be back?" said Helen.

"Sunday night, I guess," Maureen called back over her shoulder. "I've got to go to work Monday."

Helen stood with her arms folded over her big bosom, watching us from the door.

# 68

Sunday we walked down to Trav's Tavern at Glen Echo and had a beer. Maureen looked around at the place and said, "This is a real redneck bar. I like it." I told her Chief Justice Douglas used to come to Trav's and eat chilli, after a day's walk on the canal, and she said, "He *would* have liked it. He was a redneck."

"We used to walk to Holy Redeemer past a place like this," said Maureen. "Helen used to make me cross to the other side of the street."

"Good Catholic schoolgirls."

"Oh, of course. Plaid skirts and knee socks. The whole route. And field hockey. Helen and I used to change in the locker room and speculate about whether the nuns shaved under their armpits."

"What did you decide?"

"I thought they did. So they wouldn't gross out the priests when they had affairs."

"What did Helen think?"

"Helen said no. That would be vanity. And she wouldn't listen to my blaspheming the priests."

"She likes her priests on a pedestal," I said.

"Oh, you are clever," said Maureen, looking me over. "How you can ask and not really ask."

I thought I'd better be quiet. I studied my beer.

"Yes," said Maureen. "It was Tim's baby."

283

"Did he know about it?"

"No."

"But Helen did?"

"Oh, yes."

"What did she think of your abortion?"

"She feared for my immortal soul."

"So she's not happy about your continuing on with Tim."

"Neither am I, if you have to know."

"That part I can see," I said. "What I can't see is Helen. Well, that's not really true."

Maureen did not ask what I meant, so I said: "I can see it from Helen's point of view."

"See what?"

"Why you two are room-mates."

Maureen looked unhappy with the drift. Her mouth turned down and she shifted in her seat and tried to look bored and gazed over at the bar.

"I can see the attraction on Helen's part. But I can't quite see it from your side."

"What attraction?"

"You know what I mean. Her eyes are all over you."

"That's foul," said Maureen. "Just foul. Helen may be a lot of things, but she's never . . ." her voice trailed off.

"What things is Helen?"

"Nothing. She's got her problems. Obvious problems."

"But why are you still together? You don't get along."

"Don't you get tired of the same old boring questions?"

"Not until I get answers," I said. She didn't seem as angry as she usually became when I asked her about her reasons for staying with Helen.

"We go way back. Why are you so interested?"

"I'm trying to understand you. But you could be friends and not live together. Why live together?"

"Because we came to town together. Why is this such a big deal?"

"Helen seemed to think this medical problem you have might go way back to Vietnam, maybe to Moore."

"Helen said that?" said Maureen. Her surprise looked genuine enough.

"Yes. Why does that startle you?"

"I don't know. It just doesn't sound like Helen. And what do you think? Is it all something I caught in Nam, like your general?"

"You never had malaria."

"This is true. But I've got something now," she said. "At least I had something recently. Since I've been under your wing, I've been fine."

"I've noticed that."

"Meaning?"

"Think about the times you really dropped the bottom out – where were you?"

"At Houlihans . . ."

"But just before that, you were home. You have breakfast and an hour later, boom."

Maureen said nothing. Her face fell to a sombre stare, then jumped back to life, laughing. "You've got me in protective custody," she said. "Does Helen know?"

"She might."

"You thought Timothy was slipping me his Diabinese. She told me. Now you think it was Helen."

"Your urine was clean."

"Helen doesn't know that," she laughed, more to herself than for my benefit. "You're still not sure about me. You're no more sure than you were about the General. You've just got your list of possibilities."

"Does that bother you?"

"That you're suspicious?" said Maureen. "I suppose it shouldn't. You're worried about me."

She looked at me, trying to hold the corners of her mouth down, and I was sure it didn't bother her, my list and what was on it. She reached across the table and patted my hand.

"You're a good doctor," she said. "You don't leave stones unturned."

"That's the idea."

"But Helen's not slipping me anything," said Maureen. "She's got opportunity, I'll grant you, but no motive."

"She likes you," I said. "And you've been running around with men."

285

# 69

We were very quiet coming to the house, trying not to wake Helen. Maureen put English muffins in the toaster and started stirring frozen orange juice in a pitcher. I went off to the toilet in the hallway. I heard Helen pass by on her way to the kitchen and I tried to play invisible in the bathroom. I could hear them talking in there. About ten minutes later I heard Helen go by, on her way back upstairs.

"She gone?"

"Yes."

"She know I'm here?"

"She couldn't care less about you, right now."

"Why not?"

"Father Timothy Moore's asleep in the living room, on the couch."

"Moore?"

"Showed up last night, all frantic and concerned for my welfare. Heard I'd been discharged from the ward."

"Good luck," I said, kissing her good-bye.

"No breakfast?"

"I'm getting while the getting's good."

"Well, have something at least."

"What's that stuff?"

"Iced tea," said Maureen. "Helen's special spiced iced tea. Take a muffin and a jar."

I looked at the amber tea doubtfully.

"Go ahead, I can't drink it all. Give some to Mrs. Bromley."

"You going away with Moore?"

"I'll let him drive me to work. I'll call you tonight."

I took the muffin and the tea and slipped out the porch door and ran down the stairs to the car and drove to the office.

# 70

It didn't bother me much, leaving Maureen with Timothy Moore. Had I thought about it analytically, I guess I should have bothered, but after three days with Maureen, and after those nights, somehow I couldn't work myself up to be threatened.

Of course, it wasn't me who was threatened.

Mrs. Bromley hurried into my office at eight that morning and was startled to see me sitting behind the desk.

"You're back," she said. "You had calls. That small mountain of notes to your right are your calls. They missed you while you were gone."

"I should be happy."

"Did you see the paper?"

"Which paper?"

"Saturday's? No, you were on the mountain Saturday, that's right. How was the cabin?"

"Wonderful. What about the paper?"

"I saved it for you." She disappeared and reappeared with the paper.

## INVESTIGATION SUGGESTS FOUL PLAY IN VIET GENERAL'S DEATH

### BY STEPHANIE SHAW

Allegations of an insulin overdose could not be refuted, according to the report of the official investigator of the sudden and unexplained death of General Nguyen Duc

Dhieu, former Chief of Defense of the Republic of South Vietnam, who died at St. George's Hospital August 19. According to Dr. Benjamin Abrams, Clinical Assistant Professor of Medicine at St. George's, possible causes of death include the administration of excessive insulin. The General's widow has claimed the General was assassinated by the use of insulin.

There were several more paragraphs with reactions from the widow (my friend the widow), from von Dernhoffer (who said he was pleased the investigation was closed), from the Medical Examiner (who still wasn't interested in investigating the case), and finally a paragraph explaining that the District Prosecutor's office wasn't interested because the cause of death had been determined to be "natural causes." The widow and the newspaper were not satisfied, but they had no suggestions about whom to prosecute.

Mrs. Bromley stood there watching me read and when I looked up she said, "Nobody from the Medical Examiner's office has called. I've been waiting with bated breath."

"Breathe easy," I said. "They're done with it."

I had the feeling, for no good reason, that I was done with my Vietnamese followers, too. And, of course, I didn't expect to hear any more from the widow Que-Dhieu. She'd gotten what she could from me – a little inside and advance information, a little recreation. I wondered about that smash-up on Canal Road, and if it was a setup as Sumner suggested. Another item for my never-know file. The more essential item was her role in her husband's death.

But if I learned one thing in medical school, it was that there are unknowables in life – why one man is paralysed by polio virus and another just gets diarrhoea. I can live with not knowing.

Then I started thumbing through my messages. Then stopped. I sat there and looked at that pile of demands, those cries for suckling. Trouble was, I didn't feel like taking care of anybody's problems but my own just then. I considered calling Maureen. That was one call I wanted to make. She might be still home soothing Timothy Moore. Or she might be at work.

I tried work. They said she hadn't arrived yet. I considered calling her at home, but realized Helen might answer the phone.

I leafed through the pile of messages: sore backs, fevers, diarrhoeas, personal message for Dr. Abrams only (which meant "I think I have herpes"), all the things people felt required my personal consideration, things they knew were too difficult for the covering doctor.

I walked out of my office, down the hall to the lab. Mrs. Bromley was scrubbing the sink. I waited for her to step back so I could pour out the iced tea, when the phone rang. I set down the tea and grabbed the phone.

"Hey, good buddy," boomed Sumner. His voice stunned me, as if a brass kettle had lowered over my head and he had struck it with a hammer. Out of my daze I heard Mrs. Bromley say, "Ah, refreshments."

"Where you been?" boomed Sumner.

"Where are you?"

"In your waiting room, bozo. Where are you? I walk in here and nobody's on sentry and the place looks deserted."

I took Sumner down the hall and we sat in my office.

"Where've you been all weekend?" he asked. "I've been trying to get hold of you."

"I was home Sunday."

"By Sunday, I'd given up."

"Hear anything more about your friend?" I asked.

"My friend? Mrs. Que? *My* friend. I like that."

"Our mutual acquaintance."

"I saw the paper Saturday, about the General. Was that what you were so interested in the Hyporide for?"

I told him the whole story, leaving out some details about Maureen and me. He didn't ask any questions. He just listened. I emphasized Maureen's Antabuse-like reaction preceding her hypoglycemic episodes. I didn't have to point out how the blood tests suggested an oral blood-sugar-lowering drug, and how the negative urine tests suggested it was no ordinary drug.

"And this Helen character had access to Hyporide?" he asked.

289

"And Hyporide causes an Antabuse-like reaction, and hypoglycemia," I added, superfluously.

"What's this Helen's last name?"

"Sligo, Helen Sligo."

Sumner's face changed. It was as if I'd slapped him. Then a smile crept across his face.

"No fucking shit?" he said.

"You know her?"

"Do I know her? If she's the same Helen Sligo I knew about in the Forty-forty-fourth, I know her. She was Maureen Banting's tentmate until Maureen tried to punch her lights out one night."

"Why?"

"Sligo deserved it."

"Why?"

"Some of the nurses decided to finish off what the grunts had begun. Cong prisoners were dying unexplained deaths on the wards. They called me to investigate. Never could prove anything, but one or two had low blood sugars right before they died. We couldn't do autopsies out there. But everyone figured some of the nurses were knocking them off with insulin in the IV lines."

"Helen did that?"

"She was one of the ones whose name came up. There was an investigation. Couldn't prove shit."

"But you think Helen was in on it?"

"Apparently Maureen Banting did too. They had to pull her off Sligo. Maureen was a real hellcat. Sent Helen to the infirmary for a week. Got Maureen court-martialled. But they let her off with a reprimand. Everyone knew what happened."

I sat there trying to assimilate what Sumner had told me.

"Are there records? I mean about Helen and the insulin. And about Maureen punching her out?"

"Not about Helen. There were allegations, but no charges, no court-martial. Maureen was court-martialled. Judge Advocate General might have that. It'd be in her service record, too."

"Why are they still room-mates?" I asked, not to Sumner, but to the muses. "After something like that?"

Sumner said, "Nobody could ever prove Helen did anything. And I guess she convinced Maureen she hadn't, 'cause I heard they were tent-mates again before they left Nam. They kissed and made up."

"But you think Helen did it?"

"Bet your ass she did it. Everyone I interviewed had different names on their lists. Helen was on everyone's list."

I thought about that and about Helen's persisting desire to heave bricks through the windows of Vietnamese restaurants, Helen who thought Vietnam was a war we should have won. Helen the pigeon killer. Helen the protocol nurse. At Saint George's, where General Dhieu died.

Just then, Mrs. Bromley buzzed me.

"I'm afraid I may have to leave." She sounded odd.

"Anything wrong?"

"I'm just a little under the weather."

"You all right?"

"Strangest thing. Felt fine until just a few minutes ago."

I walked out front to her desk. She was several shades whiter than my lab coat and the sweat was popping out in great beads over her forehead. She put her head down on her arms.

"Come and lie down," I said, and helped her back to the exam room, wondering what I would do if she stopped breathing. I took her blood pressure which was 140/80 – high normal – and her pulse which was racing at 150. She was soaked and her eyes were dilated and rolling up into her head.

"Has anything like this ever happened to you?"

"My heart's pounding like when they gave me a shot for asthma when I was young."

Her words were slurred. I drew a few tubes of blood including one for sugar, and told her we were going to the Emergency Room. She didn't argue. That's when I knew she was in trouble.

Sumner was watching all this, and he said, "I'll bring my car around. Let's not waste time with an ambulance."

He left on the run.

"Did you feel all right this morning?" I asked.

"Yes. I felt fine. I was all right until I had that tea."

"Tea?"

"The iced tea."

I helped Mrs. Bromley to the waiting room and ran into the lab and grabbed the bottle with Helen's tea and then ran back out and grabbed Mrs. Bromley who was slumping in a chair and grabbed her under the shoulder and walked, mostly dragged, her to the lift and out the front door to Sumner's car.

Sumner took off fast and headed towards Saint George's. "What do you think?" he asked. "MI?"

"Hyporide, more likely," I said, feeling Mrs. Bromley's racing pulse.

"I want you to take the tea and Mrs. Bromley's urine and blood over to Mai Nguyen and have her run it for Hyporide," I told Sumner.

"The tea?" Mrs. Bromley said vaguely. She was on her way out.

"What about Maureen?" he asked. We were moving fast, careering around corners.

"I'll call her when we get to the ER."

Mrs. Bromley was almost unarousable when we arrived at the ER. Sumner parked in front and I ran inside for a stretcher.

A nurse saw me grab one and followed me out. We got Mrs. Bromley onto it and sped her inside.

One of the residents slammed in an IV and I called for a Bristoject of fifty-percent glucose. The nurse slapped the syringe into my hand and I drove the needle into the rubber part of the IV line and bolused the glucose in.

Mrs. Bromley looked twitchy for a few minutes and I thought: Here it comes – she's going to seize. But she brightened up and her eyes opened and she asked what had happened.

The ER resident asked me what I wanted run on the bloods they had collected when they inserted the IV.

"Stat glucose," I told him. "And give Dr. Barrington about fifty cc's of her urine when you get the Foley in." Then to Sumner, "You've got to get it to NIH warm."

"I'll call Mai and tell her I'm coming," he said. "You better call the cops. They've got to lock that maniac up."

"I better call someone else, first."

# 71

I called Maureen from the work station in the centre of the ER.

"Miss Banting's sick today," a woman's voice told me.

"Did she come into work this morning? This is her doctor."

"Yes, but she went to the health unit."

"When?"

"Just a little while ago."

"What's that number?"

The nurse in the health unit told me I'd have to call Saint George's emergency room. They had just taken Maureen off in an ambulance.

"How was she?"

"She had a seizure."

My mouth went dry and I had trouble forming words. "What did you give her for it?"

"We don't have anything. We tried to stick a blade in her mouth, but she'd already clamped down. Bit her tongue pretty bad."

"She was still seizing when they took her?"

"Yes. They tried to stop it with Valium, but it took them forever to get the IV in and she kept right on seizing."

"I've got to get in touch with that ambulance. Do they have a radio?"

"I don't know."

"What's their dispatcher number?"

I got the ambulance dispatcher on the line and she tried to raise the ambulance, until she realized they didn't have a radio.

"How long's the trip to Saint George's?" I asked.

"Forty minutes," said the dispatcher. "Twenty minutes off rush-hour peak."

Every minute Maureen's blood sugar stayed down was a minute more for brain cells to die. She was seizing because her blood sugar was vanishingly low, and once she started seizing, she'd stopped breathing for minutes on end, cutting her brain off from oxygen. No oxygen, no sugar, no brain.

All we could do was wait. We moved a stretcher out to the ambulance receiving deck and laid out the IV stuff and the fifty-percent glucose and listened for the siren.

A blaring flashing red and white ambulance turned the corner from Reservoir Road and roared up to the platform, but they threw open the door and it wasn't Maureen.

Ten very long minutes later the ambulance came screeching in. Maureen was still rigid and jerking, but they had an IV in with normal saline running. I rammed the Bristoject in and bolused in the fifty-percent glucose. Then we transferred Maureen to the ER stretcher and rolled her in. By the time she was in her ER bay, she had stopped seizing.

But she didn't wake up.

They had a neurologist see her in the ER. I watched as he went over her. He tapped her tendons with his rubber reflex hammer and rolled her head for doll's-eyes movement and pressed her sternum with his thumb. She reacted to that, but not as much as I wanted her to react. He checked her pupils with his flashlight. That's when I got suddenly light-headed and nauseated. Her pupils did not contract much. They weren't totally unreactive, but they didn't clamp right down. I'd seen pupils like that in too many people who never did wake up, and in some who had but who everyone wished hadn't.

# 72

I walked alongside the stretcher when they took Maureen up to Neurology. The nurses met us in the hallway and we manoeuvred it through the door and into the room. Two of them got on one side of her and grabbed the sheet from the other side and counted to three and lifted her dead weight from stretcher to bed.

She was floppy and pale. They had taped gauze pads over her eyes in the ER. The nurses cut away her clothes with scissors so they wouldn't have to pull sleeves past the IV. She was wearing a white blouse and a tartan plaid skirt and panty hose. They made short work of it.

I wanted to cover her, but the nurses were busy getting a Foley catheter in her bladder and doing all the things you do for a comatose patient, and when I couldn't stand to watch anymore, I walked out and sat down at the nurses' station and tried to get my mind moving again.

My beeper went off. It was the ER. They wanted to know if Mrs. Bromley could go home. I had them put her on the phone. I asked her how she felt.

"Quite better now. Was that Maureen Banting they brought in?"

"Yes. She drank the same tea you did."

"Rather more of it, looked like to me."

"Yes."

"Will she be all right?"

"The neurologist says it's too early to tell."

"What was in the tea?"

"A drug," I said.

"Who put it there?"

"That's what I'm going to find out."

"Shall I cancel the patients for tomorrow?"

"You ought to call your husband and have him drive you home and spend the rest of the day eating."

"I'll be just fine."

"Could you do one thing for me?"

"Yes."

"Call Timothy Moore and tell him Maureen's here. Don't say anything more than that."

Timothy Moore didn't wait to get the news from Mrs. Bromley. He had stopped in to see Maureen in her office and they told him. He showed up about an hour later.

He stood at the head of the bed, stroking Maureen's hair. She was breathing and she moved her arms and legs occasionally. But she was very postictal and she looked semidead.

"Postictal?" asked Moore.

"After a convulsion, people may be very unresponsive for a while, until their brain revives."

"How long will that take?"

"I don't know. Maybe never."

Moore looked very shocked.

"What happened?"

"I was going to ask you that," I said.

"Me?"

"You were with her this morning, weren't you?"

"I drove her to work."

"Did you have breakfast with her?"

"Yes."

"Did you have tea with breakfast?"

"Tea?"

"With breakfast."

"No. Why do you ask?"

"I want to know."

"No," said Moore, looking at me. "We had no tea."

"Did she bring lunch with her?"

"Lunch? Yes. A bag and a thermos."

"A thermos?"

"Yes, a thermos. What's this all about?"

"I'm just trying to figure out what happened."

296

I took a urine specimen from Maureen's Foley bag and walked downstairs to my car. It wasn't easy leaving her like that. But Tim Moore was with her and they were going to watch her pretty closely. And I had to be sure about the Hyporide.

It only took twenty minutes to drive to NIH, but it seemed much longer and I had to keep myself from speeding.

Mai was in her lab when I came in.

"I was just going to call you," she said. "I can't tell how much she has in there, but from what Sumner said, all you wanted to know was whether or not it was positive."

"Mrs. Bromley's urine was positive for Hyporide?"

"That's what I'm trying to tell you."

"What about the tea?"

"I'll run that separately. I didn't want to gook up the column with the tea."

"But the urine is definitely positive?"

"No doubt about it. How'd she get Hyporide?"

"Don't throw out that urine and keep the tea," I said.

Then I sat down and tried to think of who to call. I called Sumner who told me to call the hospital administrator and also hospital security at Saint George's so they'd send up a cop to guard Maureen.

The hospital administrator on call seemed to follow everything I said, which astonished me because it sounded so outrageous and incoherent to me.

"Her name's Maureen Banting. B-A-N-T-I-N-G? And you think she was poisoned in a homicide attempt. And you want the D.C. police and hospital security notified. And you'd like a detective here when you arrive. That about it?"

"You sound like you do this all the time."

"It happens now and again," said the administrator. "I'll have security set up a guard. No one but you and the staff will see her."

"Her friend, Tim Moore, is okay. No nurses except the neuro nurses, though."

"Got it."

I thanked Mai, and told her as much as I thought she needed to know and told her everything would be evidence and to throw nothing away.

Then I went down and got into my car and drove back to Saint George's, rehearsing what I was going to tell the cops, trying to keep my mind off Maureen and how she'd looked like a floppy doll when I left.

# 73

They interviewed me in the administrator's office. There were two of them and they were big and friendly and they called me doctor, and I tried to sound calm and cool so they'd believe me.

The one who did all the questioning was a slow-faced man with a crew cut and dark skin under his eyes. They worked like that. The one asking the questions, the other just watching me. Finally, they stepped out of the room together for a talk and then they came back in.

The slow-faced man said, "Just want to check one or two things, Doc. You say this drug that was in your secretary's urine was not available in drugstores?"

"It's a new drug. The hospital's studying it. Only a few people have a supply."

"Are they giving it to patients?"

"Yes. There's a list available, I'm sure. I read the protocol. They were trying to recruit twenty patients. I doubt they'd have that many yet."

"And this nurse, Miss Banting's room-mate, was working with the drug?"

He seemed to have the main issues sorted out. My mouth went dry and I licked my lips and said yes.

"Just one more thing, Doc," he said, half closing his eyes, as if he hadn't quite got it yet, "Did Miss Banting's urine have this drug in it?"

"They're running her blood and urine now."

"Can you find out for us?"

I called Mai. Maureen's urine was positive. The detectives talked to her. She answered all their questions about why only NIH could do the drug analysis and how it was a research drug available to only a few people.

"I want you to come with us to make a statement," said the detective. "And you say you have a protocol with Helen Sligo's name on it?"

"I've seen one in her file cabinet," I said.

"No good. We'd need a warrant."

"There are doctors, other people who must have a copy."

"We'll check it out."

Then they drove me down to the police station at Newark Street and they called in a stenographer and we went through it all again.

They were very nice to me at the station and offered me coffee and doughnuts which I couldn't eat. Then they took my address and telephone number for the third time and let me go.

## 74

Maureen was sitting up in bed. She had a hospital security guard sitting outside her door and Timothy Moore was not there. She looked very pale but she smiled when I came into the room.

"Wouldn't you know it," she said. "Three days of fasting and I go back to work and boom."

"I'm glad you're better."

"But what a shocker," said Maureen. "I mean out of nowhere. I'm just out cold. I wake up in a hospital room with no idea how I got there."

"Did you have any tea at work?"

"Tea?"

"Remember the tea you gave me? Helen's special spiced tea?"

"Sure."

She was watching me very carefully now. I tried to be casual, but I guess I had got to the tea a little too directly. I should have worked up to it. She knew something was up.

"Did anyone else?"

"Did anyone else do what?"

"Did anyone else drink Helen's tea? At work? Besides you?"

"What's the third degree for? No, I drank it all myself."

"You look a lot better now. You had me worried."

"Well, wait one minute, big boy. You don't think you're going to get away with that. What's with the tea? What gives?"

"Maureen, your urine was full of a special research drug, a drug only Helen Sligo and a few other people have access to, a blood-sugar-lowering drug."

Maureen looked at me blank-faced for a long time. Then she came back into focus and began examining my face. She was thinking fast.

"You think Helen . . . ?"

"Can you think of any other way it could be explained?"

"But how'd she know I'd drink the tea?"

"She gave it to you, didn't she?"

"Yes."

There was a long pause. Maureen looked out the window from her bed. A tear brimmed up in one eye and spilled over and ran down her cheek.

"Why would she do it?"

"You tell me."

Maureen's face filled with sudden fury, "What the hell's that supposed to mean?"

"I'm just asking," I lied. "I can think of a few reasons. A fat girl's envy. Resentment builds up. She didn't like you with Moore. It was always when you were going to be with Moore you got your dose."

Maureen studied me, not looking like she was really

listening. She was trying to see behind the words to what I was really thinking.

"You don't think that was really it, do you?"

"I can't hope to know what really motivates another person," I said.

"But you haven't listed the possibilities in the proper order, as you see it."

There wasn't much point to evasion. I said, "You're right." She waited. I said, "She'd lived through you and Tim Moore for years. She didn't like it, but Tim wasn't the threat I was."

"This is true," said Maureen.

"Helen was losing you. She was jealous. Jealous of your new lover."

"Helen and I were never lovers," Maureen said flatly. There was no heat in that, just plain unencumbered fact.

"The other times might have been warnings. Maybe warnings about Tim Moore. This last time she meant business."

Maureen put her hand to her face and her shoulders shook with a sob.

"I'm sorry," I said.

Maureen looked up at me. "Not as sorry as I am."

I walked down to the car park, feeling strange. I felt strange because, for the first time, I had heard Maureen say something that sounded hollow. She had said she was sorry, but somehow I couldn't really convince myself she was.

# 75

The next day, Mrs. Bromley was back at work and I told her the whole story.

"Have they arrested this Sligo person?"

"They said they'd let me know. I think they have to talk it over."

"Sounds like a pretty open-and-shut case, if Sligo is the only one who could possibly have got her hands on the drug."

"They haven't interviewed you yet?"

"They called last night to say they'd be by the office today," she said.

I left for Saint George's before the police could show up. Maureen was eating lunch when I arrived.

"They've got a city cop outside the door now," said Maureen. "I guess they're serious."

"Guess they are."

"Helen hasn't come in to see me."

"She can't."

"What do you think, she'll try to strangle me in bed?"

"I'm not calling the shots now," I said. "The policeman outside doesn't ask my advice."

"I've thought about what you said," said Maureen, looking down at her hands moving on her lap, then staring out the window. "There may be some truth to it." She looked over and met my eyes. "About Helen, I mean."

Maureen took in a breath and looked back at me, a little too dramatically I thought, but she was talking about a tough topic. "There were some times the same thing crossed my mind about Helen."

"When?"

"Now and then. Once in Nam. We were in the shower."

"Anything overt?"

"Not really. Just a touch – thought it was accidental."

"And later?"

"Nothing overt. She was wild when I first started up with Tim, in Nam. I thought it was just because he was a priest."

"And what do you think now?"

"Same thing. She didn't like the whole arrangement. She kept telling me I was playing with fire. I thought she meant, fire like hellfire, you know."

"Now you're not so sure?"

"Oh, stop playing Perry Mason," she said hotly. "You're the one who suggested she might have been hot for my body all along. I'm just saying the more I think about it, the more

302

things I can think of that make me think you might have something. I mean, why else would she do it?"

That was one question to which I'd given considerable thought.

"I can think of a few reasons."

"Like what?"

"Maybe she's not holding a flame for you. Maybe it was for Tim all along. When you started in with me she expected Tim to realize it was all over with you, and maybe she even thought he might turn to her."

"But Tim didn't. He just clung tighter to me," she said, averting her glance. "And I've still got that to deal with. Tim, I mean."

"But the big thing is the resentment," I said. "Anyone could see it. All those years of watching you have all the things she couldn't have – men, food, fun. Anyone could see it. That's why I kept asking you why you were still living with her. All that hostility."

"I just couldn't see it. We had fights, but then it blew over."

"I'm just glad you never came to blows," I said.

"That's what I mean," said Maureen. "We could never really do any physical harm to each other. We'd fight like cats, but never hurt each other."

"I see," I said. And for a moment I think I saw all too clearly. It was a nice little story. She was very open-minded and agreeable, too agreeable. And they had never come to blows.

The detective called me later that afternoon and told me they'd arrested Helen.

They'd interviewed Mai and Sumner and the people listed on the Hyporide protocol and they'd talked to Tim Moore and Maureen and Mrs. Bromley and thought they had a good case.

"We've got motive and opportunity, Doc. But the clincher's that drug, Hyporide. You really nailed her with that. Ordinarily, in a case like this, we wouldn't have much. Anybody could've put that drug in there, if it was something common. But to use Hyporide. She was one of four people who ever

303

touched the drug at Saint George's. None of the others had any connection to Maureen Banting. You got her, Doc. You did it."

"Thanks," I said, and hung up.

# 76

Sumner called me later.

"So they got her? Well, I guess she tried that stunt once too often," he said. "We couldn't stick her with anything in Nam. But you've got her dead to rights."

"Yeah."

"I'm glad Maureen's all right. She's a piece of work, still. Nice tight little body."

"When did you see her? You were gone when they brought her in the ER."

"I saw her a month ago, at NIH."

"NIH?"

"Sure, walking down the hall."

I hung up and pulled out some papers Sumner had sent over, with the list of all the institutions involved in the Hyporide trial: NIH was one of them.

Then I called up Tim Moore.

"How is she?" he asked.

"Fine. She's just fine."

"I can't believe this about Helen."

"That drug is the key."

"Maureen told me."

"Was Maureen assigned out to do any consulting at NIH, Tim?"

"Yes. July and August."

"Where'd she work?"

"I don't know. Clinics, I think."

"She sat around observing?"

"Yes, that sort of thing."

Helen was just as fat but she looked more drawn and her eyes looked puffy and red. She sat with her shoulders hunched over, like a caged animal, which in fact she was. She sat across from me, separated by a screen. She was wearing her own clothes.

"What do you want?" she said.

"The truth."

"Since when?"

"Helen, I'm not going to tell you I like you, or that I'm only out to help you. But I may be able to help you, if you help me."

"Yeah, you've helped me a lot, already."

"Maureen spent some time in the stockade in Nam. She struck an officer. Was that officer you?"

Helen sat there staring hate.

"I know all about the prisoners' deaths, and the investigation."

"Did she tell you about that?" asked Helen. She looked genuinely surprised.

"I found out about it, looking into General Dhieu's death."

"And now you're trying to pin that one on me? You think you can wrap everything up in a nice package and hang it around my neck?"

"I'm not accusing you of anything. I want to know if she thought you had anything to do with all that."

"I didn't do anything to anyone. I didn't ever set foot on Seven North. That gook general had nothing to do with me."

"Did Maureen think you had anything to do with those prisoners, in Nam?"

Helen looked at me, trying to decide. Finally she said, "Yes."

"She accused you of killing off patients with insulin?"

"Yes."

"Then why did you get back together? After she attacked you. After the court-martial?"

"She understood," said Helen.

"Understood what? Why you did it?"

"She understood that I had nothing to do with anything. I didn't kill them and I didn't kill that gook general. And I didn't try to kill Maureen."

We stared at each other a while, but I got nothing from that.

"Helen," I said. "You've been set up. There was Hyporide in the General's blood and urine. Enough to kill a clinic full of diabetics."

"Bullshit!" She was bright red and sweating.

"I never would have thought to look for it, of course. But someone pointed my nose in the right direction."

Even with the screen between us, my mouth tasted metallic watching her. I wasn't sure that screen could hold all her fury from me.

"Did you know Le Van Que was General Dhieu's wife when she set you up to knock off the General?" I asked, as calmly as I could.

I thought I saw something there, something in a quick movement of the eyebrows, a flash, a doubt. But then, slowly, her eyes went opaque and she smiled, "I don't know what you're talking about."

I couldn't be sure what that smile meant, but I was sure she was in control again, and I was sure I would get nothing more from her with my long bombs. I said, "Helen, are there any spare keys to your place? You know, like if you get locked out?"

"Why should I tell you?"

"Because if you don't, you'll probably spend some years behind bars."

"On the porch," she said. "Behind the couch."

The keys were there, just as Helen said. I went through the house from basement to bedrooms. I went through Maureen's room very carefully, looking under the bed and all through the closet. But I really didn't expect to find it there.

I did find her car keys though.

It didn't take too long. I looked all through the boot, and under the bonnet. It was under the driver's seat, in a plastic bag, taped to the bottom.

Thirty white pills with a number pressed into each tablet: 1321. I knew that number from reading the protocol. It was Hyporide. Maureen's car. Maureen's supply.

# 77

"You're looking very well," I said.

"Thanks to you," said Maureen. She was dressed and washed and wearing khaki slacks and a green knit shirt. Her bag was packed and on her bed. They had taken away the policeman from outside her door once Helen had been arrested.

"Can we go home to your place, Doc?" she asked, putting her arms around my neck. "You can keep me out of harm's way."

"Sure."

"Timothy Moore called," she said. "He's all broken up about Helen."

"You're not."

"I'm hurt, but not devastated. She's where she belongs."

"For the murder of Viet Cong prisoners," I said. "And for the murder of General Dhieu."

Maureen looked at me hard-eyed.

"Payment in kind," I said.

"You want to explain?" I asked. "Or do you want me to tell you about it?"

"You tell me," she said, sitting down on her bed.

"You never forgot that trouble in Nam where Helen decided to fight a little backyard war of her own. Maybe you weren't sure, or maybe you just wanted to have her in your sights. Then you heard about General Dhieu," I said. I looked at Maureen for a reaction.

She just smiled a totally impenetrable smile.

I continued, "General Dhieu would not have been one of Helen's heroes. In fact, he was one of those guys she would say lost the war for us. And when he was admitted to Saint George's he was within her grasp. Then he dies in a very familiar way – blood sugar falling out the bottom. Just like those prisoners in Binh Thuy. You read the paper and you figured Helen was up to her old tricks."

"Helen has old tricks?"

"Don't play dumb. It's just not you," I said.

She stopped smiling.

"I know all about Binh Thuy, and your punching Helen out and the court-martial. But they couldn't pin anything on Helen, and you kissed and made up."

"We didn't kiss . . ." said Maureen, chin rising.

"And when Dr. Abrams got appointed to find out what happened to General Dhieu and his disappearing sugar, you made it your business to get in touch with Dr. Abrams and put him on the right track. You were going to make sure I didn't miss Helen this time, even if you had to pin it on her yourself."

"And how did you come to this grand insight?"

"It all fell together a little too neatly. And it bothered me that Helen would use the one drug that would point to her, and only her, if it was discovered. And then I found out you'd been at NIH. You never mentioned that to me."

Maureen was bouncing her leg up and down, half smiling, eyes serious. "Nice theory," she said.

"More than that," I said. "The plastic bag's still under your driver's seat, if you want me to have the cops go fetch it."

Maureen wasn't smiling now. She stood up and went to the window, looked out and turned around. "No," she said. "That won't be necessary."

"Did you have it planned, all along, to get her someday?"

"I wound up believing Helen hadn't really slaughtered those prisoners," said Maureen. "But, as you said, when the General died the way he did I knew I'd been deluding myself all along. She got those prisoners, all right, and she got Dhieu."

She looked at me to see if I believed that. Then she said,

"Check out General Dhieu's blood or urine. They must still have some frozen. She got him. She got him with Hyporide."

"You can't check frozen anything for Hyporide. Freezing denatures it. The assay has to be on warm, fresh specimens."

"I can't believe there's no way to know it's in there."

"You can do something called gas chromatography. All that will show is if there's anything in the urine which is foreign. But it won't tell you what it is, unless there's already an established pattern for it, which there isn't yet for Hyporide. Besides you need fifty cc's and they don't have more than ten left. I called the lab before I came up here."

"It's in there. Helen put it there. That man went down with a blood sugar that no living brain could abide and Helen did it."

"So you were going to put her away for it. And in the process you didn't care whether you knocked me or Mrs. Bromley off, with the iced tea, or whether you died yourself."

"I'm so sorry about Mrs. Bromley."

"What were you trying to do with that tea, anyway? If you knocked me off who would have known to point the finger at Helen?"

"The whole problem was I didn't know the dose. Ever try to look a dose up for Hyporide? Doesn't exist yet. There's one on the protocol, but it's 'tentative.' That's what the trials are all about, establishing a safe dose."

"So you were experimenting."

"I started with the protocol dose, but that didn't do anything. So I started moving up. If I ate before I took it I got almost no symptoms, just mild jitters. That's why I handed you that muffin. I figured you'd eat it and then drink the tea and get the jitters and realize what was in it, or at least you'd know something was in it and you'd call me."

"And you'd say, 'Golly, gee, Helen must have spiked the tea.'"

"And I'd say I'd just drunk a whole jar of it and felt awful and meet me in the ER."

"But I never called you."

"I figured I hadn't put enough in your tea. I only crushed

two tablets and mixed it in a quart. That much hadn't done much to me, in the past, especially if I'd eaten beforehand."

"Well, it did quite a lot to Mrs. Bromley."

"I had no idea that would happen. I thought you'd drink it and of course you'd recognize hypoglycemic symptoms right away and you'd eat and call me."

"But when you didn't hear from me . . ."

"Once I'd given you that tea I had to do something. I didn't know if you'd swallowed it, chucked it, or fed it to a stray cat. But I couldn't wait. So I mixed up what I thought would be a reasonable dose – it was the same I'd taken the time you put me in the hospital before. I don't know why it hit me so hard. Just six tablets in a quart. But obviously, it was too much."

"Suppose I hadn't been at the ER? Suppose the ambulance had got hung up in traffic, and they didn't even have a radio. You could be a vegetable. All to get Helen."

"I read something last night. I'm not sure where it's from. It was, 'He who plans revenge should first dig two graves.' "

"And you would have gone to yours a happy martyr. For what?"

"I wasn't planning on going to any grave. I just miscalculated."

"On the dose maybe, but you figured what I'd do pretty well. You had me pegged all along. I couldn't have played my part better if you'd written the script."

"Do you hate me?"

"No," I said. "But I'm not going to help you, either."

"She belongs behind bars."

"Not for trying to knock you off."

"It's as you said," said Maureen. "Payment in kind."

"She killed people, you think, with hypoglycemia. And she's going to jail for trying to kill you the same way."

"It has symmetry," said Maureen.

"You don't know she killed General Dhieu."

"You don't know she didn't," said Maureen. "And you said yourself, there's no way to be sure now. But she killed those prisoners, all right. And I'd bet dollars to all your doubts – she got to General Dhieu, too. He was one of those guys Helen thinks lost the war we should've won."

"It may be justice," I said. "But it's not legal."

"Since when was legal ever right?"

"You admit there's a reasonable doubt Helen did anything."

"Doubt, maybe," said Maureen. "Reasonable doubt, no."

"You want to be judge and jury?"

"Someone has to be. I don't have the luxury of being a professional doubter, of just submitting a list of possibilities to my conscience."

"I'm a professional doubter?"

"Let me give you a proposition about which there is no doubt. Either Helen goes to jail, or I do, for trying to put her there."

"Not necessarily. You never accused Helen of anything. You might simply be a poor deranged woman who tried to kill herself."

"You might be able to sell that to someone. Talk about doubts, there'd be plenty on that score."

"You're not sure Helen pushed the syringe on anyone. You're only sure she'd be in sympathy. You'd put her away for wearing an American flag in her lapel, for being a superhawk."

"Looks like you're going to have to make up your mind," said Maureen, "who belongs in jail."

Her argument had a certain appeal, and I thought about it. What difference did it make whose death you paid for? Would it make any difference to those Vietnamese prisoners who died on Helen's ward, or to General Dhieu, whose name was printed on Helen's papers? But there was enough doubt about the particulars to keep me up nights. Suppose Sumner was wrong, and Maureen was wrong and all those people back at the 4044th were wrong and Helen had never tiptoed into anyone's room and sent them to never-never land with a syringe full of insulin? Suppose they just thought that because they wanted to – because Helen was over there being a cheerleader for all those killers and carnage? Helen wasn't popular in Nam because she wanted us to be there. In Maureen's eyes, and for most of us, to be a cheerleader for

311

that war was to be an accomplice. But should Helen spend several years behind bars for that? Half the country could be behind bars for that crime.

Maureen called a cab and went home to Glover Park by herself that day. I went back to the office and stared at my duck prints and my pseudo-WASP men's club furniture.

Later that day Maureen phoned.

"The bag is gone from under my car seat."

"Material evidence."

"Who has it?"

"I do."

"What are you going to do with it?"

"I'm still thinking about that," I said. "But unless I change my mind, you'd better start practising your psycho act."

"You're going to spring her?"

"Maureen," I said, "We'd better sit down and talk this out, like rational adults."

"You were there. You know what they did."

"I don't know for sure what Helen did."

"You know for sure enough."

"No."

"Ben, just do me one thing. Give me a couple of days' notice before you say anything to anyone."

"You've got it."

"You mean now?"

"I've got to get to them soon."

"It's just so quick."

I drove by her place later that afternoon, but her car was gone and the place was locked.

Then I drove to the Newark Street police station with Maureen's bag of Hyporide. I sat outside in my car staring at the bag and drove home. I'd promised to give her a couple of days. I phoned the detective who interviewed me and left a message to call me back. Then I called my answering service and told them I'd be reachable by beeper only, and then I stopped answering my pages.

Mrs. Bromley was wondering where I was.

"You've got to fend them off for me," I told her. "Stall 'em. Say anything. I'm tied up with emergencies. I'm doing a heart

312

transplant in Hong Kong. Anything. I just can't be reached right now."

"A Lieutenant Marconi called. The police detective."

"I'm especially tied up when he calls."

"Do we have new developments?"

"Nothing that you know about. In fact, you haven't heard from me at all. You're just hearing things."

"How exciting."

I signed out to one of my covering doctors. It was only Thursday, but he was very nice about it.

"Long weekend? Jesus, do I envy you," he said.

It was not a fun weekend. I signed into a motel in Bethesda, just in case Detective Marconi decided to return my call in person with a visit to my house. Watching the traffic from my window on Wisconsin Avenue distracted me for about thirty seconds. Then I started getting nervous about what I was going to tell the police. I had discovered the bag of Hyporide Wednesday, discharged Maureen and waited the whole weekend to come to them with the news?

Maureen wasn't home Friday morning. I called her at work from a pay phone.

"Miss Banting's in the hospital," said the secretary. "Has been for a week."

"Is Mr. Moore in?"

"He was called out of town."

"When?"

"Yesterday."

"I'm a friend of Tim's," I said. "But I've lost his phone number. He wanted me to call him Sunday night."

"Who did you say you were?"

"Dr. Benjamin Abrams. I'm Miss Banting's physician."

"And Mr. Moore's. I made his appointment with your secretary about a month ago."

She gave me his phone number. He wasn't home, but with his number I was able to pick his address out of the dozen Timothy Moores listed in the phone book. His landlady told me he'd left in a taxi Thursday evening.

"With his lady friend," she said. "I think they were going on a vacation. She's such a doll. I've told him that. I've told her

313

she ought to keep after him. He shouldn't live alone. And she's such a nice girl."

"They left together?"

"Thursday night. They looked so romantic. With all those bags, you would've thought they were going on their honeymoon."

I drove around for an hour and ran a few stop signs thinking too hard. Then I went to the police.

Detective Lieutenant Marconi listened gravely to my story, looking more and more unhappy as I spoke.

"You say she admitted taking this drug herself?"

I told him she admitted that.

"Why? Some kind of nut?"

"Looks that way. Suicidal. Depressive. I'm not a psychiatrist."

"And why did you look in her car in the first place?"

"One of my friends, a doctor, told me he'd seen her at NIH. And I knew the drug was being tested there. So suddenly Helen wasn't the only person I knew who could have put her hands on some Hyporide."

Marconi leaned back in his chair and chewed his pipe at me for a few long minutes.

"We'll need a new statement," he growled. "And we'll need that bag of Hyporide, you say you found all by yourself." He held my eye for a moment. "Nobody was with you when you found that bag?"

"Nobody."

"Any idea where we could find Miss Banting?"

"I haven't been able to reach her. She doesn't answer her phone. She hasn't been at work."

"Have you tried going to her house?"

"No answer."

He looked startled. "Then how do you know she hasn't really done it this time?"

I hadn't told him about my talk with Tim Moore's landlady, but his obvious alarm made me realize that Tim Moore may not have taken off with Maureen. I had not checked the rafters in Maureen's basement.

Marconi had me make a statement to the stenographer

314

again while he arranged for the warrant to enter Maureen's house. The whole time I was talking for the stenographer I was seeing Stewart Stapler's face, talking about the nurse who hanged herself.

Maureen hadn't hanged herself. Her clothes were gone, and when Tim Moore's office told me he'd resigned and left town, I stopped worrying that Maureen may have gone the way of the hanged nurse. Maureen's disappearance made it easy to get Helen out of jail.

A month later, Helen phoned me at my office.

"It's a Miss Helen Sligo," Mrs. Bromley said pregnantly. "Desires to speak with Dr. Abrams. Shall I ring her through, or call the SWAT team?"

Helen was back at work at Saint George's. She told me Maureen had not returned to Glover Park and she had no word from her. Had I heard anything? I had not.

Sumner called to say that he had managed to acquire a transcript of Maureen's court-martial proceedings. There was plenty of testimony from nurses who thought Helen had knocked off the Viet Cong prisoners. "I wouldn't want her working on my metabolic ward," Sumner said. "I bet she got the General somehow." But Helen kept her job and she kept the place in Glover Park. I asked her what she would do with the things Maureen had left behind.

"They're staying right where they are," said Helen. "Maureen will come home eventually. She's not one to hold a grudge."

Timothy Moore did not return from his honeymoon as his landlady expected. In fact, he sent her a letter with a power of attorney, asking her to sell his car and his furniture and send the money to a post office box in San Francisco. I didn't ask for the box number. I don't know what I would have done with it.

Mrs. Que-Dhieu became one very difficult widow to locate. The phone number I had for her got me a recording: "This number has been disconnected." Where do they find the voices for those recordings? The girl at General Dhieu's laundry told me the widow was out of town "visiting family" and she had no notion when she would return. Sumner told me the CID men had not visited him again about Mrs. Dhieu. He added, "No news is good news, where she's concerned."

Dr. von Dernhoffer eventually sent a formal note thanking me for my investigation of the "case of hypoglycemia," which I threw in the rubbish bin. Mrs. Bromley retrieved it, framed it, and placed it above her typewriter, despite my objections. "That is my wall, and I can hang anything there I please. That is the law. You said so." The letter is still there.

Karen Sweeney phoned to thank me. They reinstated her two weeks after my report.

Mai called to ask about the Hyporide-laden urines and blood and tea cluttering up her laboratory. The police had ordered her to keep the stuff but never collected it. I asked her if she wanted to go out for a drink sometime. She said, "Sometime. When you sound like you really want to, not just being nice."

I never saw Maureen again. A year later she sent a card. She was working in a mission clinic in Thailand. "You've never seen such beautiful children. Having a wonderful time. Wish you were here." There was no return address. She loved the clinic, but she would be leaving soon. She was applying for a visa to work in a clinic in Ho Chi Minh City.